Richard L. Rohrbaugh

DEPARTMENT OF RELIGION
LEWIS AND CLARK COLLEGE
PORTLAND, OREGON

Paul and Power

BENGT HOLMBERG

Paul and Power

*The Structure of Authority in the Primitive Church
as Reflected in the Pauline Epistles*

FORTRESS PRESS   PHILADELPHIA

To Solwieg

This book, the author's doctoral thesis at Lund University, was originally published by CWK Gleerup, the imprint for the scientific and scholarly publications of LiberLäromedel Lund.

COPYRIGHT © 1978 BY BENGT HOLMBERG

First Fortress Press Edition 1980

Library of Congress Cataloging in Publication Data

Holmberg, Bengt, 1942–
  Paul and power.

  Originally presented as the author's thesis, Lund University.
    Bibliography: p.
    Includes indexes.
    1. Church polity—Early church, ca. 30–600. 2. Paul, Saint, apostle. I. Title.
BV648.H64   1980   262'.012   79–8905
ISBN 0–8006–0634–5

8030J79   Printed in the United States of America   1–634

Contents

Introduction

One of the sore points in ecumenical discussions between Christians from different churches has always been the origin of the ministry and its exercise of authority. A reflection of this is the well-known fact that even scholarly studies in this field are often marked by the particular theological background of the scholar.[1] Every ecclesiastical tradition wishes to find its own church order confirmed by the New Testament; in fact this can in many cases be effected without doing violence to the texts due to the paucity and ambiguity of the relevant historical material.

Consequently, discussion of such questions seems to belong to the field of systematic theology and not to historical study.[2] But no serious theological discussion can in the long run do without the connection with reality that is mediated by historical investigation. Hence a discussion of the ministry and its exercise of authority within the Primitive Church is almost inevitable. Moreover, as it is a sound methodological principle to ascertain the facts of a case before starting to discuss their import, any theological analysis of the order of the Primitive Church ought to be preceded by a historical examination of the phenomena pertaining to this aspect of its life. That is what this book purports to be.

Still, there is no lack of historical investigations in this field, and it can rightly be asked what a new study can hope to accomplish that has not already been done.[3] Even if the field of investigation is narrowed to the Pauline epistles, one has to state that there exists a profusion of detailed

1. Cf. the characterizations by *Goppelt* (1966:121 n. 1) and the introduction of *Hainz* (1972:11–28).
2. Among works of this kind can be mentioned *Häring* (1972) and *Schütte* (1974).
3. For a history of the research of the last hundred years, see *Linton* (1932), *Hainz* (1972:11–28), *Brockhaus* (1975:7–94) and *Skjevesland* (1976:9–28, 109–127). See also the bibliography in *Kertelge* (1977: 565–574).

commentaries and scholarly monographs and articles on almost every single verse in these epistles. *Joseph Hainz* gives a full and balanced treatment to nearly every text of interest for this study in his massive monograph "Ekklesia. Strukturen paulinischer Gemeinde-Theologie und Gemeinde-Ordnung", (Regensburg 1972); this applies as well to *John Howard Schütz*'s penetrating "Paul and the Anatomy of Apostolic Authority", (Cambridge 1975). Moreover, to special texts and themes within the field of (Pauline) church order there exists any number of detailed investigations.

It is also apparent that there exists a considerable degree of consensus among scholars on the vast majority of details concerning philological and historical fact. But this is not accompanied by a corresponding degree of consensus as to how the facts are to be interpreted and fitted together into syntheses of historical reconstruction. This is a vital, if often neglected, part of historical study and it is here that work must be done anew in every generation.[4]

To attempt a synthesis of details of historical fact implies working with the categories of interpretation. The New Testament data are usually interpreted by means of categories from philosophy,[5] history of religions and later Christian theology, all belonging to the world of theoretical conceptions and ideas. Often a too direct and uncomplicated transition is made from isolated historical facts to their interpretation by theological categories. The facts are organized in structures or syntheses of a theological kind before the attempt is made to interpret them as parts of social structures or an organically coherent historical development. For instance, too often the material is interpreted by raising questions about "the ministry" in the New Testament—a later theological category—instead of by analysing more fundamental phenomena, such as who emits and transmits authoritative words, who has the decisive word in new situations or conflicts, who receives financial support for work in the Church or its mission, etc.

This investigation is an attempt to begin from the beginning of the ministry, order and polity. An attempt will be made to analyse the phenomena constituting the germs of the later ministry and polity, viz. the distribution of power and exercise of authority in the Primitive Church.

This type of investigation is not unlike that made by an anthropologist visiting a hitherto unknown tribe: he collects the phenomena as they appear

4. Cf. on the methodological necessity of syntheses *Riesenfeld* (1968).

5. *Bultmann's* "Theologie des Neuen Testaments", Tübingen 1953, is a well-known example of the influence of existentialist philosophy (Heidegger) on the interpretation of the New Testament.

and tries to organize them conceptually in structures of an ordinary social kind (kinship, system of customary law, financial organization, etc.). Naturally he wants to know why some people are considered wise or entitled to decide for others, i.e. why they are considered authoritative; this brings him into contact with the lore and myth of the tribe, which is a conceptual structure differing from his own. In spite of evident differences, this is the procedure used by any scholar of our century who treats the New Testament historically: he organizes the phenomena into conceptual structures (e.g. chronological order, relation to similar phenomena, probable influences between them, etc.) of which the original authors of the New Testament were either not conscious or which they did not find important enough to comment upon. Most New Testament texts, though perhaps reflecting the social structures of the Church, are not written to communicate information about them. Nonetheless they can be used in collecting such information without necessarily leading to a distortion of what they have to say on other matters.[6]

As no book of this size could comprise a full investigation of the historical phenomena pertaining to the distribution of power and exercise of authority in the Primitive Church, a limitation of the investigation must be made. Hence our concern here is with a historical study of the structure of authority in the Primitive Church as reflected in the Pauline epistles.

This means that I do not investigate the theology either of the Church, the apostolate, the divine Word, the sacraments, the worship, the church discipline or of any other phenomena of Church life. The opinions, interpretations and theologies of the actors will only be treated to the extent that they serve as evidence for the structure of authority. By "authority" is meant social relations of asymmetric power distribution considered legitimate by the participating actors. I do not analyse fully the content of the theories used to legitimate authority.[7] By "structure" is meant a totality or system of interdependent qualities or phenomena.[8]

The historical material for this investigation has been restricted to the

6. ". . . it is possible to put questions to all sorts and levels of literature—from Dickens to seaside postcards—to get it to yield information . . . which it was never written to provide. Yet it does not follow that the more it tells us of this, the less it tells us of what it is meant to be about", *Robinson* (1976:354).

7. The concept "authority" is discussed and defined in greater detail below, in Chapter 4.

8. My use of the term "structure" is not "structuralistic", i.e. postulating and analysing very general, "deep" structures of social life. Cf. *Piaget* (1971:97) and *Granger* (1973:210 ff, 228 ff) on the difference in this respect between Lévi-Strauss and sociologists such as Durkheim and Gurvitch. The structures we observe in the Primitive Church need not have been evident to the actors themselves, as they are latent organizing principles of social life, cf. *Piaget* (1971:97 f), *Naumann* (1973:4) and *Hennen-Prigge* (1977:13 f, 23 f).

genuine Pauline epistles, and as such I here consider Rom, 1 and 2 Cor, Gal, Phil, 1 Thess and Philem.[9] This means that I treat only information concerning the Pauline sphere or region of the Church. The choice is a deliberate one. It is methodologically necessary in a historical treatment of the Primitive Church to distinguish the separate regions of the Church from each other and follow one "trajectory" at a time.[10] A description of the authority structure within the Pauline trajectory would, however, be incomplete if Paul's (and the Gentile Mission's) relations with the church in Jerusalem were not treated at all. Therefore part of the investigation concerns the structure of authority in a larger part of the Primitive Church, and here the sources must be supplemented by critically sifted information from the Acts of the Apostles.

The main reason for choosing the Pauline trajectory before other possible ones is that it has been of central importance for the scholarly discussion of primitive church order since before the beginning of this century. It might not be unfair to say that, to many Protestant scholars from *Rudolph Sohm* to *von Campenhausen* and *Käsemann*,[11] and to some Catholic ones, e.g. *Küng* (1967), the Pauline trajectory is even of normative importance within the New Testament. Any new result or view-point, any valid criticism of prevailing opinions in this field thus promises to be of importance for the whole discussion of the ministry and authority in the Primitive Church.

My investigation has two parts, the first being a historical account of the distribution of power in the Primitive Church. Here I want to give a picture

9. These seven are generally considered to have been written by Paul while the authenticity of the others, 2 Thess, Col, Eph, 1 and 2 Tim, Tit has been discussed. In order to avoid burdening this investigation with a discussion of the complex questions of authenticity, and because an inclusion of at least the first three of these letters would (as far as I can see) not considerably alter the picture of authority in the Primitive Church, I have chosen to use only the first-named seven letters. If, however, the Pastoral Epistles were written by Paul, the picture of intra-church authority given in Chapter 3 would need revision.

On the historical value of the Acts of the Apostles, see the introductory remarks of Part I.

10. On the original diversity of the Primitive Church, see *Streeter* (1929), *Schille* (1966), *Dias* (1967), and on methodological conclusions from this fact see *Robinson* (1971), who together with Koester introduced the term "trajectory".

11. Protestant scholarship after the Second World War has not continued the "new consensus" of the 1930's and 1940's (on this, see *Skjevesland* 1976:17–22), but taken up again discussion, themes and opinions from the "old consensus" (of the 1880's) and from Rudolph Sohm. Bultmann's position approximates that of von Harnack and the "old consensus", *Brockhaus* (1975:22 n. 90; 31 f n. 157), *Skjevesland* (1976:22–25), while other scholars are closer to the position of Sohm: on von Campenhausen, see *Hainz* (1972:13), *Dreier* (1972:29–37) and *Brockhaus* (1975:36 f), on Käsemann see *Dreier* (1972:29–37) and *Brockhaus* (1975:41 f, 45 f), and on Schweizer see *Hainz* (1972:27) and *Brockhaus* (1975:42, 45).

of how power is distributed before I proceed to an analysis of which relations are considered legitimate and why they are so regarded.

When collecting the phenomena that constitute this picture I have of course begun by scrutinizing the sources. But I have not found it necessary to continue in the usual way of exegeting in detail every cited text. This is a practical methodological conclusion from the existence of a vast resource of reliable scholarly work on the texts. There is no point in presenting a detailed, painstaking analysis of the relevant texts when this would only amount to a repetition of well-known facts.

The practical conclusion to use and refer to the work of others when collecting and presenting historical data is, however, only a consequence of my theoretical methodological conclusion, that the important work of interpreting historical data must be reoriented. The predominantly theological interpretation of early Christian history, concentrating on the history of ideas, needs to be balanced by a different approach. I have chosen to interpret the data with categories taken from sociology, a field of scholarship seldom used by New Testament scholars.[12]

This does not need any special defence, as if the use of sociology (or economics, or psychology, or any other scientific approach) necessarily entailed a positivistic attitude toward the phenomena investigated, or any special insensitivity to the inner life of the Church.

> If and in what way a sociological examination of Primitive Christianity is feasible and to what degree it is appropriate, is possible to decide only by observing it used on the available sources, not by reflections on the "non-disposability of the faith" ("Unverfügbarkeit des Glaubens") or the "non-objectifiability of the kerygma" ("Nichtobjektivierbarkeit des Kerygmas") and other formulas, that could be abused in intimidating scientific curiosity, even if they are legitimate in other contexts.[13]

Naturally one has to be aware of the limitations of a sociological analysis of New Testament material. Such an enterprise cannot purport to be a full investigation of the reality concerned (but neither can a purely theological analysis!) and must at times appear crass in comparison with investigations sympathetically treating the opinions of the actors. But to analyse the actual distribution of power within the church of Corinth is not to deny that

12. To mention just one example where New Testament scholarship could (and should) have profited from a knowledge of sociology one can point to recent discussion on the alleged "domination-free" ("Herrschafts-freie") interaction and communication in the Primitive Church; cf. *Hoffmann-Eid* (1975:214–230) and *Löning* (1974:57–60). The latter is corrected in the same volume by *Iserloh* (1974:143 ff), who rightly stresses that charismatic communication is anything but "domination-free".

13. *Theissen* (1974c:37), my translation.

Paul is justified in defining prophecy or any other function in this church as a gift of the Holy Spirit; and to state that financial obligations are a manifestation of a power relation is not to deny that money could be given from kind and loving hearts. The sociological type of analysis represents, however, a very interesting type of analysis, revealing aspects of the Primitive Church which would otherwise have remained unknown.

As I mentioned above, Part I is a collection of historical data, most of which are familiar to everyone working in the field and largely uncontroversial. Here I attempt to give a synthetic, well-informed description of the distribution of power within the Primitive Church. In Chapter 1 I describe the relations between the leaders of the Jewish Christian church in Jerusalem and the leaders of the Gentile Christian church (especially Paul). In Chapter 2 I continue by describing the relations within the Pauline region of the Church, i.e. between Paul, his co-workers and his churches, and in Chapter 3 attention is focused on the relations within local Pauline churches.

Part II is an attempt at analysing the historical material in Part I in order to acquire a clearer understanding of the authority structure of the Primitive Church. According to the definitions given above, this means that I wish to describe the system of legitimate domination at work in the Church or, to use a somewhat anachronistic term, its (implicit) hierarchy. But a static diagram of organization showing who is over whom is not what is really interesting about a structure. We want to know something about the inner functioning of this system, what laws regulate it, how it develops and why.

This involves an analysis of how authority functions, and consequently I begin by investigating the structure of authority as such, i.e. the interdependence of the elements that constitute authority (Chapter 4). To decide to use sociology in the interpretation of authority means to discuss *Max Weber*'s classical sociology of authority, which still dominates this field. But since his death more than fifty years ago, his work has been criticized, defended and modified by numerous other sociologists, and I have tried to profit from this discussion.

Weber's theory of authority includes a typology distinguishing between traditional, rational-legal and charismatic authority, as well as many hypotheses on the inner functioning and transformations of the different types of authority. In Chapter 5 I discuss the concept of "charismatic authority" and attempt to determine the extent to which such authority functioned at different levels of the Church. This has been done to a certain extent by *Schütz* (1975), who uses *Weber*'s sociology, interpreted by *Parsons* and

Shils, to interpret Paul's theology of his own person and authority.[14] My own approach to *Weber* differs from *Schütz's,* mainly in that I use sociology in interpreting social phenomena concerning the authority of Paul and others.[15]

In *Weber's* terminology the Primitive Church should be described as manifesting the "routinization of charisma"; this is the subject of Chapter 6. I begin this by discussing the relation between this concept and the concept of "institutionalization" in modern sociology, and then try to analyse the development of the exercise of authority in the historical material with the help of these sociological categories.

Chapter 7 contains a short summary of the preceding discussion, and an attempt at drawing some methodological conclusions from what has been found to be the structure of authority and its nature in the Primitive Church.

14. *Schütz* (1975:16–20, 264–278).

15. The sociological approach to New Testament history is being increasingly used, after having made a start (that was never fulfilled) as early as sixty years ago with the form-historical approach, *Gewalt* (1971). The work of *de Haas* (1972) is mainly a treatise in systematic theology although it uses Weber and other sociologists to criticize Käsemann's views on Early Catholicism (pp. 87–110). Among other New Testament scholars using Weber's sociology can be mentioned *Gager* (1975, esp. pp. 67–76) and *Theissen* (1975a), who however confuses Weber's and Paul's conceptions of charisma in this essay (1975a:211, 215). Otherwise *Theissen* has given excellent discussions on questions of methodology concerning the use of sociology in New Testament research (1974c and 1975b), and his works generally manifest the fruitfulness of this approach. *K Berger* provides methodological discussions of a general kind, taking as his starting point the sociology of knowledge (1977b:218–241 and 1977c).

PART ONE

The Distribution of Power
in the Primitive Church

Before beginning to describe the distribution of power at different levels in the Primitive Church a preparatory discussion on what is meant by "power" is in place. This is not intended to be a technical discussion of theoretical sociology but will be limited to some remarks on the phenomena to be looked for to get a picture of how power is distributed within a social group which is not a formal organization in the modern sense.[1]

Social scientists are not unanimous in their definitions of "power",[2] but at this stage I do not want to go into the finer distinctions between different definitions of the concept. As a preliminary definition I have chosen that by *Etzioni*: power is "an actor's ability to induce or influence another actor to carry out his directives or any other norms he supports".[3] This broad, inclusive definition of power will be used throughout Part I, as it will permit me to treat a large range of power phenomena, including supernatural powers in human beings and power relations of which the participants are unaware or only partly aware.

Indications of this "ability to induce or influence another actor, etc." are in the first place phenomena belonging to relations of explicit superi-

1. Etzioni, following Parsons, defines organizations as "social units devoted primarily to attainment of specific goals" and elucidates by adding that in his book the term stands for "complex bureaucratic organizations", *Etzioni* (1961:XI n. 1). Bearing in mind the great difference between a modern complex organization and the aggregate of small local churches we call the Primitive Church, I have taken care to use only Etzioni's most general and abstract terminology, and to use his discussion of modern phenomena as heuristically useful but not directly transferable to the period I am examining.
2. Cf. *Bachrach-Baratz* (1972:29–50), *Hennen-Prigge* (1977:1–7) and any major dictionary of social science.
3. *Etzioni* (1961:4). Another attempt to conceptually structure the field of "power" is made by *Hartmann* (1964), who takes "influence" as his general category within which "power, force, manipulation, authority, etc." are placed.

ority and subordination. When we see that orders, admonitions, decisions and rebukes coming from one person (or group of persons) to another person (or group of persons) evoke a positive response we can state that there is an asymmetric distribution of power, i.e. one person exercises power over another.[4] If a particular person regularly exercises power we say that he has a power position.[5]

When all phenomena of this kind have been collected one can try to fit them together into a meaningful pattern, e.g. see whether there is more than one level of subordination or, in other words, an enduring hierarchical structure of power positions.

The degree of subordination can vary from very close control in almost every sphere of the life of the subject, to the other extreme where there is virtually no control and what there is of control is exercised only in one sphere of life.[6] There can be a high degree of subordination without formal organization. (The question of how power is legitimated does not belong to the strictly phenomenological field and will be discussed in Chapter 4.)

Related to the phenomena of explicit superiority and subordination and not easily distinguished from them are phenomena that indicate what can loosely be termed "word-power". This term refers to the fact that in most groups the exchange of verbal communication is asymmetric, not only as regards frequency but also as regards kind. Some people are listened to more than others, not primarily on account of their loquacity but because their words are considered to yield better information or judgement and are generally regarded as being wise and weighty. This may be "codified" in a set of rules about who may speak and where. (E.g., "Children should be seen and not heard". Women must be silent in the congregation, 1 Cor 14:34. After a general discussion the important men have the final and decisive word (Acts 15:5–22). Or the reverse, as in the Qumran community (1 QS VI:8–12): everybody may take part in the discussion, but the important men speak first and then the rest in a strictly descending order of rank.) Another universal phenomenon is the fact that sacred words, oracles, prophecies and revelations of divine wisdom are generally received as genuine only from certain kinds of people, "word-bearers" chosen and legitimated according to specified criteria, so as to ascertain that what is spoken really comes from a transhuman source.

Thus if we look at the flow of communication of authoritative words

---

4. *Etzioni* (1961:4). This does not mean that the subordinate actor is devoid of power, only that he has less.

5. *Idem*, p. 5.

6. *Idem*, p. 17.

(words listened to with respect)[7] and note that this flow is asymmetric (most of it comes from a small group of persons), there is reason to regard the "senders" as being the élite of the group. There is generally a close identity between the group that sends authoritative words and the group of power-position incumbents. The man with "word-power" can make willingly met demands on other members of his group or society that they shall "hear" him, which comes close to meaning "obey" him. They willingly accept and submit to his influence, which is normally not manifested in the form of explicit orders but rather in the form of teaching, instruction, recalling and interpreting the holy tradition, defining the situation and so on.[8]

Although I have now distinguished between verbal and practical behaviour denoting explicit superiority and subordination on the one hand and more general "word-power" corresponding to a readiness to be influenced by certain "senders" on the other, it is obvious that these two kinds of phenomena are better seen as lying at two different points on the same continuum. At one end of the continuum we have an asymmetric power relation of extreme explicitness and intensity (formal command, unquestioning and prompt obedience), at the other end a relation where the influence of one actor over another is discernible but not intense and not explicitly expressed. Thus I cannot concentrate my investigation of the distribution of power in the Primitive Church on expressions of explicit, more or less formalized power relations alone. I must also take into account what can be learnt about the more informal and hidden yet effective power structure by looking at the distribution of influential, authoritative words.

A third class of phenomena which we have to consider is the behaviour of subordinate actors when specifically oriented towards superior actors. The relation between actors in a power relation can be described as an unbalanced exchange relation. One party gives the orders, makes demands, speaks authoritative words and the other gives in return obedience, service, personal support and money. The subordinate actor has to "pay" in some way.

To get a clear picture of how power is distributed one must investigate not only the stream of authoritative words from the "senders" or superior actors but also the stream of service, support and money in the opposite

7. This is of course not an exact definition of "authority, authoritative". This concept will be discussed in greater detail in Chapter 4.

8. In a social system (a group or organization, for example) the direct order is not used in everyday relations ("ein Arbeitsmittel des Alltags"), but is a forceful, boundary-defining and boundary-enforcing measure, used in more extreme and precarious situations, and then only by superiors. Ordinarily, relations are upheld and the system made to function by communications of a less stringent type, *Luhmann* (1964:151 f).

direction from the "subjects" or subordinate actors. The mere existence of "payment" (a transfer of money or other goods) indicates the presence of influence in the social field. But to keep this within the phenomenon of power as defined above I shall restrict the investigation of "payment" to those situations where we have some indication that this is a response to a tacit or expressed demand from an actor whom we on other grounds have found to have some sort of power position.

Now we know in broad outline what will be treated in the following: explicit and implicit relations of superiority and subordination. And we shall expect to find them by collecting and interpreting phenomena of two kinds: (a) the stream of authoritative words and (b) the stream of obedience and support. The question I apply to the New Testament texts is to begin with simply this: Who is subordinate to the other, and in what degree? And I attempt to find the answer to that question by investigating who is at the receiving end of the two streams. By doing this I shall be able to establish the main facts of the power structure of the Primitive Church.

Not until this has been done (in Part I) can the investigation proceed to an analysis of what kinds of power we find in this community and why the power is distributed as it is or, in other words, to an analysis of the *authority* structure. This secondary analysis will constitute Part II of this work.

SOURCE-CRITICAL REMARKS

Our sources of information on the Primitive Church in the times of Paul are mainly the letters of Paul and the Acts of the Apostles. As is nowadays generally recognized the letters of Paul are primary sources, Acts secondary. The tendency to regard Acts as little more than a piece of romantic fiction from the end of the first century has, however, been decisively countered during the last decade.

Among the number of surveys of the literature on Acts published lately[9] *Grässer*'s survey in "Theologische Rundschau" 1976 and 1977 is the most up to date and gives a full account of what has been done in the field since 1960.

According to Grässer there seems to be a new tendency emerging. Scholars such as *Dibelius, Haenchen, Conzelmann, Klein, Schmithals* and *O'Neill* tend to see Acts as a late, strongly idealizing and theologizing literary composition reflecting the ("frühkatholisch") outlook which came to the fore around the end of the first century, and containing a slender amount of accurate historical information. Now a new generation of schol-

---

9. E.g. *Dupont* (1967), *Marshall* (1970) and *Gasque* (1975).

ars, *Burchard, Jervell, Löning, Marshall, Stolle* and *Wilson,* have continued the redaction-critical work of their predecessors but arrived at different results.

Luke is now no longer regarded as primarily a systematic theologian, still less a "frühkatholisch" one (*Wilson, Grässer*). His history of the Primitive Church is based on historical tradition, sometimes of a very fragmentary kind; he makes real mistakes here, but they are not intentional reinterpretations. The work of separating tradition from redaction has revealed a larger amount of factual, historical information than was formerly thought to be there. This applies to both Luke's information about facts and circumstances in contemporary history, politics and geography[10] and his knowledge of what happened in the earliest times of Church history.

A number of works on Paul in Acts exhibit the new tendency, e.g. the works of *Burchard* (1970) on the conversion of Paul in Acts, of *Stolle* (1973) on Paul on trial and of *Wilson* (1973) on the Gentile Mission in Acts.[11]

This shift towards a view of Acts which credits it with a generally higher degree of reliability as regards historical information seems to permit of a greater confidence in the use of information about Paul from Acts. I shall not, however, attempt a full analysis of those texts from Acts which are cited in the following as corroborating and sometimes supplementing the information from Paul's own letters, but shall content myself with referring the reader to scholarly discussions on them.

Of course this also applies to some extent to what will be said on the Pauline texts. The literature dealing with Paul's letters is boundless and I do not presume to do more than draw some conclusions from this discussion. It seems to me that there is something of a consensus on the main facts and lines of interpretation of Pauline texts, and it would be presumptuous not to acknowledge and make use of this.

When using texts from the letters of Paul as the main sources for historical reconstruction one must take account of both the special character of Paul's thinking and reasoning and the special, often controversial situations for which his letters are written (this applies in particular to Gal and 2 Cor). The character of Paul's thinking and the way he reasons has been described as dichotomizing, generalizing and simplifying, ruthlessly drawing out the consequences of underlying principles.[12] It is not unusual to find

---

10. This was pointed out early in this century by W. Ramsay, and lately by the classical scholar A.N. Sherwin-White.

11. Cf. *Grelot* (1971:465 f), *Hengel* (1972b:17 n. 11a) and *Mussner* (1974:127 n. 1, and 132 n. 13).

12. *Eckert* (1971:22–26), with numerous examples.

him engaged in putting forward his theological or practical view in marked contrast to what his readers think and practise.

Another fact of importance for the assessment of the historical value of these sources is the fact that Paul's relation to Jerusalem does not remain unchanged throughout his life as a Christian. Having begun as a persecutor of the Church he is still very much an outsider and a newcomer, especially to the Jerusalem church, during the first part of his life as a Christian. This he spent partly alone in distant regions (Gal 1:17b, 21) and partly as one of the "prophets and teachers" leading the Antiochene church.[13] We may presume that the two-week visit to Cephas c. A.D. 35 (Gal 1:18) convinced Cephas and James that Paul's conversion was genuine and that he had seen the Risen Lord and received His call to "evangelize". But not until about thirteen years later, at the Apostolic Council in Jerusalem is there any mention of recognizing Paul as apostle of Christ to the Gentiles, the equal of Cephas (Gal 2:7 f).

When we meet him in the major epistles the situation has changed. He is no longer a member of the leading gremium of Antioch, nor a missionary under Antioch accompanying Barnabas.[14] He has struck out on a great, independent, and successful missionary enterprise of his own, which has established beyond doubt his God-given grace as apostle to the Gentiles. He is now an independent and powerful leader with his own team of assistants, his own contacts in numerous local churches that he himself has founded, his own expansive planning (cf. Rom 15:19 ff) and a theological diction of great originality and depth.[15] With *Holtz* and many other writers I believe we must regard the Apostolic Council (Gal 2:1–10) and the Antioch Incident that followed close on it (Gal 2:11–14) as forming something of a watershed in Paul's development.[16]

---

13. *Idem,* p. 178. Cf. *Gerhardsson* (1961:262 f) about which characteristics Paul must have been lacking in the eyes of the Jerusalem church.

14. On the relation between Paul and Barnabas, see Chapter 2.

15. It is only after the Council and the Antioch Incident that Paul develops his habit of using letters as a medium for apostolic work, *Holtz* (1974:147 n. 5).

16. *Holtz* (1974, passim), *Stuhlmacher* (1968:106 f), *Maly* (1969:77 f), *Mussner* (1974:187).

CHAPTER 1
The Distribution of Power
within the Church—Paul and Jerusalem

A. FROM THE CONVERSION TO THE ANTIOCH INCIDENT

1. The Tendency of Paul's Report

Paul writes Gal 1-2 in the latter part of his life. The events he treats of belong to the earlier part of his Christian period[17] and have been given a very unfavourable interpretation by people in Galatia who, as Paul well knows, have the hearing of his "own" Galatians. This is a contributory cause of the tendentious record of what happened in Paul's earlier life, especially in connection with the church in Jerusalem.[18] The word "tendentious" does not mean that Paul is making deliberately false statements. That is precluded for instance by Gal 1:20 where Paul takes God as witness to the fact that he is speaking the truth.[19] But it means that his perspective is strongly dominated by his own (later) theological interpretation of his own apostolate and his need to explain and defend this.

Commentators do not agree as to what it was Paul was accused of by his opponents in Galatia. Either it was said (a) that he had showed too great a measure of independence (by treacherously concealing the necessity of

---

17. *Haenchen* (1965:61 et passim) has argued the importance of this.

18. *Stuhlmacher* characterizes Paul's description as throughout tendentious ("durchaus tendenziös"), (1968:85). *Schlier* calls the report "die auf das apologetisch Notwendige konzentrierten Berichte" and says that it is formed "unter dogmatisch relevanten Gesichtspunkten", even if dates and facts are correct (1971:112). Cf. *Theissen* on another polemical Pauline text (2 Cor 10-13): "Seine (sc. Pauli) Objektivität bei der Wiedergabe der Aussagen anderer muss bezweifelt werden" (1975c:206).

19. *Kasting* (1969:77 n. 71), *Nickle* (1966:41) and *Robinson* (1976:36). Like most of the commentators, *Sampley* (1977) limits the reference of 1:20 to the preceding two verses, but argues that the oath is made at the most sensitive point of Paul's argument: the first contact with the Jerusalem apostles. The taking of a voluntary oath in a conflict was regarded as a very significant action in Roman legal custom; it could sometimes close a lawsuit before it was opened.

circumcision, thus "pleasing men", Gal 1:10),[20] or (b) that he showed too little independence to be considered the equal of the other apostles (cf. Gal 1:11 f).[21] In any case it seems clear that his "gospel" and his person were thought to be incomplete and lacking in full authority. Paul's answer to this defamation is a vigorous explanation of his own position as an apostle against suspicions, misunderstandings and false reports.[22] *Stuhlmacher* summarizes:

> Paulus hat aus der Rückshau ein Ereignis zu interpretieren, welches in stärkstem Masse für seine Gegner und zu seinen eigenen Ungunsten zu sprechen schien.—Die paulinische Tendenz ist offensichtlich auch in Gal. 2 die, Eigenständigkeit und Unabhängigkeit seines Apostolates und seiner Botschaft zu erweisen.[23]

Although this tendency is obvious we should beware of oversimplifying Paul's intention in Gal 1-2. On the one hand it is quite clear that from Gal 1:1 to 1:12 and through the report of 1:18—2:14 Paul is stressing the God-given independence of his apostolate. On the other hand it is also quite clear that he does not repudiate other authority than his own nor is he out to minimize his contacts with Cephas and the other "pillars" in Jerusalem. He is careful to point out to his opponents and detractors the incontrovertible fact that he was officially and irreversibly acknowledged by the Jerusalem "pillars" as Apostle to the Gentiles, with a competence and a "gospel" of his own (Gal 2:6-9).[24] The dialectic between being independent of and being acknowledged by Jerusalem is the keynote of this important text and must not be forgotten.

2. Paul, Antioch and Jerusalem Up to the Apostolic Council

It cannot be denied that the first part of Paul's report on his dealings with Jerusalem is dominated by what has been called "alibi-reasoning" ("I was not there"). From his conversion and onwards he has been utterly inde-

---

20. *Georgi* (1965:36 n. 113), *Roloff* (1965:66), *Kasting* (1969:121), *Eckert* (1971: 217), *Holtz* (1974:116), *Schütz* (1975:130) and *Wilckens* (1974:132): "Er habe die nötige Subordination seiner Mission unter die Jerusalemer Autoritäten aufgegeben".

21. *Gerhardsson* (1961:264), *Stuhlmacher* (1968:65–68), who thinks Paul was accused of being a mere delegate or missionary from the Antiochene church, and *Schlier* (1971:22).

22. *Linton* (1949) considered that the need for Paul to give a scrupulously true account of his dealings with Jerusalem to the Galatians points to their knowledge of another and different version of the same events, a version that influenced Luke's picture of Paul in Acts. This much-cited hypothesis has lately been criticized by *Burchard* (1970:159 f) on methodological grounds.

23. *Stuhlmacher* (1968:85). Cf. *Bonnard* (1956:26, 35), *Gerhardsson* (1961:263 f), *Eckert* (1971:177 and 210) and *Mussner* (1974:126).

24. *Holtz* (1974:118), *Wilckens* (1974:133).

pendent, and this is shown by what happened to him immediately after. In Gal 1:16 f he points out three things: (a) he did not confer with any human being, (b) he did not go up to Jerusalem but to Arabia and (c) even when he returned he did not go up to Jerusalem but went back to Damascus (where his conversion had presumably taken place). Nobody asked him to go to Jerusalem and he had no need to do so, that must be the conclusion Paul wanted his readers to draw. Even in these introductory verses we sense the importance of Jerusalem: the very fact of not having been there is of significance.

But three years later (or rather, as inclusive reckoning is probably intended: in the third year after this) Paul did go up to Jerusalem, and the choice of the verb ἱστορῆσαι in Gal 1:18 is anything but unintentional. The verb means "to visit, to get to know, to inquire about, to gather information (from someone)",[25] and is chosen to stress the fact that Paul did not go up to Jerusalem in order to make a report to Cephas or anything like that. "Der Anschein soll entstehen, dass sich die beiden Apostel als gleichberechtigte Partner begegnen".[26] Yet not only lexical but also historical reasons indicate that Paul really did get information from Cephas during these two weeks, even if this was not the purpose of his journey.[27] *Gerhardsson* has shown that in the Jewish context where both Cephas and Paul belong there was a custom when two teachers met (or pupils of teachers who were doctrinal authorities): "the word of the Torah 'was between them' ",[28] and they exchanged information about doctrinal statements from their own teachers and predecessors.

> —if Paul in Jerusalem were the same man as the Paul of the epistles, we can almost guess what the two men did. A Paul does not go up to Jerusalem to Peter, 'the Rock', merely in order to talk about the weather (Dodd). And a man with Peter's commission does not waste a fortnight talking rubbish. It can be little doubt that during this time the word of Christ 'was between them'—.[28]

In other words tradition about Jesus was passed on from Cephas to Paul.

25. The meaning "to get information from" has been stressed especially by *Kilpatrick* (1959).
26. *Roloff* (1965:67). Cf. *Stuhlmacher* (1968:84), *Bonnard* (1953:33), *Eckert* (1971:179). *Mussner* even calls it a kind of "courtesy visit", without any intention of seeking association with the other apostles (1974:95). This may be going a bit too far in de-dramatizing the visit.
27. *Brown-Donfried-Reumann* (1973:23 f n. 52).
28. *Gerhardsson* (1961:298), who also mentions that this is a more probable source of Paul's knowledge about Jesus (not all of it, though) than "that more or less hypothetical entity 'the Hellenistic Community' ", p. 299. See also *Cerfaux* (1965: 355). For a criticism of the concept of "Hellenistic Community", see *Larsson* (1964), *Hengel* (1972a:47–57) and *Marshall* (1972/73).

Roloff has remarked that it is not Paul's foremost intention to make little of this meeting[29] and describe it as devoid of significance in which case he could have refrained from mentioning the number of days at all. On the contrary he wants to emphasize that for a whole fortnight he stayed with Cephas, and, it is implied, talked as one Apostle with another, having ample time to confirm the complete agreement that existed between them.[30]

Of the period following Paul's first visit to Jerusalem we know very little. He tells us that he went to the regions of Syria and Cilicia (the province where he was born) "and was still not known by sight to the churches of Christ in Judea" who, however, heard about his missionary work in the north, Gal 1:21–23. Paul thus does not "evangelize" on orders from Cephas or the church in Jerusalem, nor does he do it in regions under their supervision as would have been the case had he preached in the "churches of Judea". If he had stayed in Jerusalem or Judea as an apostle, which would not have been an unnatural thing to do, he would have been in a subordinate position vis-à-vis Jerusalem. Just to quench any possible rumours or suspicions, Paul makes quite clear that he was engaged in independent apostolic work, which was gladly recognized by the Jewish Christian churches.

The rest of the information we have about Paul from this period is supplied by Acts. As this does not touch directly on his relations with the church in Jerusalem, I shall not go deeply into this. We can note, however, that a number of scholars find historical truth in Acts 11:25 f, which tells how Barnabas came from Antioch to Tarsus in Cilicia and took Paul with him back to work in the church of Antioch,[31] and in Acts 13:1, where Paul is counted (as the last) among the "prophets and teachers" of this church. The close association between Barnabas and Paul is witnessed by the report in Acts 13–14 on "the first missionary journey", which they undertook together, and by Paul himself (Gal 2:1, 9, 13; 1 Cor 9:6). It is difficult to ascertain how much correct historical information we have in Acts 13–14[32] —this and other "journeys" have been thought of as Lukan constructions —but it does not seem rash to state that during part of the forties Paul was one of the leaders of the Antiochene church and that together with Barnabas he was sent out by this church as their "apostle" or missionary.[33]

---

29. So e.g. *Oepke* (1973:63 n. 46), *Schlier* (1971:60).
30. *Roloff* (1965:68).
31. *Pieper* (1926:82 f), *Dix* (1953:32), *Goppelt* (1966:62), *Maly* (1969:73), *Bornkamm* (1969:51 f), and *Holtz* (1974:111 n. 1). Against this: *Haenchen* (1971: 367).
32. See *Catchpole* (1977:438 f) for a discussion of the historicity and location in time of the journey.
33. More about this period in Paul's life in Chapter 2.

3. Paul at the Apostolic Council

We find Paul and Barnabas together also at the Apostolic Council from which we have reports in Gal 2:1–10 and Acts 15:4–29.[34] The former text is undoubtedly our only source of primary evidence of what happened at the Council, and yet this report "is not distinguished by its dispassionate objectivity".[35] This means that we have to use this text with some caution, aware of the necessity of sometimes distinguishing between Pauline account and historical reality (cf. my initial remarks).

(a) What was the position of Paul at the Council?

Anybody reading Paul's report in Gal 2:1–10 must get "the impression that he stood quite alone before the 'pillars', their equal and a match for them. This impression is deceptive".[36] Paul was in reality, together with his equal Barnabas, a delegate from the church of Antioch.[37] The only sign of this in Paul's report, apart from the "with Barnabas" in v 1, is the mention of the fact in v 9 that the "pillars" gave to him *and Barnabas* the right hand of fellowship. This signifies, not just a cordial farewell at the end of the proceedings or a personal acknowledgement of the two Gentile missionaries (with Barnabas probably enjoying the higher status in both Antioch and Jerusalem[38]), but the making of a formal agreement between two churches. The question that was discussed at the Council was not primarily the nature of Paul's or Barnabas's apostolate but whether the Antiochene church could continue its practice of not circumcising Gentile converts.[39]

The church of Antioch at the time of the Council does regard itself as bound to the mother church in Jerusalem. The fact that it sends delegates[40]

---

34. With most commentators I take Acts 15 to be a description of the same event as that in Gal 2:1–10, but still inferior to the latter as a historical source. I refer to *Mussner's* excursus on the "Apostelkonzil" (1974:127–132) and the literature he cites there.

35. *Gerhardsson* (1961:263).

36. *Haenchen* (1971:465).

37. This seems to be a rather common opinion today. See *Haenchen* (1965 and 1971), *Georgi* (1965:14), *Stuhlmacher* (1968:67, 85, 98), *Kasting* (1969: 106), *Holtz* (1974:114, 128) and *Schütz* (1975:138).

38. Acts 4:36 f and 9:27 indicate that Barnabas was well-known in the Jerusalem church before Paul's conversion. And 11:22 ff together with the list of names in 13:1 permit the same conclusion for their respective positions in Antioch.

39. *Haenchen* (1965:62).

40. Many commentators are of the opinion that no antithesis exists between Paul's assertion that he went up to Jerusalem "by revelation" κατα ἀποκαλυψιν (Gal 2:2a) and the statement in Acts 15:2 that he was sent with Barnabas as a delegate of the Antiochene church. See *Bonnard* (1953:36 n. 3), *Stuhlmacher* (1968:85, 87), *Eckert* (1971:184), *Haenchen* (1971:464), *Schlier* (1971:66), *Oepke* (1973:83), *Mussner* (1974:102), *Schütz* (1975:139) and *Larsson* (1976:8). *Nickle* points out (1966: 42 n. 5) that ἀποκαλυψις is never used by Paul of any communication mediated by another human being, for which reason Paul's assertion must not be made to mean

to Jerusalem in order to present its missionary preaching and practice for approval is clear evidence of this.[41] The Antiochene Christians saw in Jerusalem the salvation-historical centre of the Church, which obviously had certain legal consequences.[42] This seems to have been the common opinion among the first Christians, that Jerusalem was the centre of the rapidly growing Church.[43] This was owing to its role as the Holy City and theologico-juridical centre of Judaism, and to the fact that this was the place where Christ had died and risen, where the Spirit had been effused, and where the Apostles of Christ resided, they being the guardians of the divine Word, that tradition of and from Jesus which had gone out from Jerusalem.[44] This Antiochene attitude is corroborated by Gal 2:12 f as we shall see further on.

> Damals verdankte er (sc. Paulus) seine Autorität der Gemeinde Antiochias; seine Autorität war—um es einmal überscharf auszudrücken—abgeleitet von der Antiochias. Auf dieser ruhte sie im Grunde.

This is *Haenchen's* conclusion [45] and although drastically worded it expresses a fact that is normally not realized by the numerous scholars who share the opinion that Paul was a delegate for the Antiochene church: the nature of Paul's presence and influence is not defined by himself. The limits for his action are determined by the church of Antioch, which moreover is represented in Jerusalem quite as well by Paul's older colleague Barnabas. Whatever interpretation Paul put on the nature of his commission, then or later, it is a historical and sociological fact that this was primarily defined by the other actors in the situation: Barnabas and the church of Antioch with their expectations and Cephas, James and the Jerusalem church with theirs.

(b) What was actually agreed on at the Council?

In spite of the fact that we have two different accounts of the Council

---

only an utterance from a prophet during a prayer-meeting, as *Georgi* (1965:16) and *Stuhlmacher* (1968:87) understand it.

41. See especially *Stuhlmacher* (1968:87). *Georgi* is of the contrary opinion when he calls the two churches "partners" and refuses to see any inequality implied in the proceedings (1965:17).

42. "Für die Antiochener wäre also Jerusalem immerhin der (heilsgeschichtliche?) Vorort der Kirche gewesen, und diese Auffassung hatte offensichtlich auch gewisse rechtliche Konsequenzen", *Stuhlmacher* (1968:87), cf. *idem*, p. 282, "Jerusalem geniesst einen heilsgeschichtlichen und sakralrechtlichen Vorrang vor seinen Tochtergemeinden".

43. *Bultmann* (1953:62), *Lohse* (1964:333), *Eckert* (1971:215, with n. 1), *Brown-Donfried-Reumann* (1973:45–49).

44. *Gerhardsson* (1961:274–280).

45. *Haenchen* (1965:63). Cf. *Schütz* (1975:155) Paul "derived his 'authority' from that relationship (sc. the relationship with Antioch)".

which agree in the main, it is not easy to state exactly what the agreement between the Jerusalem and Antioch churches did comprise.

The majority of scholars place the origin of the so-called "Apostolic Decree" (Acts 15:29) at a later date than that of the Council, as Paul does not seem to know about it when writing Gal or 1 Cor.[46] It is probable that this Decree did not form part of the original Council agreement.

We can limit ourselves to the decision on or, more exactly, to the mutual acknowledgement of the Antiochene practice—new or old[47]—of not circumcising those Gentiles who became Christians.[48] But it is not easy to say exactly what this entailed as it does seem to have been open to interpretation. Paul himself sees it as an irreversible approval of his own law-free "gospel", including his missionary methods and their consequences.[49] Paul's Judaistic opponents in Galatia gave a radically different interpretation of the same events:[50] they regarded Paul as preaching a gospel that had been accommodated to what men (i.e. the Gentiles) could accept (Gal 1:10 f). He had left out the absolutely vital condition which had to be met when a Gentile was to become a Christian, namely circumcision. Somehow he had managed to talk the Jerusalem leaders, the real Apostles with full authority, into condoning this concession to the Gentile mission of Antioch. But the subsequent conflict in Antioch concerning Jews and Gentiles eating together had unmistakably shown that this concession had been grossly over-interpreted by Paul as entailing abrogation of the Law.

This conflict (which will be discussed in greater detail below) indeed supplies the clearest evidence that the question of whether Jewish and uncircumcised Gentile Christians could eat together or not was not part of the agreement in Jerusalem. This seems to have been aimed rather at separating Christian Jews and Gentiles from one another than at uniting them as a single body of believers.[51] The question of what amount of Torah-

---

46. For a discussion on the Decree see *Brown-Donfried-Reumann* (1973:51–54) and *Fitzmyer* (1970a:§72–77). *Strobel* (1974) argues that Gal is written against the background of a knowledge of the Decree in Galatia, and *Hurd* (1965) thinks that it was known in Corinth when Paul wrote 1 Cor. For a more detailed discussion of this I must refer to my forthcoming article on the relations between Jewish and Gentile Christians before A.D. 70.

47. *Holtz* argues (contrary to the usual view) that the policy of not circumcising Gentiles was rather a *novum* in Antiochene missionary practice and not something that had been silently tolerated by the Jerusalem church for more than a decade (1974:130–141).

48. The acknowledgement of Paul's apostolate as being equal to Cephas's and the agreement on the collection for Jerusalem will be treated further on.

49. *Haenchen* (1965:64).

50. We may dimly perceive them behind Gal 1:7, 2:4 and the whole argument in this letter. My description of their views follows the reconstructions of *Kasting* (1969:121 f), *Eckert* (1971:203 f) and *Jewett* (1971b:208).

51. *Eckert* (1971:221).

observance was to be demanded from the Gentile Christians if common meals were to be permitted was in all probability not discussed at all. The mere acknowledgement of Antiochene non-circumcision missionary practice among Gentiles strained the tolerance of the Jerusalem church to its utmost limits.[52] Anything beyond this concession, which really does speak well for the courage and openness to the Spirit among the Jerusalem leaders, would have been absolutely unthinkable at the time. It is not surprising that the question of what this decision would eventually entail for the Jewish Christians did not concern the leaders in Jerusalem at that time.[53] To the Jerusalem leaders this was a concession made to Antioch and an acknowledgement that this church had a "Sendungs- und Interessensphär"[54] of its own. It was a large concession, but made no difference to their own situation. Paul, who was a more thorough and logical thinker, sees that this agreement will and must have far-reaching, fundamental consequences even for the Jewish Christians themselves, at least in their dealings with the Gentile Christians. As it was this concession was of immense consequence for the future (*Mussner* calls the result a "theological victory for Paul"[55]). But even Paul cannot summarize the result of the proceedings as anything like "freedom from the Law was fundamentally and generally conceded".

We thus have at least three different interpretations of the Jerusalem agreement: (a) Paul's, at the "liberal" extreme, (b) the "rigorist" interpretation of Paul's Judaistic opponents who unlike Cephas and James did not concede anything to Paul and (c) the interpretation of Cephas, James, and Barnabas[56] and the Jerusalem and Antiochene churches behind them. The last interpretation was the "middle", reasonable and generally held interpretation, while Paul's version is a "radical" (but as history was to show, theologically legitimate) over-interpretation of the agreement, and the Judaistic version a strongly "conservative" and distorting under-interpretation. The agreement was made between two churches and dealt with an important but limited question, namely whether the Antiochene church should continue its practice of not circumcising those Gentiles who were baptized into the Christian fellowship. As is revealed to the Antioch

---

52. *Haenchen* (1965:66), *Kasting* (1969:122).
53. *Kasting, ibidem, Nickle* (1966:63), *Oepke* (1973:86 f).
54. *Stuhlmacher* (1968:99).
55. *Mussner* (1974:127 n. 131) "Theologisch gesiegt hat in der Urkirche Paulus". This assertion is substantiated at length in *Mussner* (1976:77–121).
56. *Holtz* concludes that the separation between Paul and Barnabas (*cum* Antioch) essentially was a consequence of the Jerusalem agreement and the fact that they interpreted this differently. The Antioch Incident merely revealed the existing difference (1974:114).

Incident there was no discussion of any general, clearly defined freedom from the Law for the Gentile Mission in its relations with Christians of Jewish descent.

(c) Paul's interpretation of the Council

Paul states the purpose of his journey to Jerusalem in Gal 2:2b: "I laid before them (but privately before those who were of repute, οἱ δοκοῦντες,[57]) the gospel which I preach among the Gentiles, lest somehow I should be running or had run in vain" (Barnabas has already dropped out of the picture!). The meaning of "laid before" ἀνατιθέναι in this context is more exactly rendered by "presented for approval".[58] The following μὴ πως clause ("lest somehow . . .") strengthens this interpretation. All other uses of μὴ πως in Paul's letters (1 Cor 9:27, 2 Cor 2:7, 9:4, 11:3, 12:20, Gal 4:11, 1 Thess 3:5) refer to a real, not hypothetical, possibility which makes improbable a translation of this clause by an indirect hypothetical question "lest they somehow dare say I had run in vain".[59] Paul entertained some apprehensions about his own work and how it would be looked upon in Jerusalem, and that, according to his own words, was why he went there, ordered by God "by revelation". We shall return to the question of what he may have feared.

In v 3-5 Paul describes somewhat obscurely the decision made on the central question of circumcision. Titus, who was a Greek, had been brought to Jerusalem by Paul perhaps to use him as a provocation and a test case. If he was obliged to be circumcised the Judaists would have won their case, but if not then the case would be resolved in favour of Antioch and the Gentile Mission. To judge from Paul's vocabulary the contention was a sharp one. These few verses contain quite a number of terms belonging to the semantic field of power and subordination "compel, to spy out our freedom, bring into bondage, yield, submission" (ἀναγκάζειν, κατασκοπεῖν τὴν ἐλευθερίαν ἡμῶν, καταδουλεύειν, εἴκειν, ὑποταγῇ). The demand of those "false

---

57. *Kasting* gives a list of the scholars who identify "those of repute" οἱ δοκοῦντες with "the pillars" (οἱ στῦλοι): Barrett, Lietzmann, Oepke, Bornkamm, Foerster, Hahn, Dinkler (1969:98 n. 82). To these can be added: *Mussner* (1974:120) and *Schütz* (1975:141 n. 1). *Kasting* himself suports the group of scholars who think that οἱ στῦλοι is the inner circle of a larger group of δοκοῦντες (ibidem, n. 83): Bonnard, Jülicher-Fascher, Käsemann, Schlier, Zahn.

58. So *Bauer* (1958:123) "zur Begutachtung vorlegen", *Stuhlmacher* (1968:87), *Schlier* (1971:66) and *Holtz* (1974:121). *Gerhardsson* specifies "presented his gospel for the approval of the highest doctrinal court" (1961:276).

59. *Brown-Donfried-Reumann* (1973:28, with n. 64) discuss and turn down this translation, as do *Kasting* (1959:117 n. 166), *Schlier* (1971:67 f) and *Holtz* (1974: 121 n. 5), with criticism of *Georgi*'s misleading paraphrase (1965:19).

brethren"[60] that Titus be circumcised is described as an attack on "our" (the Gentile apostles', and included therein the Gentile Christians')[61] freedom. Any attack on the missionary practice of Antioch is in itself an attack on the truth of Paul's and Barnabas's gospel and an attempt to disqualify their authority as apostles.[62] Any concession here would entail submission and slavery. We notice that for Paul the contention does not merely concern doctrine (as if such pure questions existed), but is also inseparable from the question of spiritual supremacy and distribution of power. Truth and authority are intertwined.

More light is thrown on the factual dependency relation, which 2:2 witnesses, by the terminology in 2:6 "those of repute imposed nothing on me" (ἐμοὶ γὰρ οἱ δοκοῦντες οὐδὲν προσανέθεντο). The verb here has the meaning "to impose something on someone",[63] which forces us to the conclusion that "Paulus durchaus mit der Möglichkeit einer rechtskräftigen Auflage von seiten Jerusalems für die Arbeit der Antiochener rechnen kann".[64]

We have no formulated theory in Pauline texts stating why and to what extent the Apostles of Jerusalem can give legally binding injunctions to other churches and their apostles, but this does not do away with the fact that, at the time of the Council, this power did exist. It may seem superfluous to state that fact often precedes theory about that selfsame fact, but this is nevertheless overlooked by those who try to draw conclusions about power allocation in the Primitive Church only from the theology of Paul.[65]

60. *Schmithals* (1963:89–99) and *Nickle* (1966:46–49) have advanced the hypothesis that the "false brethren" were not Christians but nationalistic Jews, who on false premises had been brought into the proceedings of the church by their Jewish Christian sympathizers. This proposal has not met with general approval.

61. *Mussner* (1974:108 f). *Georgi* thinks that this Judaistic attack was the real cause of the Council, and that Paul and Barnabas were sent to Jerusalem, not because Antioch harboured any doubts about the rightness of non-circumcision of Gentiles, but because this church wanted the (majority of the) Jerusalem church to draw up a clear line of demarcation with the Judaists (1965:15 f).

62. *Schlier* characterizes the attitude of the opponents as "Instanzenbewusstsein" (1971:71 f). On the intimate connection between the gospel and the apostle, and how the validity of the one affects the authority of the other, see *Stuhlmacher* (1968:56–108) and *Schütz* (1975:35–53).

63. *Bauer* (1958:1411), *Bonnard* (1953:40) "prescribe", *Gerhardsson* (1961:279), *Schlier* (1971:74) and *Oepke* (1973:79) who gives a thorough discussion.

64. *Stuhlmacher* (1968:91), "ein Hinweis darauf, dass wir uns im Rahmen einer rechtlich orientierten Denkweise befinden". Cf. *idem*, p. 87 f, 98, 100, 103 f and *Schütz* about Gal 2:6 ff, "Here the tone and vocabulary suggest more the official and ecclesiastical than the personal dimension of such recognition" (1975:147).

65. *Mussner* criticizes Gerhardsson's comparison of the relation between Paul and Jerusalem with the relation between a rabbi and his rabbinical college (cf. n. 58 above) on account of Paul's own view of himself in Gal 1:1, which does not permit any superior authority (1974:115 n. 84). This amounts to an avoidance of the historical question of what the distribution of power really was by transforming it to a question concerning what Paul thought of his own apostolate.

A careful reading of our text shows that Paul's attitude to "those who were apostles before me" (Gal 1:17) is somewhat ambivalent. On the one hand he implicitly recognizes their authority to judge his gospel (2:2), but on the other he is expressly independent and declares that he has his gospel directly from a divine revelation, which nobody, not even himself, has control over (e.g. 1:8, 12). This ambivalence is seen in his way of referring to the other apostles with "mild irony"[66] and generally in his report of the Council. In spite of his consciousness of the exalted prestige of the original Apostles in the Church, he has not simply accepted this or regarded their earlier commission as Apostles as a source of higher authority.[67]

A phrase that has been much discussed as witnessing Paul's independence is the parenthesis he makes in 2:6, "what they were . . ." (ὁποῖοί ποτε ἦσαν). Perhaps Paul wants to keep his distance from the (exaggerated or wrongly reasoned) high esteem in which "those of repute" were held especially in Jerusalem. Either his intention was to show that he is not inferior to them[68] (and the facts of the case do indeed give this impression[69]), or else his intention is to remove the question of the prestige of the other Apostles from the really relevant perspective of the whole course of events. This perspective is the truth of the gospel, to put it shortly. The Jerusalem Apostles did not impose anything on him; in this they obeyed the Gospel, and it is in this, and not in some rank or prestige, that their true importance lies.[70] A third possibility is that the phrase refers to a certain part of the past lives of the "pillars", viz. their custom of circumcising converted Gentiles, a custom that Paul's opponents in Galatia knew of and had declared to be normative. Paul dissociates himself, and the Apostles, from this fact of the past, by his parenthesis and by his reference to what was agreed upon

---

66. *Barrett* (1973b:31) and (1953:3, 17), cf. *Eckert* (1971:188). All commentators do not agree on interpreting οἱ δοκοῦντες as irony, see e.g. *Burton* (1921:71 f). *Roloff* speaks about the "schillernde Zweideutigkeit" of the phrase (1965:71), and *Käsemann* considers it was used in earnest first and only later ironically (1942:43 n. 82).

67. *Stuhlmacher* (1968:88), *Mussner* (1974:91 n. 64).

68. *Georgi* (1965:20), *Stuhlmacher* (1968:92). *Kasting* objects that this is improbable in a context where it is important for Paul to use the fact of their recognition of his gospel (1969:118 f).

69. *Stuhlmacher* states that the "pillars" stood *between* the two fronts (1971:86), and this may be a correct description of their attitude to the point at issue before the Council. But in the process of decision at the Council nothing could be more obvious than the fact that "the pillars" stand *over* the two fronts and from this position decide the point at issue to the advantage of Antioch.

70. *Schütz* (1975:142), *Mussner* (1974:114), *Oepke* (1973:78), *Pedersen* (1977: 114).

in Jerusalem.[71] It is difficult to draw conclusions with certainty about how Paul regarded the Jerusalem Apostles just from his way of expressing himself here. This question should be answered in the context of a broader and more fundamental question: Was unity with the Jerusalem Apostles a *theological* necessity for Paul or only a *pragmatic* necessity? We touched on this problem when discussing the meaning of Gal 2:2b and can take this clause as our starting-point. What did Paul fear? Some think that he feared that the non-approval of "his (and the Antiochene) gospel" would split the Church into two, a Jewish Christian church observing the Torah and a Gentile Christian Church without the Torah and without any deeper communion with its origin.[72] On the other hand it can be objected that the Antioch Incident shortly after the Council shows that the unity of the Church is not of supreme value for Paul (the supreme value is the truth of the Gospel).[73] And although Paul does not seem to have entertained doubts about the truth of his gospel and what he was doing as a missionary to the Gentiles,[74] is it really unthinkable that Paul at this (rather early) point in his apostolic career could have felt some uncertainty or hesitation about the correctness of his own, new interpretation of the revelation he had received from the Risen Christ?[75] His apprehensions may have been of a serious, theological nature, and not only consisted of a hope that there would not be too many difficulties or compromise proposals in the acknowledgement process.

Holtz has shown that Phil 2:16 is the key to a correct understanding of Paul's fears in Gal 2:2. His commission from Christ is to found churches that will stand on the Day of Judgement. If they do not do this the apostle will be shown to be a failure, then he has "run in vain". This is what Paul feared at the Council: to have failed in his task of building churches.[76] Of course he knows that his work has resulted in communities of Christ-believers, but his question in Jerusalem was:

71. *Kasting* (1969:120). Against this interpretation stands the fact that it leaves the second half of the parenthesis unexplained. προσωπον λαμβανειν ("show partiality") seems to have something to do with a person's prestige rather than with a past demeanour.

72. Closest to this pragmatic interpretation come *Haenchen* (1971:465) and *Kasting* (1969:117).

73. *Holtz* (1974:123).

74. *Schütz* (1975:140). Cf. *Burton* (1921:72 f), *Bonnard* (1953:37 f), *Mussner* (1974:103).

75. "But at the period of his second visit to Jerusalem, some years before he wrote to the Galatians, was he so certain of his interpretation of that revelation (sc. Gal 1:12) that he did not have to fear a rejection of it by men who had known Jesus personally?" *Brown-Donfried-Reumann* (1973:28 n. 62). *Nickle* considers that Paul may have entertained doubts about whether he started the Gentile Mission too early (1966:43), i.e. whether he had interpreted his revelation correctly.

76. *Holtz* (1974:122). The same interpretation by *Schlier* (1971:68).

ob solche Gemeinschaft dann auch wirklich Gemeinde des Jesus Christus ist, der Ursprung und Inhalt des Evangelium ist. Diese Gemeinde wird allein durch das Evangelium konstitutiert.[77]

As there is only *one* Gospel (Gal 1:6–10) it is absolutely vital that Paul's missionary preaching and practice are in accord with the Gospel—if not, he has run in vain. And this question can only be answered in Jerusalem, by the other apostles:

Vom Ursprung seiner (sc. Pauli) Berufung her gehört zu ihr wesenhaft die Identität des ihm erschienenen Auferstandenen mit dem, den die Auferstehungszeugen vor ihm als den Auferstandenen bezeugen.—So war Jerusalem der Ort, an dem die Identität des Evangeliums, zu dem sich Paulus berufen wusste, mit dem, zu dem er sich berufen glaubte, festgestellt werden konnte und musste.[78]

In whatever way it was formulated (if it ever existed outside Paul's mind at all), the question from Paul to the notables of Jerusalem was whether *his* gospel was identical with and conformed to the one and only Gospel.[79]

The apostles of Jerusalem, and especially the Twelve, had an "eschatological uniqueness", consisting in the fact that they were the "indispensable connecting links between the historical Jesus and the community of the New Age. As such they must be consulted, and fellowship with them must be maintained, at almost any cost".[80] Of course Paul considers himself as an apostle of Christ, subordinated to the Gospel as are the others, but as he neither can nor will deny that the other apostles have been commissioned directly by the Lord, unity with them is of fundamental significance for his own apostolate.

Man kommt darum nicht an der Erkenntnis vorbei, dass Paulus Gal 2,2 neben 1,1 stellt, *weil sein Apostolat beide Gesichtspunkte erfordert:* er ist Apostel, weil ihn der Auferstandene berufen und gesandt hat, aber er ist

77. *Holtz* (1974:126).
78. *Idem*, p. 145. Cf. *Roloff* (1965:73).
79. Hypothetically it could have been the other way round: Paul feared a rejection of his gospel, because this would irremediably separate the Jewish Christian part of the Church from the rest of the Church. *Stuhlmacher* comes close to this interpretation when he writes: "Wäre sein Evangelium in Jerusalem auf Ablehnung gestossen, so müsste Paulus sich in der Tat eingestehen, umsonst gelaufen zu sein. Seine Missionsfahrt gilt ja, wie Röm. 9–11 zeigen, der einen Kirche aus Juden und Heiden, und in diesem heilsgeschichtlichen Rahmen kann die Entschränkung des Heiles auf die Welt der Heiden nicht *den endgültigen Ausschluss der Juden* meinen" (1968:90, my italics). As *Holtz* points out in his sharp criticism of this interpretation (1974:126 n. 1) there can hardly have been any discussion at the Council on whether the *Jews* had any part in the salvation or not. Had Jerusalem delivered a negative answer to Antioch about the non-circumcision of Gentiles it is not difficult to guess which party would have been regarded as excluded from God's saving act in Christ.
80. *Barrett* (1953:17 f).

es nur, indem er das Evangelium gemeinsam mit den übrigen Aposteln bezeugt. Gäbe es diese Gemeinsamkeit nicht, so wäre er in der Tat 'ins Leere gelaufen' (2,2).[81]

We must draw the conclusion from Gal 2:1–10 that the Gentile Mission of Antioch (Paul and Barnabas) is in fact dependent on what decision is taken by the Jerusalem authorities.[82] Paul and Barnabas, and through them the Church of Antioch, cannot decide the issue for themselves, because only the apostles (and notables, if James the brother of the Lord is not an apostle) in Jerusalem are in a position to decide for the Church as a whole. Of course the agreement between the churches of Jerusalem and Antioch is mutual, but this does not mean that the relation is a symmetric one. The Jerusalem apostles did not go to Antioch, and still less to Paul to make sure of the unity of the Gospel. That was done at the point where the Gospel originated viz. the Jerusalem church, and that is why "Antioch" has to go there. This is not mere coincidence nor is it mere tradition and custom. As *Stuhlmacher* has made clear, the role of the Jerusalem apostolate as the highest doctrinal court of the Church is part and parcel of Paul's salvation-historical conception of his own apostolate.[83]

When we take a closer look at the whole of Gal 1:18—2:21 we see that this is not primarily a report of Paul's contacts with the church in Jerusalem, but more precisely a description of Paul's three meetings with a particular person, viz. Cephas.[84] Perhaps with his conflict with Cephas in Antioch in mind (and here he really did stand out alone against him), Paul has "personalized" the proceedings in Jerusalem. They were of an ecclesiastical nature, but Paul has made them part of his autobiography in order to effect an equality between himself and the most important man in the whole Church,[85] and with him the "pillars".[86]

This concentration on Cephas may be due to the fact that the "different

81. *Roloff* (1965:73). On this, see also the balanced statements of *Kuss* (1971: 109), and cf. *Pedersen* (1977:110–113). See also *von Campenhausen* (1969:33), *Schlier* (1971:68 n. 3) and *Brockhaus* (1975:121 f).
82. *Bultmann* (1953:304), *Haenchen* (1971:465).
83. *Stuhlmacher* (1968:87 f). See further below, B:2.
84. *Roloff* (1965:67). Paul calls him Κηφᾶς, except in Gal 2:7 f, where he calls him Πέτρος. I consider *Fürst* (1963) gives a satisfactory explanation of this change: Cephas is the usual name, even in the Greek-speaking church. Petros is Paul's translation of what the name means, because at this exact point he wants to stress the unique role of Cephas: he is "the Rock" of the Church, appointed by the Lord Himself—and this is the man that Paul is acknowledged as being the equal of.
85. *Haenchen* (1965:63), *Mussner* (1974:145), "der massgebende Mann". Cf. *Gerhardsson* (1961:266–270).
86. *Schütz* considers that Paul's reason for this "personalization" of the events is that he wants to stress the fact that he and the Jerusalem notables are all personally subordinated to the Gospel (1975:140, 143 ff). "Such personalization effects an

gospel" in Galatia was somehow associated with Cephas, or to the fact that he had been involved in two of Paul's previous conflicts with Judaists.[87] But it probably also has something to do with the clarification of Paul's relation to the Jerusalem church. When he wants to prove the truth of his "gospel", which does not require circumcision of Gentiles, he has to prove the independence of his apostolate and show that he is not subordinate to the church in Jerusalem or inferior to its foremost apostle, Cephas. And according to Paul every apostle is subordinated to the Gospel and is authoritative because and insofar as he is a faithful preacher of this one and only Gospel—not because he knew the historical Jesus or has access to old and reliable traditions about Him.[88] The essential criteria of apostleship are common to all the apostles and they are qualities which Paul has in the same degree as any other apostle, even Cephas himself.

As *Schütz* points out, "this pattern of movement and attraction" (meaning that Paul adapts the Jerusalem leaders to his own pattern of apostolic experience)[89] "is not a cunning and aggressive defense in the guise of an offense. It is the logical way for Paul to conceive of the problem of his relationship to the Jerusalem Church."[90] Logical it may be (or rather theological), but the Jerusalem church and Cephas are not identical.[91] By answering the question about his own equality with Cephas from a markedly theological perspective Paul in fact evades the "legal" or sociological question of his dependence on the Jerusalem church. He has not proved his full independence in relation to Jerusalem even if he proves that he is not inferior to or subordinate to Cephas. But does he prove even this?

(d) Was the mission work divided at the Council?

We noted above Paul's intention in Gal 1:18 f to stress that he was the equal of Cephas, and we meet it again in 2:1–10. Paul seems to be the only person acting from the Antiochene side and the argument that leads up to the agreement in v 9 explicitly treats the relationship between the two

---

equilibrium between Paul and the 'pillars'. Parity is achieved not by clarifying Paul's claim to apostolic status but by clarifying Jerusalem's subordination to the gospel's authority . . .", p. 145.

87. *Brown-Donfried-Reumann* (1973:25 f).

88. This intensively held perspective is seen to dominate his account by a number of scholars, *Roloff* (1965:72 f), *Stuhlmacher* (1968:68), *Eckert* (1971:193, 204), *Holtz* (1974:126) and *Schütz* (see above, n. 86).

89. So also *Haenchen* (1965:64).

90. *Schütz* (1975:143).

91. *Eckert:* Paul's relation to the Jerusalem church is not identical with his relation to the Jerusalem Apostles; the church is something of an "eigenständige Grösse" (1971:215 f). Cf. *Brown-Donfried-Reumann* (1973:27 n. 59).

apostles. Both have been entrusted by God with the Gospel, both exercise their apostolate in the power of God, Cephas among the Jews and Paul among the Gentiles. Paul clearly stands as the counterpart of Cephas and is obviously the *primus inter pares* among apostles on the Gentile side, as Cephas is in the Jewish Christian Mission. According to Paul it is this insight into the fundamental parallelism between Cephas and himself that is the basis of the subsequent agreement.[92]

But what is meant by the agreement "that we should go to the Gentiles and they to the circumcised"?[93] It can hardly have aimed at a division on strictly ethnic lines, by which the missionaries from Antioch were to go only to non-Jews, while those from the Jerusalem (and Palestinian) church were to go to all Jews in the whole world.[94] The evidence in Paul's own letters and in Acts witnesses to the fact that Paul acted as a missionary in synagogues and among Jews even after the Council.[95]

It is more probable that the Jerusalem agreement implied a division of the missionary responsibility into two geographically distinct areas.[96] This division meant that the mission to the Jews of the Holy Land (which was roughly Palestine) fell to the lot of the Jerusalem church with its leader Cephas, while the Antiochene church with its two "apostles" Paul and Barnabas was entrusted with the responsibility for all Christian mission outside this area, including the Jews in the diaspora. "Circumcision" ($\pi\epsilon\rho\iota\tau\omicron\mu\eta$) in v 9 would then signify "the mission field belonging to Jerusalem" or "the Holy Land".[97]

Considering the context (with Paul's need to keep to incontrovertible

92. *Eckert* (1971:190), *Mussner* (1974:116).

93. The hypothesis advanced by Cullmann, Dinkler and Klein that v 7–8 reflect the wording of the official minutes has met with general disapproval. See *Georgi* (1965:14 n. 10), *Munck* (1954:55 n. 62), *Stuhlmacher* (1968:93 f), *Kasting* (1969: 78 n. 75), *Haenchen* (1971:467), *Mussner* (1974:117 n. 93), *Holtz* (1974:119 n. 1) and *Schütz* (1975:147).

94. Proponents of this interpretation are *O'Neill* (The Theology of Acts in its Historical Setting, London 1961:104), cited after *Wilson* (1973:185), *Schmithals* (1963:36–51) and *Suggs* (1967:295 n. 1).

95. See e.g. the discussion of texts such as 1 Cor 9:20, Gal 1:13, 5:11, 2 Cor 11:24 ff and the evidence of Acts in *Stuhlmacher* (1968:99 n. 5), *Bornkamm* (1966:155) and *Wilson* (1973:186 f).

96. So *Barrett* (1964:294), *Schlier* (1971:56), *Oepke* (1973:85) and the authors mentioned in next note.

97. *Fridrichsen* (1947:12, 22 n. 25), and after him *Gerhardsson* (1961:280 n. 1, 307, 318). *Munck* extends the area of responsibility of Jerusalem to include Syria and Cilicia with their large Jewish colonies (1954:112). Against this speaks the fact that the agreement was made by two churches and not primarily between two persons or groups of persons, and Jerusalem's district cannot very well have included the capital of the Gentile Mission. Fridrichsen's views have to be modified with reference to the ecclesiastical nature of the agreement.

facts) it is hard to dispute the existence of an agreement such as Paul outlines, but its meaning could not have been as clear as crystal even to those involved. The agreement has a solemn and binding form and its associations with sacred law ("Sakralrecht") and salvation-history have been noted and emphasized by commentators.[98] But this character also makes the agreement difficult to put into practice, as its content will tend to differ according to how one interprets salvation-history, sacred law and ecclesiology. It was primarily a compromise aimed at making possible "the simultaneous coexistence of two missionary enterprises relatively independent of each other",[99] and its weakness and obscurity appeared the moment it was put to the test by conflict between the parties. Had the agreement been understood by all parties to entail full independence for the Antiochene church to continue its practices the Antioch Incident could never have arisen. But obviously the division was not so strictly geographical as to prevent Jerusalem from intervening in these practices. It may be that Paul attached more importance to the agreement as a definition of boundaries than anybody else did (cf. below on 2 Cor 10:12–18 as evidence of this interpretation of the Jerusalem agreement), and so made it more precise than it was.[100] Anyway, because of its obscurity and impracticability, it soon fell by the wayside,[101] and the practical solution of the problem of independence from Paul's point of view was to move his own missionary work to areas where he could act in complete independence (cf. Rom. 15:20).

The question of the "two gospels" in Gal 2:7 f must also be seen in this context. *Fridrichsen* interpreted this text as referring to two different forms of the one Gospel, based on the same historical tradition about Jesus. The two gospels differed not only in the role they ascribe to the Torah, but also in their christology.[102] *Schütz*, for instance, has criticized this theory, and pointed out that the phrase "my gospel" is used by Paul to underline his own, specific involvement in the process of the "evangelizing" of the world, and not to refer to a special formulation of the Christian message.[103] The

98. Especially by *Stuhlmacher* (1968:99).

99. *Nickle* (1966:45). Nickle does not consider this agreement to be a kind of surrender (cf. *Cerfaux* (1965:357): "cette politique de resignation"), but an agreement reached in a positive, perhaps even enthusiastic spirit by both parties. On the content of the agreement see also *Bonnard* (1953:41) and *Schütz* (1975:147).

100. *Haenchen* even regards 2:7 f as purely a Pauline construction (1971:467), while *Georgi*, who thinks that the mutual recognition comprises differing theology, organization, way of life and mission (1965:22) approaches the opposite extreme.

101. *Gerhardsson* (1961:271 and 1963:130), *Wilson* (1973:187).

102. *Fridrichsen* (1947:8–12).

103. *Schütz* (1975:71–78, 148–150).

term "gospel" (εὐαγγέλιον) is used in two different senses in Gal 2:2 and 2:7. In the former case it has full, theological significance and refers to the content of Paul's (and the Antiochene missionaries') preaching, which of course was not identical with what was preached to the Jews,[104] but sufficiently in accord with it to win the unqualified approval of the Jerusalem authorities. But in 2:7 εὐαγγέλιον is used as a *terminus technicus* for the apostle's actual function of preaching to the Gentiles, his calling. Paul's apostolate is not primarily distinguished by his own message, but by his own sending; the phrase in 2:7 might just as well have been "apostolate to the Gentiles" (ἀποστολὴν τῆς ἀκροβυστίας).[105]

The above discussion leads to the conclusion that the somewhat diffuse distinction between two "districts" or "apostolates/gospels" with Paul and Cephas one at the head of each has greater theological than sociological-legal validity. The wording of Gal 2:7–9 does not permit us to state the existence of a clear-cut and equal distribution of competence between the two apostles. And this conclusion seems to be amply borne out by the subsequent Antioch Incident.

4. Paul, Antioch and Jerusalem in the Antioch Incident

Gal 2:11–14 tells of the third meeting between Paul and Cephas, and we can presume that Paul wrote about this to the Galatians to stress his equality with Cephas, or even his superiority: Paul was after all more faithful to the Gospel than Cephas! These verses abound with biting criticism of Cephas: he "stood condemned" (scil. by God),[106] he was "fearful", he is characterized as a "hypocrite", he is not "on the right road toward the truth of the gospel".[107] In relation to that fundamental norm, to which both Cephas and Paul are subordinated and by which they are to be judged, Cephas out of cowardice acted against what he knew to be right, whereas Paul stood the test.

What caused Paul to criticize Cephas so harshly? Probably only a short time after the Apostolic Council[108] Cephas was a guest in the "district" of Paul and Barnabas, in the centre of Gentile Mission, the mixed congregation of Christian Jews and Gentiles in Antioch.[109] At first Cephas con-

---

104. *Gerhardsson* (1961:271), *Stuhlmacher* (1968:97), *Eckert* (1971:190).

105. See *Roloff* (1965:90–93) and *Schlier* (1971:76–78).

106. *Roloff* (1965:74).

107. The translation by Kilpatrick, cited from *Schütz* (1975:151).

108. So the majority of commentators. See e.g. *Roloff* (1965:73 n. 109) and *Eckert* (1971:193).

109. On "districts", see *Gerhardsson* (1961:307 ff; cf. p. 187 for rabbinical parallels).

formed to the prevailing (and revolutionary) custom of eating together with Gentile Christians, thereby sanctioning it. But when "certain men" or delegates of James came from Jerusalem and wanted to discontinue this custom Cephas gave in to their demand for some reason.[110] The result was that the church in Antioch was divided into a Jewish and a Gentile section, each observing its own eucharist. Indirectly this compelled the Gentiles to live as the Jewish Christians ('Ιουδαιζειν, v 14) whether this was intended by Cephas or not. Probably Cephas's behaviour neither was in effect a breach of the Jerusalem agreement nor was regarded as such as this is not even hinted at by Paul in his strongly worded accusation. Barnabas would surely have reacted against any flagrant violation of an earlier agreement, for which he and Paul had contended side by side in Jerusalem.[111] The only possible conclusion is that it did not contain a word about mixed eating. But if Cephas's behaviour did not go against the letter of the Council agreement it undoubtedly was a departure from the custom of the Antiochene church and a violation of the spirit of the agreement, or in other words the Gospel, as Paul understands it.

And here we see a difference not only between Jerusalem and Paul, or Cephas and Paul, but between the old colleagues Barnabas and Paul. The latter is rigidly consistent in his views as to what a law-free gospel must entail, while Cephas and Barnabas, who naturally also embrace the law-free gospel as regards the Gentiles, cannot share his views. And *Schütz* has convincingly shown that "it will not do to regard the argument as a clash between expediency represented by Peter, and principle represented by Paul".[112] Instead we see here a "conflict between two principles: the singularity of the gospel and the unity of the Church",[113] both of which had been decisive in forming the Council agreement and both of which were now defended with perfectly good conscience, but by persons taking opposite sides in a concrete controversy.[114]

The conflict throws light on issues touched upon above, for instance the content of the Jerusalem agreement. But it also tells us that the Jerusalem church could well exert pressure through delegates in order to introduce stricter order as regards shared meals. And we see no sign that Cephas, Barnabas or the church in Antioch (at least its Jewish section) did resent

110. This will be discussed in greater detail in my article mentioned above in n. 46.
111. *Schütz* (1975:151).
112. *Idem*, p. 154.
113. *Ibidem*.
114. Cf. *Koester* (1971:121 f).

this as an illegitimate intrusion into Antiochene affairs from a distant sister church. Our conclusion must reasonably be that Jerusalem had the right to intervene ("Einspruchsbefugnis")[115] even in such a distant and independent church as that in Antioch.

Another thing the Antioch Incident demonstrates is the strength of Cephas's authority. "Peter's position as halakic authority was so strong that Jewish Christians followed his practice even in Antioch, which lay in Paul's 'district' ".[116] The only person who did not yield to the authority of Cephas was Paul. He objected, and objected strongly, with express reference to the norm of the Gospel. Thereby he demonstrated (a) that the authority of the Gospel is superior to that of the apostolic halakah, and (b) that he, unlike Barnabas, for example, was not subject to the halakic authority of Cephas. But even if this shows that Paul does not take orders from Cephas it does not make him his equal. Paul, who does the right and customary thing could apparently not command a following in his "own" church! This Cephas could, with infuriating ease, and also without words, by sheer force of example. The conclusion must be that as regards status and power Paul is indeed the inferior of Cephas.

Most scholars do *not* think that Paul managed to reverse the decision of Cephas and the delegates from Jerusalem.[117] It is hard to believe that he would not have mentioned such a resounding triumph, had there been any to report, especially as the question of "Judaizing" was highly relevant in the Galatian situation.

The break with Barnabas and the Jewish Christian part of the Antiochene church effected a separation between the parties, at first theological, and then also geographical. After the Antioch Incident we see Paul emerging as an independent missionary and apostle, striking out far west into areas wholly his "own".

---

115. *Stuhlmacher* (1968:87). Cf. also *Gerhardsson* (1961:279 f), *Nickle* (1966: 64), *Eckert* (1971:195 f), *Holtz* (1974:125), *Schütz* (1975:152) and *Larsson* (1976: 9 f). Cf. the material on "General Sessions" and the supremacy of Jerusalem in doctrinal matters from Qumran and the rabbinical literature collected and discussed in *Gerhardsson* (1961:245–249).

116. *Idem*, p. 318. By "halakic authority" is meant the power to promulgate author- itative and normative teaching of a doctrinal, ethical, and legal nature, something we observe Paul doing in his letters, p. 307 ff.

117. Among those who think that Paul "won" in the conflict with Cephas in Antioch are *Munck* (1954:86 f, 94), *Roloff* (1965:75), *Hainz* (1972:125, 248) and *Oepke* (1973:88, 99). *Maly* (1969:77) is undecided.
Among those who think that Paul "lost" are *Schmithals* (1963:64), *Georgi* (1965: 31 n. 92), *Nickle* (1966:66 f), *Stuhlmacher* (1968:106 f), *Kasting* (1969:122), *Eckert* (1971:227), *Haenchen* (1971:476), *Koester* (1971:122), *Holtz* (1974:124, with n. 2), *Mussner* (1974:186 f) and *Catchpole* (1977:439 f).

To summarize the discussion to this point: Up to and including the Apostolic Council and the Antioch Incident Paul has to receive authoritative words from the leadership of the Jerusalem church, which enjoys undisputed superiority of status. This arises from the fact that during this time Paul, whatever else he may be, is one of the leaders of a local church (that in Antioch) which regards the Jerusalem church and its leadership as being the highest doctrinal and legal authority within the whole Church.

B. PAUL AS AN INDEPENDENT APOSTLE TO THE GENTILES

Following the principle of primarily using concrete historical facts and processes as evidence of the distribution of power in the Primitive Church, I shall first try to analyse the Great Collection to find out what it has to say on Paul's relations with Jerusalem. I shall then study some of the indications of influence from the Palestinian church in Pauline areas, and lastly see if my findings are corroborated by Paul's own attitude to Jerusalem during this period.

1. The Collection

In Gal 2:10a we have, in Paul's own words, the latter part[118] of the Jerusalem agreement: "Only they would have us remember the poor" (μονον των πτωχων ίνα μνημονευωμεν). Grammatically, this is the continuation of 2:6b "those . . . who were of repute added nothing to me", but some commentators argue that 10a cannot be interpreted as a qualification of "added nothing" (οὐδεν προσανεθεντο), in which case the Collection would have been regarded by Paul as an imposition on the part of the Jerusalem notables.[119] That Paul took the task seriously we can see, not only from v 10b, but also from 1 Cor 16:1-4, 2 Cor 8-9 and Rom 15:27-29.

What was the meaning of this assignment to remember the poor? Was it no more than a charitable action or did it have a more far-reaching, fundamental significance for relations between Jerusalem and Antioch?

It is an undisputed fact that the "poor", whom Paul and Barnabas undertake to "remember" are the poor of the church of Jerusalem. This church seems to have been in a difficult financial situation with a number of poor members to take care of. Perhaps the experiment of living in a "communism of love" (to use *Troeltsch*'s term) for almost twenty years had also brought about the impoverishment of those who had owned something at

118. "historisch fast als die wichtigste Bestimmung des Konvents zu bezeichnen", *Bultmann* (1953:94).
119. As qualification of v 6 it is taken by *Holl* (1928:61). This is disputed by e.g. *Bonnard* (1953:43) and *Mussner* (1974:124).

the start.[120] Presumably the church had a large proportion of Galileans who had left their jobs and homes and gone to Jerusalem to await the advent of Christ Jesus in the Holy City.[121] Moreover persecution by the Jewish authorities may have added to the poverty of the church.[122] These circumstances have led commentators to assume that this "remembering" is meant primarily as a charitable act, designed to help the Jerusalem Christians in their distress. Paul's expression in Rom 15:26 ("Macedonia and Achaia have been pleased to make some contribution for the poor among the saints at Jerusalem") must refer to real poor, and this impression is strengthened by his manner of arguing for the Collection in 2 Cor 8:13 f and 9:12.[123]

In a famous essay *Karl Holl* set out to show that this collection is not only an expression of Christian love for needy brethren but also the expression of a certain understanding of the Church, more exactly the self-understanding of the church in Jerusalem.[124] It is evident from the justification of the Collection in Rom 15:27, that the Gentiles are thought to be in a debt of gratitude, not to the poor but to the whole church of Jerusalem from which they have received spiritual treasures. *Holl* infers that not only "the saints" (οἱ ἅγιοι) but also "the poor" (οἱ πτωχοι) was a well-known self-designation of the Christians in Jerusalem.[125] This "holiness" and God-pleasing "poverty" were the foundation of the legal claims of these Christians on other churches. Both Antioch (see Acts 11:25 ff) and later the churches of Paul are regarded by Jerusalem as being under an obligation to support their mother church, and this legal obligation is evident even in Paul's language.[126] Jerusalem is the permanent centre of the Church, where

120. The expression "religiöse Liebeskommunismus" is found in *Troeltsch* (1912: 49). *Nickle* cites Dodd "They carried (the system of partial and voluntary communism) out in the economically disastrous way of realizing capital and distributing it as income" (1966:23 f, n. 42). *Gewalt* (1971:92–96) and *Haenchen* (1971:233) are among those who doubt the existence of any "Liebeskommunismus". See the balanced discussion in *Braun* (1966:1, 143–149 and II, 155–157).

121. *Goppelt* (1966:33), *Gewalt* (1971:93), *Theissen* (1974a:269).

122. *Nickle* (1966:24).

123. *Idem*, p. 110.

124. I cite this essay as *"Holl* (1928)" and give the page-numbers from this publication, as is customary.

125. *Schlier:* "of the saints" (των ἁγιων) is not genitivus partitivus but genitivus epexegeticus (1977:436).

126. "Paulus bezeichnet die Abgabe bald mit erbaulichen Ausdrücken als κοινωνια und διακονια, χαρις, εὐλογια, bald mit mehr rechtlich klingenden als ἁδροτης, λειτουργια, λογια", *Holl* (1928:60).

Davies seems not to have considered the latter group of terms when he characterizes Paul's terms for the collection as non-juridical, and draws the conclusion that this shows the collection to have been quite voluntary and not a tax (1974:199). The terminology Paul uses cannot of itself supply proof of the degree of voluntariness,

the apostles of Christ reside, the "pillars" of the Church, and "the holy"; and for this reason Jerusalem has a certain right to supervize the rest of the Church and to receive taxes.[127]

Most scholars consider that *Holl* (and later *Stauffer*)[128] goes too far when he uses terms such as "right of taxation" about the Collection. But on the other hand, it is now generally admitted that it was more than an act of charity. As is seen from 2 Cor 8–9 and Rom 15:25 ff, Paul sincerely wishes to create by this collection a concrete expression of the unity of the Jewish and Gentile sections of the Church.[129] By this means the Gentile churches are to be brought to recognize their continuity with the church in Jerusalem and through it with Israel and to acknowledge their enormous debt of gratitude. And presumably the Collection will also have an effect on the Jerusalem church and be an impressive sign to the Jewish Christian church that God has also called the Gentiles to faith in Christ Jesus and given them a share in his grace. This "ecumenical" or unifying purpose is inherent in the action as such, and has been stressed and underlined by Paul himself.

We can thus state that the significance of the Collection is connected with ecclesiology or the conception of what the Church is.[130] And this leads us to the decisive question: which understanding of the Church does the Collection express, Jerusalem's or Paul's?

Many scholars choose the latter view, probably because almost all the evidence we have about the Collection is found in Paul's letters. The purpose and the meaning of the Collection is then analysed from Paul's utterances, without taking up the question of whether the apostle might be bound by, or at least reflect, the opinion of the receiving party (Jerusalem).[131]

---

as is obvious from 2 Cor 8–9. Here Paul insists on the voluntariness of the collection, but at the same time puts such strong moral pressure on the Corinthians to participate (generously) in it that the alternative of not participating is virtually excluded.

127. It is to be observed that *Holl* does not make any analogy between the Pauline collection for Jerusalem and the Jewish temple-tax, but merely cites this opinion from Pfleiderer and Holtzmann in his note 28 (on p. 58). On p. 62 he talks about "ein gewisses Besteuerungsrecht".

128. *Stauffer* calls the collection "Kirchensteuer" (1960:366). For a criticism of his view, see *Georgi* (1965:17 n. 28).

129. Thus a majority of scholars, e.g. *Munck* (1954:285), *Knox* (1955:41 n. 23), *Nickle* (1966:111–129, et passim), *Cerfaux* (1965:220 f), *Hainz* (1972: 101 f), *Oepke* (1973:85), *Barrett* (1973b:27), *Davies* (1974:200), *Mussner* (1974:126).

130. *Georgi* summarizes the discussion after Holl by stating that his hypothesis of the collection being a centralistic church-tax has been abandoned, and then continues "Dafür hat sich aber allgemein die Einsicht durchgesetzt, dass Kollekte und Kirchenverständnis aufs engste miteinander verknüpft sind" (1965:10).

131. So also *Georgi* in his history of the research in the field: "Die Frage nach den Intentionen der Jerusalemer ist geschwunden.—liegt der Ton doch auf den paulinischen Intentionen, wobei die praktische, um nicht zu sagen pädogogische Absicht des Paulus—stark herausgearbeitet wird" (1965:10).

According to certain writers the Collection must be interpreted from the context of Pauline missionary strategy and ecclesiology as we find it in Rom 9–11.[132] From its beginning as an act of charitable support the Collection is thought to develop to be more and more connected with the Pauline mission to the Gentiles. The ultimate purpose of this is to provoke the Jews to conversion through envy of the Gentiles and their obvious participation in salvation (Rom 10–11). The Collection becomes part of this scheme. The full representation of the Pauline churches coming to Jerusalem is designed to remind the Jews (and not only the Christian ones) of the prophecies concerning the pilgrimage of the nations to Jerusalem (Is 2, Mic 4)—a powerful sign that the last days are dawning, which will revitalize the mission to the Jews (which mission Paul knew had stagnated, Rom 9:30, 10:1–3, 16 ff)[133] and make an impression upon Judaism at its centre.

Some parts of this interpretation are less well founded than others,[134] but it is probable that the Collection has eventually come to acquire a significance for Paul himself that it did not have from the beginning. The real significance of the Collection is not the money as such or the amount of help it will bring, but the demonstration of unity between Jews and Gentiles within the Church. In this sum is included money from a great number of (perhaps all of) Paul's churches, which in addition are personally represented by a (unnecessarily) large delegation of Gentile Christians.[135] Even if no "pilgrimage of the nations" or "eschatological provocation" were intended by Paul, it is reasonable to assume that it was of the utmost importance to him to show Jerusalem what God had effected among the Gentiles through him and so "seal to them this fruit" (Rom 15:28, my translation). The delivery of the Collection is no mere fulfilment of an assignment undertaken to help Jerusalem and manifest Church unity, it is also a proof of the value of Paul's work as Apostle to the Gentiles. Why else did he change his mind from when he wrote 1 Cor 16:4 ("If it seems

132. *Munck* (1954:283–300), *Georgi* (1965) and *Nickle* (1966).
·133. *Munck* (1954:295).
134. Cf. *Bultmann*'s review of *Munck*'s book (1959) and *Schmithals*'s review of *Georgi*'s book (1967). *Davies* (1974:202–217) has shown that the apostle's ties with the Holy Land weakened and that his interest in the eschatological role of Jerusalem and the mission to the Jews lessened as the years went by, while at the same time his own part of the Church came definitely into the fore as the foremost field for God's eschatological action. Besides, Munck (and Nickle) have a too rigidly and literally "apocalyptic" understanding of Paul's eschatology.
135. See *Munck* (1954:288–292) and *Nickle* (1966:68 f) for a discussion on the historical value of Acts 20:4.

advisable that I should go also . . . ") and decide to risk his life by coming in person to Jerusalem?[136]

But to see the Collection in historical perspective we must also investigate what the Jerusalem church thought about it. The leaders of Jerusalem can hardly have shared, or even known of, the Pauline view.[137] Why did they find it fitting and proper that the Gentile Christians in Antioch and its environs should help to relieve the distress in Jerusalem? Must we not assume that the Collection right from the beginning had the character of an obligation, given and undertaken in the form of a solemn and binding agreement?[138] And of course this obligation is not simply a formalization of the Christian duty of neighbourly love—as if the Christians in Jerusalem were absolutely and permanently the most distressed within the whole Church. Rather, the element of obligation is connected with the Jerusalem church's theological understanding of itself. It is generally agreed that the church in Jerusalem thought of itself as a holy and elect group within Israel with an eschatological task of witnessing to and expecting the second coming of the Risen Messiah Jesus.[139] And often it is considered that this high-strung, apocalyptic self-understanding was incompatible with a concern for everyday, practical problems and with a legal way of thinking. Thus the agreement about the Collection is considered not to have contained any legal element.[140] But as a fact legal and eschatological thinking are not incompatible; instead the sacred-legal ("sakral-rechtliche") element is an integrating part of the election-historical and salvation-historical perspective that can be found both in Jerusalem and in Paul's concept of the "Gospel".[141] The church in Jerusalem is in its own and Paul's eyes entitled

---

136. *Bornkamm* (1971:137), *Käsemann* (1974:392).

137. *Nickle* concedes that Paul never explicitly says that he anticipated that the collection would provoke the conversion of Israel, and has to produce some clever (but unpersuasive) reasoning to make this silence plausible (1966:140–142). Cf. *Schmithals* (1967:671).

138. *Stuhlmacher* shows, with the help of Jewish and Hellenistic texts, that "obligation", ὀφείλημα, ὀφειλέτης (Rom 15:27) and "remember" μνημονεύειν (Gal 2:10) have a legal and eschatological-spiritual content. The latter term stands for an inner commitment together with a corresponding external or concrete obligation to a person, an attitude S. finds corroborated by Paul's argument in 2 Cor 9:12 f (1968:103 f).

Cf. the terminology used of the collection by some recent commentators: "cette sorte de vassalité", *Cerfaux* (1965:357); "Vertragsklausel, Pflicht", *Stuhlmacher* (1968: 100, 103); "Verpflichtung", *Eckert* (1971:191 f); "Auflage, geschuldete Verpflichtung", *Hainz* (1972:242 f); "rechtliche Verpflichtung", *Schlier* (1977:436).

139. See e.g. *Georgi* (1965:23–30), *Käsemann* (1974:386).

140. See *Mussner* (1974:124 f, who cites others of the same opinion), *Oepke* (1973:85) and *Georgi* (1965:17, 30).

141. *Stuhlmacher* (1968:69, 87 f). See below on Paul's view of Jerusalem.

to support from other Christian churches and not primarily on moral grounds but on theological grounds, viz. its unique salvation-historical role. If this is not given its proper place in the understanding of the Collection, the element of utilitarian exchange (money versus recognition of Gentile Mission) will tend to be overstressed.[142]

We should not forget that the agreement about the Collection is part and parcel of the agreement that the church in Antioch and its apostles have a missionary responsibility and a "sphere" of their own. But the centre of the Church and the somewhat independent periphery must be united by concrete measures now that the observance of the Torah is no longer a common feature of the whole Church. As *Klaus Berger* has argued[143] the Collection should be seen in this perspective and understood as analogous to the institution of "alms for Israel". Uncircumcised, God-fearing Gentiles used to give alms to the poor of Israel in order to express their wish to belong to the righteous people and share their confession of the one God. There are even indications that through alms-giving a God-fearer could become regarded as belonging to God's people without being circumcised.[144]

The Collection for the Jerusalem church is thus to be understood as a sign that the Gentile Christians have been converted to the same faith as the Jewish Christians and are incorporated into the same new covenant, although their road to righteousness does not go via the law. Connection with the centre of the Church is indispensable for the Gentiles and is consequently safeguarded by an obligation which cannot be characterized as anything less than legal.

This juridico-theological interpretation of the Collection agreement was not very easy to convey to Gentile converts, although it expresses what were vital interests even for Paul: a confirmation both of the independence and intrinsic value of Gentile Christians and of their essential solidarity with the centre of the Church.[145] This is why we find Paul working out the secondary reasons for the Collection in his letters (brotherly love, the norm of reciprocity, κοινωνια as obedience to Christ's gospel, etc.), though the primary reasons are sometimes apparent (as when he uses terms such as "service" (διακονια or λειτουργια) for it).[146]

Against the postulated legal or compulsory character of the Collection one could point to the fact that it is expressly said to be voluntary (2 Cor

142. As in *Gewalt* (1971), *Ehrhardt* (1969:72 f, 85 f) and *Chadwick* (1959:5).
143. *K Berger* (1977a).
144. *Idem*, p. 187 ff.
145. *Idem*, p. 202 ff. Cf. *Chadwick* (1959:13) on the implication of a dual structure of the Church.
146. *K Berger* (1977a:199), *Hainz* (1972:242–245). Cf. above, n. 126.

8:8,10; 9:7), and that this was an important feature of it in Paul's eyes.[147] But to cite 2 Cor 8–9 as evidence actually cuts both ways, as it is obvious that these chapters are a veritable battery of arguments against the somewhat lax and unwilling attitude towards the Collection in Corinth. It is true that no orders are given about the extent of individual contributions (see, however, 2 Cor 9:5–6), but the moral pressure on the Corinthian church is so formidable that it is difficult to believe that it could have refused to participate if it were to continue its relationship with the apostle at all. The Collection cannot very well be described as voluntary for the Pauline churches, or for the apostle himself (cf. Gal 2:10a), even if the arguments for it are ethical and theological and not strictly formal or legal.[148]

Although the task of collecting money for Jerusalem was probably recognized as a solemn and binding obligation by both parties of the agreement, it is not improbable that they interpreted it differently. The church of Jerusalem understood it is a "duty" that documented its spiritual supremacy, while Paul gave it a more theological interpretation as an acknowledgement of Jerusalem's actual importance in God's election- and salvation-history.[149] The existing differences in interpretation deepened in time with the historical development of the parties. The Jewish nationalistic movement and its suspicion of Gentiles grew steadily during the fifties. This made every contact or collaboration with Gentiles, and especially the work of a "traitor" like Paul (who certainly had a bad reputation in Jerusalem, cf. Acts 21:21, 28) a real danger to the Christians in Jerusalem. And the Antioch Incident had damaged relations between Paul and Jerusalem—not only on the part of Paul, but also on the part of Jerusalem. The agitation of Judaists from Palestine (cf. below) in Paul's own churches is indirect evidence of this. Perhaps the Jerusalem church as a whole harboured a slight suspicion: Was Paul really to be trusted any more?[150]

---

147. *Nickle* (1966:125–127).

148. It is important not to be so sociologically naive as to think that there is only one alternative here: (a) a giving under strict formal, legal obligation, which if necessary can be enforced, or (b) free, spontaneous giving from a good and loving heart. "Non-juridical" does not mean "voluntary". The reference to theological arguments and ethical norms can, in the correct context, constitute a strong pressure—and I consider that this is the case here.

149. *Stuhlmacher* (1968:105). Cf. for similar distinctions between Jerusalem's and Paul's interpretations of the collection *von Campenhausen* (1957:69 n. 81 and 1969: 34), *Wilckens* (1964:735 f), Mundle and Wendland as cited by *Hainz* (1972:242 n. 1) and *Schlier* (1971:80 n. 5).

150. On growing Zealotism, see *Goppelt* (1966:40, 54 f) and cf. *Bornkamm*'s remark about "zunehmende Judaisierung der Urgemeinde" (1959:663). On how the relations between Paul and Jerusalem developed after the Council, see *Stuhlmacher* (1968:102 n. 1), *Käsemann* (1974:384, 392) and *Catchpole* (1977:443 f).

On the other hand Paul's successful work in the years succeeding the Council and his separation from Antioch eventually gave the Collection something of a new accent. Without going to such lengths as *Munck* et al. we can reasonably presume that when Paul turned towards Jerusalem after having completed his work in the east (Rom 15:23), the Collection appeared to him more as an expression of his successful work among Gentiles and of the independence of the Gentile section of the Church than as a humble tribute to the supremacy of Jerusalem. But would the increasingly "Jewish" church in Jerusalem accept the *result* of the Council agreement? The success of the Gentile Mission was greater than they had ever thought possible in A.D. 48–49; perhaps it was also greater (and more menacing) than they wished now?[151] With all these factors in mind it is not surprising that Paul feared that the Collection may not be "acceptable to the saints" in Jerusalem (Rom 15:31b) and beseeched the church in Rome to intercede for him (v 30).

We read the end of the story about the Great Collection in Acts 21:17–26, and see that Paul's misgivings proved to be justified.[152] There can be no doubt that, but for the political situation in the Jewish capital, the money Paul and his delegation of Gentile Christians had brought with them would have been exceedingly welcome. But it could not be received in the way Paul would have liked: openly, officially proclaimed to (the church of) Jerusalem. That would have been an impossible provocation of Jewish feelings. And besides there was already a cloud of suspicion hanging over Paul and all his work, which must be removed (v 21 f). A compromise was proposed which enabled the church to receive the Collection from the Gentiles (thereby acknowledging them as fully Christian and a work of the Lord) without antagonizing the zealous Jews in the same city: Paul was to undertake the cost of paying the expenses of four men who had made Nazirite vows. As the vulnerable party the Jewish Christian leaders had every cause to ask for and be granted such a special form of the transmission of the Collection as would not condemn them in the eyes of devout Jews. And so the money was delivered, as a result of these negotiations, partly in the form of payment for sacrifices in the Temple—a delivery as silent as possible and a "crashing failure" as far as Paul's plans were con-

151. Cf. the remarks of *Theissen* (1977:106) on why Paul's (or the Gentile Mission's) success simply had to antagonize the church in Jerusalem.

152. I follow *Haenchen* (1971:606–614), *Georgi* (1965:88 f, with n. 340), *Bornkamm* (1966:160 f) and *Wilckens* (1974:137 n. 70) in the opinion that this pericope contains reliable information about what happened when Paul came to Jerusalem to deliver his collection.

cerned.[153] His secondary, theological interpretation of the Collection had to yield to the way the Jerusalem church wanted it to be interpreted and treated. We are forced to conclude that Paul's intention and interpretation were not sufficiently strong to change the course of the underlying historical process. The Great Collection had begun as a manifestation of the Jerusalem leaders' conception of the Church; and their interpretation of it must be seen as its enduring definition.[154]

We do not know how the Collection was received by this church. Some think that it was well received and healed the threatening cleft between the two sections of the Church.[155] But the arrest of Paul a few days later must have caused a storm of antipathy to break out against all Christians in Jerusalem and will in all likelihood have discredited "his" Collection in their eyes. This may account for the remarkable silence about it in Acts (cf. the veiled reference in 24:17): being something of a missionary and diplomatic catastrophe, it was best to pass over it in merciful silence.

The conclusion of the above discussion of the Great Collection is that the apostle Paul is a little more dependent on historical facts such as the original decision in Jerusalem and the compulsory character of the assignment to collect money for Jerusalem than is realized when one first reads his statements about them. And this is confirmed by the outcome of his undertaking, where once again the Jerusalem church manifests its superiority and reduces Paul's role to that of being the one who collected money for them. In view of this it could be discussed whether the often-made modern distinction between the "spiritual" and "legal" supremacy of the Jerusalem church is based on any historically discernible phenomenon.

2. Jerusalem Influence in the Pauline Region

We saw in the previous section that the obligation to make a collection under which Paul and Antioch had placed themselves at the Council constituted a permanent influence on the part of the Jerusalem church on Paul's work as an independent apostle to the Gentiles, roughly during the period A.D. 49–56 (58).[156] This was, however, an obligation which the apostle

153. *Nickle* (1966:155 f). Cf. *Georgi* (1965:89). Both Nickle and Georgi maintain that Paul viewed and intended the collection as a salvation-historical provocation, and both of them admit that in this intention he failed completely.

On the "compromise" character of the agreement to undertake the payment for these sacrifices, see *Ehrhardt* (1969:107 ff) and *Maly* (1969: 93 f).

154. *Hainz* (1972:243, the final paragraph).

155. E.g. *Nickle* (1966:70–72). None of his arguments is compelling.

156. On Pauline chronology, see *Fitzmyer* (1970b:§ 4–9), *Robinson* (1976:31 n. 1, and Chapter III passim), and *Suhl's* detailed investigation (1975).

himself had willingly undertaken to extend to all "his" churches (which at the time of the Council must have been thought of as an extension of the Gentile Mission from Antioch). But there are some indications of the influence of Jerusalem and the Jewish Christian church in Palestine reaching Pauline churches without his initiative or even agreement.

A number of Paul's letters witness to the fact that Jewish Christian missionaries or agents followed in the footsteps of the Apostle, in the sense that we see them turning up in churches he has founded.[157] Unambiguous examples are the churches in Philippi (Phil 3), Galatia (Gal) and Corinth (1 and 2 Cor). But the existence of Jewish Christian missionaries in these churches is not sufficient evidence of an (intentional) influence from the Palestine church. We must look more closely at each of these cases.

(a) "The evidence of 1 Corinthians shows the certain influence, and probable presence, of Peter in Corinth", *Barrett* thus sums up his essay on "Cephas in Corinth", where he follows and elaborates an earlier essay by T.W. *Manson*.[158] In their view, some of the questions treated in this letter seem to reflect the disturbing influence of Jewish Christian activity in this church. This has not consisted in preaching another Christ or another Gospel, but rather (in *Manson*'s words) in a "concerted move to instil Palestinian piety and Palestinian orthodoxy".[159] It stressed points which Paul passed over lightly, e.g. *kosher* food, payment to missionaries, thereby adding to the confusion of the Corinthians.

But how intentional was this? Can we really talk about "a concerted move"? The Corinthians had been converted and brought up by Paul, who was a Jew of the diaspora with a rabbinical training from Jerusalem and a revolutionary attitude to the Torah. He had been followed by Apollos, a cultured and rhetorically skilled Jew from Egypt, "Hellenistic" both in his Judaism and his Christianity. Lastly Cephas, personally or in some other way, had made a deep impression on at least some of the Christians in Corinth; and he was a Galilean, presumably more conservative and cautious in his attitude to the Torah when not urged from above to act otherwise, and having vivid personal memories from the years together with the

157. *Staab* comments on Phil 3:2: "Er nennt sie 'Hunde', wohl deshalb, weil sie immer bellend und beissend hinter ihm herliefen" (1969:191), and this might be a general description of the behaviour of the Judaists in Pauline areas.

158. *Barrett* (1963), see esp. pp. 6–8 with an account and commentary of Manson's work. Cf. *Ehrhardt* (1969:106), *Vielhauer* (1975) and *Hyldahl* (1977:27), who also find the personal presence of Cephas in Corinth probable. *Goppelt* represents those who did not believe in a "counter-mission" from Palestine, but rather find the background to the Judaistic opposition against Paul in the gnostic Judaism of Asia Minor (1966:69).

159. *Barrett* (1963:8).

Lord some twenty years previously. When strong personalities as unlike as these three made their influence felt in a spiritually immature (1 Cor 3:1-3) and impressionable church, it is not surprising that there arose differences of opinion concerning the Christian way of life.[160]

These differences and schisms were probably not contrived by the missionaries themselves (1 Cor 3-4 and 16:12 make it almost certain that Paul and Apollos were on good terms), and there is no need to think of Cephas's activity in Corinth as "a concerted move" to instil Palestine piety in the Gentile churches. This would imply a deliberate Petrine (or Palestine Jewish Christian) plan to visit Gentile churches in order to correct possible mistakes and complement some vital points that had been neglected in the teachings of Paul. But this is surely more than can be concluded from our sources in 1 Cor. If we have Jewish Christian influence in Corinth, and if this was transmitted by Cephas himself (which is denied by a number of scholars), it is more likely that this influence was exerted more or less unintentionally, mainly by sheer force of example and the mere presence of a highly authoritative person—as in Antioch, for example (Gal 2:11-14).

(b) In 2 Cor we have a different situation: the presence of rival Jewish Christian "apostles" and the success they enjoyed is an established fact. The question of the identity of Paul's opponents in 2 Cor 10-13 has been discussed in detail throughout the years and cannot be presented here.[161] I will simply admit that I find *Käsemann's* brilliant analysis, elaborated by *Barrett,* the most plausible solution.[162] The intruders are Jewish Christians from Jerusalem, provided with commendatory epistles from the highest authorities in that church. Their task is to inspect the church and strengthen the ties between the Gentile church and the mother church, but this commission was seriously abused by the envoys (*sch^eluchim,* ἀπόστολοι) when they attacked and rejected the authority of Paul, the founding apostle, violently denigrating his character, conduct and spiritual competence and established themselves as the real authorities in Corinth.

Paul did not want to break the peace with Jerusalem and the leaders there, but on the other hand could not tolerate having the Corinthian Church wrecked by their envoys. This accounts for his strained, tortuous way of arguing and of defending himself in 2 Cor 10-13: Paul wants to distinguish between the "superlative apostles" in Jerusalem (11:5, 12:11;

160. This view on the divisions in the Corinthian church was proposed by Prof. Karl Heinrich *Rengstorf* in a lecture given in Lund 14 Nov. 1975. *Hyldahl* sees Apollos as behind the division and the opposition against Paul (1977:27 f).
161. For the history of the discussion see G. *Friedrich* (1963), *Georgi* (1964), *Barrett* (1971) and *Betz* (1972).
162. *Käsemann* (1942), *Barrett* (1964, 1970, 1971).

notice the mildly ironical tone) and the "false apostles" (11:13, vehemently denounced), who assert that they are acting on behalf of the former —and have letters to prove this.

> But . . . had they (sc. the Jerusalem leaders) given them authority to do what they were in fact doing, or were the intruders acting *ultra vires?* Evidently Paul hoped, and perhaps believed, that they were.—This . . . however compelled him to fight in Corinth with one hand tied behind his back[163]

I shall not delve into the details of 2 Cor 10–13, but merely note the important fact that, if *Käsemann* and *Barrett* are right, the Jerusalem leaders may not have interpreted the agreement of Gal 2:7–9 in the same way as Paul did. There can be no doubt that Paul is referring to this in 2 Cor 10:12–18, where he talks about "the measure (το μετρον) of the province (του κανονος) God dealt out to us as our measure".[164] The meaning of κανων has been much discussed,[165] but the "geographical" (in the sense "appointed areas of work", not necessarily strictly geographical) connotation of the term cannot be excluded. This connects the text with Gal 2:7–9 and Rom 15:17–20, where Paul states the norm of not building upon the work of others. This consequence was not drawn from the agreement by the Jerusalem authorities, as is obvious from the way they sent their envoys to already existing churches. Perhaps these agents were not sent to do missionary work at all, not even among the Jews of the diaspora, but rather to build a network of contacts, consolidating the internal ecclesial relations between the "old", original Jerusalem church and these newly founded churches, fruits of a mission which originated in Jerusalem (Gal 2:7–9, Rom 15:19). Paul certainly hoped, and perhaps believed, that this was what lay behind the Jerusalem action, but its effect was to disrupt the foundations of the church in Corinth.[166]

---

163. *Barrett* (1973b:31).
164. *Barrett's* translation (1973b:265).
165. *Käsemann* argued against the too restricted interpretation of κανων as denoting Paul's God-given district of missionary work (Lietzmann, Windisch, Bauer) that the concept also includes the whole of Paul's apostolic calling and the grace visible in his work (1942:59–61). In *Lønning* (1972:17–23) the geographical reference of the term is totally excluded, and it is thought to denote "the gospel" of Paul. *Stuhlmacher* locates the background of the term in the Jewish Apocalyptic concept *qan*: "endzeitliches, gerichtlich einklagbares Mass des Schöpfers" and thus interprets Gal 2:9 as a piece of that "Sakralrecht" which is at the same time part of God's election and sending of Paul to the Gentiles and part of human church history (1967:6–7). *Barrett* (1973b:264–268) argues for an interpretation of κανων as denoting "province", comprising both the geographical reference and the assignment from God to Paul to preach the Gospel to the Gentiles.
166. See *Barrett* (1971:238 f) on the "disobedience" of the intruders as regards the "concordat" between Paul and the Jerusalem authorities, notably Cephas.

It seems probable that the Jerusalem church took an active interest in and responsibility for the Gentile Mission of Paul (and others). Acts gives us some indications of the same interest and active measures from this church towards other and successful missions, in Samaria (8:14–25) and Antioch (11:22, 27–30, 12:25), even if we must count with a Lukan tendency to stress the unity of all Christian mission with the source and origin in Jerusalem. It is also a fact that Silas (Silvanus), who was Paul's colleague on the "second missionary journey" which penetrated far into Greece, was a respected member of the Jerusalem church.[167] If we accept the hypothesis advanced by *W.L. Knox, Nickle* and *Hainz* Paul was accompanied on his "third" journey, too, by agents from the Judean churches (ἀπόστολοι τῶν ἐκκλησιῶν (sc. τῆς Ἰουδαίας), 2 Cor 8:23), who were commissioned to function as controllers of the Collection and living signs of unity with the recipient mother church.[168]

Paul did not resent the presence of representatives from the Palestine Church in his area as long as they accompanied him or were otherwise his collaborators. When working together with them he had no difficulty in asserting the full apostolic authority that had been acknowledged by the notables at the Council. To send Jewish Christian envoys, who were obviously suspicious of Paul from the start, without first having made sure that they knew and intended to respect the Council "concordat" must have seemed to Paul to have been a wilful disregard of the agreement on the part of the Jerusalem authorities. But he put all the blame on the intruders.

There existed a vigorous conservative or rigorist wing in the Palestine church which actively distrusted Paul (much in the same way as the Jews did, Acts 21:21, 28) and took measures to counteract his harmful work in the diaspora. His opponents in Corinth (2 Cor 10–13) certainly belonged to this wing, although they did not insist that the Gentiles should be circumcised or that they should observe the Jewish sabbath and feasts. As we can see from Gal 2:11 ff there were "Judaizers"—notably Cephas— who had no thought of demanding the circumcision of Gentile Christians (especially not after the Council), but wished them to conform to certain minimum requirements of Torah-observance concerning food.[169] Some of

167. See below, Chapter 2 A.

168. The two "apostles" mentioned in 2 Cor 8:18–24 have probably been sent out from the churches of Judea (i.e. Jerusalem and environs). They are to act as controllers or witnesses guaranteeing to givers and receivers that everything in this action is rightly done, and they visibly manifest the unity of the Gentile and Jewish Christian churches. This is the interpretation of *Hainz* (1972:149–157) and *Nickle* (1966: 18–22). The latter even suggests their identity: the one mentioned in v 18 is Judas, and that in v 23 is Silas, *idem*, p. 21 f.

169. *Barrett* (1973b:30).

them, unlike Cephas and James, had no respect for Paul as a person and felt free to censure all his apostolic work. But the difference between the Corinthian intruders and Paul was not primarily doctrinal but concerned apostolic authority and legitimacy.[170] And their attitude to Paul clearly indicates that Paul's standing in Jerusalem was neither secure nor unambiguous. This was probably the result of two things: the recognition given to Paul at the Apostolic Council had been deficient in some respect[171], and the outcome of the Antioch Incident had weakened his standing even more.

c) In Phil 3 Paul addresses some pungently phrased warnings for Judaistic missionaries ("dogs") to the church at Philippi. We have no indication of whether they have any connection with the Palestine Jewish Christian church. There is a faint similarity between Phil 3:4–6 and 2 Cor 11:18, 22,[172] where Paul compares himself with the apostles from Jerusalem, but it is not sufficient proof of the origin of the Judaists in Philippi.[173]

d) Galatians shows us a situation where Judaistic agitators urge Gentile Christians to adopt the practice of circumcision. The identity of these agitators has been the object of much scholarly discussion[174] and the answers to this question are numerous: *Munck* considered them to be Gentile Christians, *Schmithals* Gnostic Jewish Christians and *Fitzmyer*[175] and *Schütz* Hellenistic Jews influenced by their background (close to the "Colossian heresy"). A number of authors suggest some relation between

170. Cf. *Käsemann* (1942) and *Schütz*, who give an analysis of the subtle yet profound difference between the two conceptions of the apostolic "I" (ἐγω) (1975:165–186).

171. *Dix* (1953:48 f).

172. E.g. the term 'Εβραιος' which can mean "able to speak Hebrew" and thus be an indication of Palestinian origin occurs in both texts. But here it probably means "full-blooded Jew", see *Barrett*'s discussion on 2 Cor 11:22 and the literature cited there (1973b:293).

173. *Goppelt* thinks that the "workers", (ἐργαται) of Phil 3:2 and 2 Cor 11:13 signifies the same group of "Missionare und Visitatoren der palästinischen Kirche" (1966:69). I do not consider this applies to the former text (cf. *Kümmel* (1973: 287 f), *Wikenhauser-Schmid* (1973:500), but even if it does not we may have a piece of information about Judaists in general in Phil 3:15, where Paul ironically uses the term "the perfect" or "mature" (RSV) (οἱ τελειοι). Probably Paul is referring to a common Judaistic distinction between "perfect" Christians, i.e. such Christians as kept the whole of the Torah, and ordinary Gentiles, who to be sure were exempted from keeping the Torah but on the other hand could not be regarded as "perfect" Christians, *Linton* (1970:193). This suggestion fits in with the picture *Klaus Berger* gives (1977) of how the Jerusalem church assessed different sorts of Christians within the same Church.

174. See *Kümmel* (1973:260–263), *Rohde*'s paragraph added in *Oepke* (1973: 30–36) and *Schütz* (1975:124–128).

175. *Fitzmyer* (1970c:§ 7).

the agitators and the church of Jerusalem. This cannot have applied to the leaders, but to the losing party of the Council (the "false brethren", Gal 2:4 f) who rejected any thought of a law-free Gentile Mission.[176]

If this last view is correct, and the need for Paul to give an accurate report of his contacts with Cephas and Jerusalem indicates that his Galatian opponents were far from sparsely informed about what happened in Jerusalem, we can note the existence of at least two variants of Judaistic opposition against Paul. One type of opposition comes from the extremist, pro-circumcision sector of the Jerusalem (or Judean) church, cf. Gal 2:4 f and 6:12; Acts 15:1. This was by no means condoned by the leaders in Jerusalem, cf. Gal 2:4 ff and Acts 15:24. Another type of opposition came from quarters in closer contact with the leaders; they adhered to the Council agreement, but naturally interpreted it on the basis of a strong, self-confident trust in the superiority of the Jewish Christian church—an attitude that could easily lead to abuse, as 2 Cor shows.

The apparent strength of this anti-Pauline (and in part also anti-Council) Judaistic opposition in Jerusalem must be explained by the support it drew from the historical situation: the rise of a strong nationalistic movement among the Palestine Jews. The leaders, such as Cephas and James, are at least theologically *less* Judaistic than any of Paul's opponents, but they have to take into account the growing political pressure from without. A good example of this "Judaizing" tendency that was forced on the Jerusalem church by its historical context is the reception of the Pauline collection, as we saw above.

To sum up: Cephas did visit Antioch and perhaps also Corinth, and in both places this led to a decline in Paul's authority. It is probable that the Judaistic intruders we see Paul counteracting in Gal and 2 Cor came from the Jewish Christian church in Palestine and that they, unintentionally or wilfully, ignored the principle of non-intervention which for Paul was so natural (2 Cor 10:14, Rom 15:20). It is a fact that Paul had difficulties in defending himself and his cause against the weight of Cephas's example in Antioch (and Corinth) and the whole of his "gospel" and apostolic work against the Judaists in his "own" churches (Gal and 2 Cor). All this indicates that we cannot interpret the agreement in Gal 2:7–9 as being a declaration of equality between Jerusalem and Antioch, or between Cephas and Paul. There seems instead to be good reason to believe that the Jewish Christian church in Palestine, with the Jerusalem leaders at its head, en-

176. *Goppelt* (1966:54), *Kümmel* (1973:262), *Oepke* (1973:212 f), *Schoeps* (in "Urgemeinde—Judenchristentum—Gnosis", 1956, cited by *Rohde*, p. 35 f), *Wikenhauser-Schmid* (1973:417).

joyed an undisputed superiority of status in relation to the Gentile Christian church and its apostles.

3. Paul's Attitude to Jerusalem[177]

The foremost evidence of Paul's attitude to Jerusalem is of course his dogged determination to bring the Collection to a completion and thus fulfil his obligation in spite of sorely trying opposition and defamation from Jewish Christians. But we can easily find this corroborated by what he says about the church in Jerusalem.

In 1 Thess 2:14 Paul compares the harassment the Thessalonians had suffered at the hands of their countrymen to the persecution of the "churches of God in Christ Jesus which are in Judea". This comparison comes more naturally to Paul than that of the nearby Beroea (Acts 17:13), and is obviously meant to be complimentary[178]—an indirect witness of the high regard in which Paul held the church of Jerusalem.

In 1 Cor 11:16 and 14:34 we see the apostle correcting practices in the Corinthian church with regard to the "practice" ($\sigma\upsilon\nu\eta\theta\epsilon\iota\alpha$) of the Jewish Christian church.[179] Here he took his lead from Jerusalem and 1 Cor 14:36 indicates the reason for this: Paul saw the "Word of God" as proceeding from Jerusalem which to him (as well as for contemporary Judaism and Christianity) is the divinely chosen centre for doctrinal decision.[180] Paul's own expression when he surveys his own apostolic work in retrospect ("from Jerusalem and as far round as Illyricum I have fully preached the gospel of Christ", Rom 15:19) shows how natural it was for Paul to regard Jerusalem as the source of the word of God, and to take this, somewhat unhistorically, as the starting point of his own apostolic work.

1 Cor 15:3–11 bears ample witness to the fact that Paul aligns himself with the resurrection witnesses and apostles of Christ. He is the last and least of a closed group of people who have met the Risen Lord, and from one point of view[181] an unworthy member of this group. But through the

---

177. Cf. *Gerhardsson* (1961:274–280) and the description he gives of the Primitive Christian attitude as presented by Luke, p. 214–220.

178. " 'Judäa' meint hier Jerusalem mit dem zugehörigen Land . . . die Stadt, welche die hochgeachtete Muttergemeinde barg. Mit ihr auf die gleiche Stufe gestellt zu werden, war für die Adressaten zweifellos ein hohes Lob", *Staab* (1969:20). Cf. *Stanley* (1959:867 f).

179. "Les 'Églises de Dieu' sont les églises de Palestine, celles dont la pratique fait loi", *Cerfaux* (1965:217). Cf. "Les traditions de Jérusalem font loi", p. 219.

180. *Gerhardsson* (1961:275 f), where this is shown to be an argument using the Scriptures (Deut. 17:8 ff, on which see *idem*, p. 214 f).

181. "Menschlich gesehen ist er der letzte, d.h. geringste Apostel", *Conzelmann* (1969a:306). Only "menschlich"? *Barrett* rightly comments, "In this statement worthiness is reckoned from the standpoint of Christ himself, not from that of Paul's critics.

grace of God he has worked more than any other apostle (Paul "boasts" here of the results of his labour, as in other places in 1 and 2 Cor). We see here how Paul's awareness of his inferior[182] rank as an apostle is paradoxically mixed with unflinching self-confidence. But here it is not Paul who constitutes the standard—he was added, as an afterthought of the Lord Himself, to an already existing group or institution, the apostolate.[183]

This pre-eminence of Jerusalem is not primarily a matter of chronological priority, nor is it a grudgingly made concession to circumstances not in Paul's power to change. Rom 15:27 tells us very clearly what the real nature of the relation was in Paul's eyes: The Gentile churches (in Macedonia and Achaia) are said to be in debt or under an obligation ($\dot{o}\phi\epsilon\iota\lambda\epsilon\tau\alpha\iota$) to the "poor among the saints" (i.e. Jerusalem), "for if the Gentiles have come to share in their spiritual blessings, they ought also to be of service to them in material blessings".[184] Now the question is what Jerusalem had actually done for the churches in Macedonia and Achaia. As far as we know it was Paul himself who founded them and he did by no means regard himself as a missionary sent from the church in Jerusalem. Nor is it likely that he regarded the intrusions in Galatia (Philippi) and Corinth as spiritual blessings. The answer to the question must be that "Jerusalem" is not understood in a purely historical sense, but in a distinctly theological perspective as the source of the Word of God, the Gospel, whose servant Paul is.

This Pauline view of Jerusalem is confirmed by the way Paul describes the collection in 2 Cor 9:12-14, where obedience to God is proved by contributing money to the Christians in Jerusalem, and $\kappa o\iota\nu\omega\nu\iota\alpha$ with them naturally entails supplying their needs (the same terminology is used in Phil 2:30 about the Philippian church's obligations towards its apostle). There can be no doubt that Paul sees the Collection as a form of exchange according to the principle of reciprocity expressed in Gal 6:6, 1 Cor 9:11 and Rom 15:27: he who receives spiritual gifts is to requite with material gifts (of the kind at his disposal).

But, it may be objected, Paul's acknowledgement of the unique role of

---

As far as they are concerned he is ready to insist that he is in no way inferior to the superlative apostles (2 Cor 11,5, 12,11)", (1973a:345).

182. *Brockhaus* (1975:121).

183. See *Cerfaux* (1965:211–221). "Sur un point, toute humilité à part, il se trouve vis-à-vis de ces apôtres en état d'infériorité. Il doit recevoir d'eux les prémières traditions; car il n'a pas connu le Christ et n'a pas assisté aux premiers pas de l'Église", p. 212. C. speaks about Paul being joined to an institution which was formed by the Lord Himself during his Galilean mission (p. 353–358, esp. 355 f). Cf. *von Campenhausen* (1969:30).

184. Cf. *Stuhlmacher* (1968:103 f).

and importance of the church in Jerusalem does not diminish his independence as an Apostle of Christ, which he clearly considered himself to be. And as an Apostle of Christ he is subordinate to no one else in the Church. This remark necessitates a brief discussion on the apostles of the Primitive Church.[185]

In the Primitive Church there existed at least two different kinds of apostles: the Jerusalem Easter apostolate constituted when the Risen Lord appeared to his disciples and commissioned them, and a wandering missionary apostolate, especially in the Syro-Palestinian sections of the Church (as in Acts 11:27, 13:2-5, 14:4, 14, 21:9, Rev 2:2, Did 11:3-6 and even in 1 Cor 4:9, 9:5 f).[186] It seems that the latter group of apostles could also be called prophets and they exhibited a "charismatic" character, i.e. they were regarded by themselves and others to have special, pneumatic gifts (power to work miracles and exorcise, the gift of inspired speech in glossolalia, prophecy). They also lived a markedly "charismatic" life, without salary, home, family. Recruitment to this group of free-lancing missionaries was unrestricted, determined only by the Spirit, although some sort of recognition (and later even testing, cf. Did) by local churches probably was necessary. To the extent that they were called "apostles" we may surmise that they were sent out by a local church on a commission, as we see in Acts 13:2-5 and 14:4, 14, where Barnabas and Paul are clearly apostles of the Antiochene church (cf. Phil 2:25 on Epaphroditus and the "apostles of the churches" in 2 Cor 8:23). The proximity to the Jewish "schaliach" institution is here obvious,[187] and we do not need to assume that this "church apostolate" ("Gemeinde-apostolat") borrowed the term "apostle" from any other context (the Jerusalem Easter apostolate, for example).[188] The decisive difference between this type of apostle and the Jerusalem Easter apostolate is that only the latter was regarded as being sent by the Risen Lord Himself, without mediation, while the former represented a

185. What follows is only a sketch, which leaves many vital aspects undiscussed that I hope to treat in more detail in a coming article. In this section I use the capital 'A' to distinguish Apostles of Christ from other apostles.

186. *Kretschmar* (1964), *Theissen* (1973 and 1977:14–21), *Roloff* (1977:515 f). *Lemaire* thinks that the term originated here, and that Paul and Barnabas were among the first to be called "apostles" (1971:180, 195 f). *Kasting* (1969:71–80), *Hengel* (1972b:33 f), *Delorme* (1974:290 n. 6) and *Hahn* (1974) all find a Jerusalemite origin more probable.

187. *Gerhardsson* (1963:109 n. 28). Cf. on these wandering missionaries also *Georgi* (1964:46 f), *Goppelt* (1966:24), *Lemaire* (1971:180, 195 f), *Oepke* (1973:64 f), *Hahn* (1974:73 f), *Brockhaus* (1975:117 ff) and *Rohde* (1976:183 n. 19).

188. *Brockhaus*, ibidem. I cannot here go into the discussion on the relations and possible influences between the two apostolates.

human sender (a local church).[189] The "Apostles of Jesus Christ" form a group of their own, comparable only to the great leaders and prophets of the Old Covenant (Moses, Isaiah, Jeremiah, etc.), and the difference between them and the other apostles was well known and recognized in the Primitive Church.[190]

Against the background described above we must now ask to which category Paul was regarded as belonging.[191] It cannot be denied that he once was sent out as a missionary together with Barnabas and that he participated in the Apostolic Council together with Barnabas as a delegate from the church in Antioch. It is not improbable that these well-known historical facts contributed to the accusation of his opponents (e.g. in Galatia) that he was only an apostle authorized "by men", an apostle of a local church (Antioch), cf. Gal 1:1, 11 f, 2 Cor 11:5, 12:11.[192] Compared with the Jerusalem Apostles he is an apostle of the second class, whose gospel naturally must be scrutinized, complemented and perhaps also corrected to conform to the one authoritative Gospel in Jerusalem.

Paul himself never refers to any Antiochene apostolate of his,[193] but refers always to his calling as being directly from Jesus Christ (Gal 1:12, 1 Cor 9:1, 15:8). He is an "Apostle of Jesus Christ" (Rom 1:1, 1 Cor 1:1, 2 Cor 1:1, Gal 1:1), the equal of Cephas himself and acknowledged as such by the others at the Apostolic Council in Jerusalem (Gal 2:7-9).[194] In relation to this his Antiochene apostolate probably meant no more to Paul than an incipient confirmation of the Lord's commission—at least in retrospect.

But which apostolate was Paul considered to belong to by the "pillars" in Jerusalem? According to Paul's own words they acknowledged him as an Apostle (of Christ) to the Gentiles, the equal of Peter, "the Rock"; and it is not possible to invalidate this statement as pure or partial imag-

---

189. On this see *Gerhardsson*'s momentous article (1963), whose fundamental thesis had not attracted attention until *Hahn* made it the foundation of his article in 1974.

190. *Gerhardsson* (1963), *Kasting* (1969:61–71), *Hahn* (1974:56–59). Cf. *Roloff* (1965:81) and *Brockhaus* (1975:114, 121).

191. The following perspective on Paul's relation to Jerusalem is taken from *Brockhaus* (1975:120–123).

192. *Stuhlmacher* (1968:67), *Brockhaus* (1975:121), and note 21 above.

193. He is surprisingly silent on this important period of his life and almost conceals that he went to Jerusalem on behalf of the Antiochene church (Gal 2:1). In Rom 15:19 we find "Jerusalem", where "Damascus" or "Antioch" could have been expected, *Hengel* (1972a: 50 n. 23). Is this a reflex of the unpleasant separation from Antioch?

194. *Kasting* (1969:77f).

ination. But two factors in the context of this recognition served to qualify and modify it:

(A) At the same moment as Paul is recognized and acknowledged as an Apostle of Christ to the Gentiles, he is assigned the task by the Jerusalem leaders to collect money for Jerusalem. And, as *Brockhaus* points out,[195] this places him surprisingly close to the "apostles" of 2 Cor 8:23 and Phil 2:25, agents for churches, concerned with money on behalf of their senders. Thus he is at one and the same time defined as an Apostle of Christ (preaching the gospel to the Gentiles) and an apostle of the Jerusalem church (with the task of collecting money from the Gentiles to manifest their solidarity with the centre of the Church: Jerusalem).

(B) Paul was probably not acknowledged as Apostle publicly, but "privately" (Gal 2:2b), since "a formal public recognition of an 'Apostolate to the Gentiles' in A.D. 49 no doubt seemed to S. Peter and the others an impossible provocation to the Jews".[196] This withholding of public approval not only hurt Paul's feelings but made it possible for his opponents to attack him, his personal authority and his apostolic work even after the Council, which they did.

Indirectly this confirms how dependent Paul is on the confirmation of his apostleship by the other Apostles of Christ. He had not been a disciple of Jesus, nor had he known Him personally; instead he had been a persecutor of Jesus's disciples. He was called at the "wrong" place (Damascus, not Jerusalem) and at the "wrong" time (perhaps as much as two or three years after the others), and he is well aware of being an "afterbirth" to the apostolate of the Risen Lord (1 Cor 15:8). "For this monstrous begetting he paid the price all his life long",[197] and part of the price was his dependency, on Barnabas and Antioch, on Jerusalem and the "pillars". Materially he had been fully recognized by them and refers to this as a fact against his opponents in Galatia. But the formal deficiency of this recognition lessens its value. And then the connection between the apostolate to the Gentiles and the Collection for Jerusalem combined to situate Paul, as it were, somewhere half-way between the two categories of apostles. Assuredly he was more than a "church apostle" of the ordinary kind, but in the same measure he was also inferior to the group of original "Apostles of Christ" in Jerusalem. The greater closeness of the other Apostles to Christ simply was part of Paul's definition of his own apostolate (1 Cor 15:5-11).[198]

195. *Brockhaus* (1975:122).
196. *Dix* (1953:49). Cf. the remarks of *Cerfaux* (1965:212 f, 359 f).
197. *von Campenhausen* (1969:30).
198. Cf. *Schlier* (1971:68 f).

The picture sketched above of Paul's oscillation between the two definitions of apostle is related to how he was regarded by others. Whatever he thought of his own apostolate he was forced to take account of the hard historical facts; and other people's definitions of him and his standing in the Church were of course historical facts at the time. This is exemplified by the situation in which Paul writes his letter to the Christians in Rome when he is about to set off on his final journey to Jerusalem. *Bornkamm* and *Jervell* have pointed to the similarity between Paul's situation at the Apostolic Council and his situation at the point where he is about to complete his work east of Rome by delivering the Collection to Jerusalem.[199] Once again the whole of the Apostle's work is at stake—his authority and the authenticity of his apostolate, the justification and acknowledgement of the Gentile Mission and the churches it has brought into existence, the unity of the Church.[200] Paul always regarded his work as ultimately aimed at the conversion of Israel,[201] and therefore must have regarded the impending visit to Jerusalem as extremely important. Should this church refuse to accept the Collection, this would imply that it refused to acknowledge his apostolate and the fully Christian status of the Gentile churches.[202] And this would be a rejection of his (and God's) work among the Gentiles, which could not but result in a destruction of the unity of the Church. Still, Paul is by no means sure that the Collection will be accepted. Political pressure from the Jews in Palestine, the loss of confidence in Paul on the part of Jerusalem after the Antioch Incident which had so painfully been demonstrated by repeated attacks from Jewish Christian quarters in Galatia,[203] Philippi and Corinth—all this served to increase his apprehensions about his reception in Jerusalem. And this is what we see reflected in the apostle's passionate plea to the church of Rome "to strive together with me in your prayers to God on my behalf, that I may be delivered from the

---

199. *Bornkamm* (1971:137 f), *Jervell* (1971:66).

200. *Jervell* (1971:67), *Wilckens* (1974:137 f), *Käsemann* (1974:387, 392). There exists quite a discussion about the question to which degree the letter to the Romans should be understood as written with the Jerusalem visit in mind. *Jervell* names Rom "der Brief nach Jerusalem" (the title of his article from 1971), and this perspective is found also in *Bornkamm* (1971:136–139) and *Suggs* (1967). *Käsemann* gives an account of the discussion (1974:387–392), and so do *Wilckens* (1974), who sides with the Bornkamm-Jervell position, and *Schmithals* (1975:32–35) who does not.

201. *Munck* stressed this perspective strongly (1954:277, 280, 300).

202. A possibility that cannot be excluded, according to e.g. *Schlier* (1977:438).

203. *Wilckens* even thinks that the conflict in Galatia resulted in a triumph for the Judaistic agitators, which impaired Paul's standing in Jerusalem, (1974:136). This hypothesis necessitates the dating of Gal before 1 Cor, and makes it difficult to understand why the letter was preserved by the addressees at all (as it must have been, if we are not to assume that Paul took a copy before he sent it), *Wikenhauser-Schmid* (1973:417).

unbelievers in Judea, and that my service (διακονια) for Jerusalem may be acceptable to the saints (εὐπροσδεκτος τοις ἁγιοις)", Rom 15:30 f.

The conclusion is obvious: The relation between Paul and Jerusalem is much the same at both the Apostolic Council (A.D. 48 or 49) and at the time of Paul's final visit to the Holy City (A.D. 56–58).

He is not subordinate, not an emissary of the Jerusalem church, but fully aware and proud of his independence as an Apostle of Jesus Christ and the magnificent results God's grace has brought forth through him in the Gentile world. But he and his work are still dependent on the recognition of the church which is the source and centre, not only of the Palestine Jewish Christian church but of *all* churches. Paul is certainly eager that this dependence should not be misinterpreted (as it had so consistently been by his opponents during the years preceding the final visit), but he is neither willing nor able to deny the fact of this dependence.

CHAPTER 2

The Distribution of Power within the Pauline Region of the Church

A. PAUL AND HIS CO-WORKERS

1. Paul's Most Important Co-workers and His Relations to Them

From Acts and the Pauline letters we know that Paul did not usually work alone but had a team of co-workers.[1] More than one hundred names are associated with the apostle in Acts and the Pauline letters. *Ellis* has placed thirty-six of them in one or more of nine categories designated "brother, apostle, minister, (co-)servant, companion, labourer, co-prisoner, co-worker, fellowsoldier" (ἀδελφος, ἀποστολος, διακονος, (συν)δουλος, κοινωνος, ὁ κοπιων, συναιχμαλωτος, συνεργος, συστρατιωτης).[2] Twelve of these people stand in a long-term relationship with the apostle, and nine of them continue in close association with him till the end of his life. They are: Mark and Titus (from the Antiochene period, or the first missionary journey), Timothy, Prisca-Priscilla, Aquila, Luke and Erastus (from the mission to Greece, or the second missionary journey), Tychicus and Trophimus (from the final period as they are mentioned only in Eph and Col). Of these nine five, according to *Ellis,* "stand in an explicit subordination to Paul, serving him or being subject to his instructions",[3] namely Erastus, Mark, Timothy, Titus, and Tychicus.

In making these groups *Ellis* has taken care to remove all names that either appear in Acts only or that lack a precise designation. Nevertheless

---

1. According to *Pieper* (1926:154) this is one of the principles underlying Paul's missionary work. Paul does not mention any co-workers in association with his sojourns in Arabia and Cilicia (Gal 1:17, 21). The commentators generally believe that he preached the Gospel even at this time, at least in Cilicia, *Bonnard* (1953:32, 34), *Schlier* (1971:58, 63), cf. *Holtz* (1974:141 n. 1).
2. *Ellis* (1971), see the chart on p. 438.
3. *Idem,* p. 439.

he includes the testimony of the Pauline antilegomena (Eph, Col, 1 and 2 Tim, Tit) on the grounds that they probably contain historical information even if Paul did not write these letters.[4] This is not unreasonable as the Pauline "school" or tradition must have preserved vivid memories of the group of close collaborators whose names we find mentioned in both the genuine Pauline letters and Acts and who must thus be historical persons (this applies to Mark, Timothy, Prisca, Aquila, Luke and Erastus). I should also accord Trophimus and Tychicus the verdict of historicity as their association with Paul is supported by two distinct lines of historical and literary tradition, Acts and the Deutero-Pauline letters. It is possible that one or more of this group survived Paul by as much as twenty or thirty years, and all through these years could possibly have served as a source of information on who Paul's closest collaborators were.

I prefer, however, to make more cautious use of the Pastoral epistles than *Ellis* does, as the historical distance separating them from Paul seems to be greater than that between Paul and Eph and Col.[5] Thus I do not consider we can say with certainty who remained with the apostle till the end of his life. This is why I should like to modify *Ellis*'s list of Paul's closest co-workers:

Erastus is designated "minister, servant" (διακονος) in Acts 19:22 and, together with Timothy, he is given an independent task on Paul's account in far-off Macedonia. If the identification of Erastus as the high official (οἰκονομος, *quaestor*) of Corinth known from an inscription from this city is correct,[6] he cannot very well have followed Paul on his travels or been his assistant for a long time.

Tychicus is not mentioned in any of the letters generally agreed to be genuine, but the picture given of him in Eph 6:21 and Col 4:7 as a conveyor of Paul's letters agrees with the information in 2 Tim 4:12 and Tit 3:12 stating that he was "sent" by the apostle. This is, however, a doubtful basis on which to build a reconstruction of Tychicus as one of Paul's full-time assistants.

Mark, the nephew of Barnabas, is designated co-worker (συνεργος) in Philem 24 and Col 4:11, and in Acts 12:25 and 15:37–39 he is expressly characterized as an assistant of Paul and Barnabas; he is always "brought along" (συμπαραλαμβανομενος). This impression is strengthened, not only by

4. *Ibidem,* n. 2.
5. See the introductions to the New Testament for the dates of the respective letters, and the growing opinion that the Pastorals are pseudepigraphs of a rather special kind and not really comparable to Eph and Col, *Brox* (1969:22–60), *Wikenhauser-Schmid* (1973:515–537). Cf. *Grelot* (1971:455 n. 9).
6. *Theissen* (1974a:241–246).

2 Tim 4:11 ("useful in serving me"), but also by Col 4:11 where he is treated as a somewhat junior assistant who needed a commendation. Philem 24 witnesses to the duration of this relationship, which was not broken for good by the conflict with Barnabas, Acts 15:37 f.[7]

Epaphras must have been a close collaborator of the apostle, as he is his "coprisoner" when Paul writes the letter to Philemon (v 23). This lends credibility to the information in Col 1:7 f, which seems to signify that Epaphras was the founder of the church at Colossae; and there he is given the honorific designations "our beloved fellow-servant" (σύνδουλος) and "faithful minister (διάκονος) of Christ" (cf. 4:12). If this information is correct (which may well be so, even if Paul did not write Col) Epaphras must have been a capable and trusted assistant of Paul and must be counted as belonging to his staff.

Timothy was undoubtedly the co-worker closest to Paul's heart and seems to have been his assistant for a period of about fifteen years. During the "second journey" Paul takes him along as an assistant to Silvanus and himself, after having had him circumcised (Acts 16:1–3).[8] He was subsequently "sent" by Paul as his authorized representative to the churches in Thessalonika (1 Thess 3:2), Corinth (1 Cor 4:17, 16:10) and Philippi (Phil 2:19 ff). The first and last of these visits proved successful, but this does not seem to apply to his visit to Corinth.[9]

Titus was "brought along" (συμπαραλαβών) by Paul (and Barnabas?) to the Apostolic Council in Jerusalem as an uncircumcised Gentile Christian. Demands were made that he should be circumcised, but he probably left Jerusalem as Greek as he was when he came (Gal 2:3 f).[10] We see him most clearly as the representative of the apostle, when he was asked to go to Corinth. He apparently discharged his commission to satisfaction, the Corinthian church repenting from its earlier improper conduct towards

7. Among persons who served Paul for a short time only, but still receive generous designations may be mentioned Epaphroditus (Phil 2:25 ff) and Onesimus (Philem 10 and Col 4:9). See also below, note 55.

8. *Fascher* (1937a:1346 f), *Barrett* (1969:4 f) and *Spicq* (1969:49) think with the majority of scholars that the circumcision of Timothy arranged by Paul is historical.

9. *Fascher* (1937a:1345, 1347). He explains the failure of Timothy in Corinth as being due to the fact that he was probably too Jewish and too Pauline (cf. Phil 2:20–22), including a certain shyness and meekness in personal appearance (cf. 2 Cor 10:10). See also *Spicq* (1969:52).

10. As *Oepke* points out, the highly improbable opinion that Titus was circumcised at the Council, only not *forced* to it, would probably never had been advanced if it were not for the influence of the absolutely impossible reading that leaves out οἷς οὐδέ in v 5. Acts 16:3 concerns the half Jewish Timothy and cannot be adduced as a parallel, even less Gal 5:11, *Oepke* (1973:75 f).

Paul and receiving Titus "with fear and trembling" (2 Cor 7:6–16). Then Paul urges him to return to Corinth immediately and complete the Collection (2 Cor 8:6), and it is this second visit of Titus on which the apostle looks back in 2 Cor 12:18.[11]

It is possible that Titus held a more independent position in regard to Paul than did Timothy—in spite of the συμπαραλαβων of Gal 2:1, which does imply a less than collegial relationship. Two facts speak in favour of this assumption: (a) the terminology of Paul in 2 Cor 8:6, 17 and 12:18, "I urged Titus to go and sent the brother with him": note the difference between "urge" (παρακαλειν), which more or less presupposes the consent of the object, and "send with" (συναποστελλειν) which does not.[12] (b) Titus is never mentioned again in Paul's letters which may indicate that he parted from Paul and worked independently like Barnabas and others.[13] (Here we see a marked difference between Timothy and Titus[14]). The reference to Titus in 2 Tim 4:10 and in Tit 1:5 where it says that he worked in Dalmatia and Crete may reflect a historical tradition in Pauline circles.[15]

This survey of some of Paul's co-workers permits us to draw the conclusion that Paul did have a staff of collaborators, who lived, travelled and worked with him. They served, at least for a time, as his full-time assistants when they were entirely at his disposal enabling him to use his more trusted assistants as a distance medium for his own presence in his churches. This witnesses to the degree of authority he exercised within this group of missionaries. But it is also necessary to keep in mind the fact that the relationship was deeply personal (cf. the use of the father-son analogy, and the many occurrences of "faithful, trusted, beloved" and "brother" when Paul speaks of his co-workers), if we are not to get a wrong impression.[16]

Paul also collaborated at times with persons whose time, travels and missionary capacity were not at his disposal. The three most important missionaries in this category are, in order of appearance, Barnabas, Silvanus (Silas) and Apollos. An examination of Paul's relationships to these three brings out the facts of Paul's authority in his own mission field in full relief.

11. See *Barrett* (1969).

12. *Idem*, p. 11 with note 30. He points out that Paul's request "might have seemed a somewhat unreasonable request", which of course can have influenced the form of it. Cf. *Spicq* (1949:54 n. 1).

13. So *Fascher* (1937b:1582).

14. Timothy is co-sender of Col and Philem (letters sent from prison), and is mentioned warmly in Phil 2:19 ff (written from prison). According to Acts 20:4 he also accompanied Paul on his last voyage to Jerusalem.

15. *Fascher* (1937b:1583).

16. *Grelot* (1974:52).

Barnabas. As was previously mentioned it is true that Paul mentions himself first in Gal 2:1 and makes himself the central figure of his report, but even in this account Barnabas is a colleague and not a subordinated assistant (cf. Titus).

Barnabas is the older of the two and at this time probably had a higher status than Paul, both in Antioch and Jerusalem. It has been suggested that Barnabas who was a Levite from Cyprus, and thus a Greek-speaking Hellenistic Jew, came from Antioch and was one of the founders of the church in this city; then in Acts Luke "moved" him to Jerusalem in order to be able to use him as a mediator between Jerusalem and Antioch, which Luke considered necessary.[17] Another hypothesis is that he belonged to the "circle of Stephen", those Hellenistic Jewish Christians who had to flee from Jerusalem after Stephen's death and later (Acts 11:20) founded the church in Antioch.[18] Most scholars, however, find the notice Acts 11:22 creditable, i.e. that Barnabas lived in Jerusalem even after the persecution of the "Hellenists" and that he was sent by the church in Jerusalem to Antioch after the mixed congregation of Jewish and Gentile Christians already had begun to exist.[19]

Barnabas played an important part as intermediary between Jerusalem and the Primitive Gentile Christian Church ("die heidenchristliche Urgemeinde", in *Bousset's* words) in Antioch.[20] After arriving in Antioch he gave his unqualified assent to the practice of not circumcising converted Gentiles and became an advocate of "law-free" Gentile Mission. Thus a missionary practice, which at first might have seemed to be of local and even incidental occurrence, received authoritative support and eventually universal recognition.[21] From Acts 13:1 we can infer that Barnabas became "the leading man" among the leaders of the Antiochene church,[22] and in this capacity he brought the young and gifted Saul to Antioch where he became one of the prophets and teachers leading this church.[23] Barna-

17. *Weiss* mentions this hypothesis in a note (1917:126 n. 1), and *Schmithals* makes it his thesis (1963:23 n. 6).
18. *Haenchen* (1971:370).
19. *Weiss* (1917:126, but cf. n. 1), *Pieper* (1926:90), *Dix* (1953:35), *Nickle* (1966:28 n. 54), *Conzelmann* (1969b:138), *Burchard* (1970: 160 n. 107) and *Holtz* (1974:133 n. 1).
20. Cf. *von Harnack* (1923:58 n. 1), *Pieper* (1926:91).
21. Even *Haenchen* believes that in this respect Barnabas did not have a walk-on part in missionary history. His courage and insight are decisive in the question of non-circumcision in Antioch (1971:371). Cf. *Maly* (1969:75).
22. *Conzelmann* (1969b:51, 138: "der führende Mann").
23. Cf. Chapter 1, n. 31. Some authors also consider Acts 9:26 f to be historically correct: *Schmiedel* (1899b:486), who otherwise sees Acts 9–14 contradicted by Gal 1, *Maly* (1969:73) and *Burchard* (1970:160 n. 107)—provided that Paul in 1 Cor 9:6 does not count Barnabas as one of the "apostles", of which he only met Cephas (and James, if he was an apostle) on his first visit to Jerusalem. Here Burchard pre-

bas is named first, Saul last, which indicates their difference in status in Antioch.[24]

Acts 4:36 is commonly taken as an indication that Barnabas was known in the Primitive Church as a person who had sold land and given the money to the church of Jerusalem.[25] This may well have been the preliminary to a consistent practice, that Barnabas followed while working as a missionary—to support the Church financially by not using his right to get his living from it (cf. 1 Cor 9:6).

This is not the only principle Barnabas followed. He also took pains to maintain good relations with the church in Jerusalem (Acts 11:30, 12:25, 15:2 seem to reflect this kind of attitude, and are indirectly corroborated by the testimony of Paul in Gal 2:1-10 and 13), but also accepted and defended with all his authority the non-circumcision practice of the Gentile Mission.

These same three principles for apostolic work: to receive no support from the church but to work for one's own living, to maintain good relations with the church in Jerusalem and to maintain a law-free Gentile church were adopted by Paul, who elaborated them theologically and kept to them faithfully all his life.[26] This indicates that there was a time when Paul was taught by Barnabas and learned the "trade" of being a missionary to the Gentiles.

> Un da Barnabas der Ältere ist, ist er der Lehrmeister des Paulus: Barnabas und Paulus verzichten auf das Recht der Missionare, sich von den Gemeinden unterhalten zu lassen.[27]

Acts 13–14 describes Barnabas and Paul as colleagues on the first missionary journey, when the church in Antioch made a missionary thrust into new territory by sending specially equipped and "ordained" missionaries (cf. 13:3).[28] At this time Paul was not a missionary in his own right, as he was later to become, but received his commission from the church in Antioch (or: from the Spirit through the church) and probably also acted

---

supposes a uniform concept of "apostle". But Paul may here (Gal 1) be thinking of the "apostles of Christ" or "apostles of Jerusalem"; Barnabas may not have belonged to either category, as it is not certain that he was regarded as an apostle before he was "sent out" by the church of Antioch (Acts 13:3 and 14:4, 14).

24. *Haenchen* believes that Luke deliberately placed Barnabas and Paul at the top and bottom of the list, in order to emphasize their being brought together as a pair of missionaries in 13:2 as being the work of the Holy Spirit (1971:401). This is an ingenious suggestion, but hardly necessary, as Paul, in spite of his remarkable gifts, was in fact a young man and a newcomer.

25. *Idem*, p. 233.

26. *Conzelmann* (1969b:138).

27. *Ibidem*. Cf. *Cerfaux* (1965:360) and *Theissen* (1975a:200 n. 2).

28. *Catchpole* discusses the historicity of Acts 13–14, (1977:438 f).

as assistant to Barnabas, who was the leader of this missionary enterprise.[29] It has long been noted that Acts refers to the two missionaries a "Barnabas and Saul" (in that order) up to the occasion (13:9) when the latter begins to be called "Paul". From this point on they are spoken of as "Paul and Barnabas", with a few explainable exceptions.[30]

This account of the relationship between Barnabas and Paul does not seem to be tendentious, as if the intention had been to depreciate Paul and make him appear inferior to Barnabas. On the contrary, if Acts has depicted Paul as the instigator and founder of the Gentile Mission we would have had cause to consider the account tendentious. But it is just what we can expect—that Paul, like other humans, grows up and reaches full stature gradually. It would be anachronistic to transpose the "full-grown" Apostle to the Gentiles we meet in Paul's letters to this first appearance.[31] Besides, even Acts shows us Paul as the active preacher and missionary, the person who is most exposed (13:16, 14:8 f, 12 "he was the chief speaker", 19 f). Presumably this is a historical touch and not just an idealizing tendency of Luke's. This growing importance of Paul, which came from his capacity of theological analysis and effective address is manifested at the Apostolic Council, where we can sense from Paul's own report ("tendentious" as it is) that he was the active and leading one of the two Antiochene delegates.[32]

Later the Antioch Incident caused a break in the relations between Barnabas and Paul (Gal 2:12 ff, Acts 15:36 ff) and the development of an increasingly independent missionary enterprise on the part of Paul. Apparently this did not diminish the respect Paul felt for Barnabas as an apostle,[33] and the plural in 1 Cor 9:4 ff signifies that Paul is not thinking only of himself as having the same rights as "the other apostles", but also includes Barnabas in this "we".[34]

29. *Weiss* (1917:152): "der eigentliche Führer der Unternehmung", *Maly* (1969: 74), *Oepke* (1973:66).
30. *von Harnack* (1897:410 f).
31. *Weiss* (1917:130). He is followed in his opinion that Barnabas was originally the leader but is outgrown by his younger colleague, by *Pieper* (1926:155), *Fascher* (1937b:1579), *Goppelt* (1966:46), *Conzelmann* (1969b:139), *Maly* (1969:74 f) and *Hengel* (1972b:18).
32. *Conzelmann* (1969b:139), cf. *Bonnard* (1953:36). *Dix* presents Paul's contribution at the Council as the decisive one: he was the one to put the question of the relation of the Gentiles to the law in such a fundamental way (cf. Gal 2:14–16) that the Jerusalem church in its faithfulness to the Gospel had no other choice but to acknowledge the Gentile Mission—and this, they knew, would eventually ruin their own chances of converting Israel, (1953:46–49).
33. *Weiss* (1917:33, 526), *Roloff* (1965:61, possible), *Kasting* (1969:65) and *Ellis* (1971:439) think that Barnabas was regarded as an apostle.
34. *Barrett* (1973a:204).

As Gal 2:7 ff indicates some sort of division of the missionary responsibility had been agreed upon at the Apostolic Council, the parties to the agreement having been on the one hand "the pillars" and on the other Paul and Barnabas. These two thus were the primary representatives of a special *type* of apostles, viz. apostles to the Gentiles (ἀποστολοι εἰς τα ἔθνη) while the others were apostles to the circumcised (ἀποστολοι εἰς την περιτομην). Now we know that both Barnabas and Paul (and probably their collaborators as well, cf. 2 Cor 12:18) followed the practice of not using their apostolic right to support from the churches, while the Palestinian missionaries did avail themselves of this right. This difference is probably one of the causes for the criticism of Paul we glimpse in 1 Cor 9:2 and 12.[35] The reference to Barnabas, a person known and respected in Jerusalem, Antioch and also in the Pauline churches, is not made merely to gain esteem by association, but above all in order to connect Paul's abstention from his rights with a practice common to *all* apostles to the Gentiles.[36] This warns us not to exaggerate the seriousness of Paul's separation from Antioch and Barnabas. In 1 Cor 9 (and Gal 2) he still sees himself connected with Barnabas in that special relationship to Jerusalem and its apostles which was the result of the agreement at the Council.

Silvanus (Silas). Today there is common agreement that the Silas mentioned in Acts 15—18 and the Silvanus mentioned by Paul in 2 Cor and 1 and 2 Thess are one and the same person.[37] According to Acts 15:22 ff, Silvanus (I will use Paul's name from now on) was one of the delegates that the church of Jerusalem sent with the Apostolic Decree to Antioch and other places. Silvanus (Silas) and Judas are there described as "leading men among the brethren" (ἀνδρες ἡγουμενους ἐν τοις ἀδελφοις),[38] probably they were "members of the original circle of Christians there".[39] Somewhat

---

35. Cf. *Theissen* (1975a).

36. *Barrett's* conjecture that 1 Cor 9:6 is "evidence that he (sc. Barnabas) rejoined the Pauline mission" (1973a:204) is not only unfounded, but also builds on the false assumption that the conflict between Barnabas and Paul caused Barnabas to abandon Paul's mission. The truth is quite the opposite: it was Paul who left the church of Antioch and his senior colleague Barnabas. Cf. *Holtz* (1974, esp. p. 125).

37. A thorough discussion of the identity of Silas-Silvanus can be found in *Schmiedel* (1903) and *Selwyn* (1969:9–17). The latter argues that Silas-Silvanus after his collaboration with Paul eventually became the co-worker of Peter and co-operated in the writing of 1 Peter, cf. 5:12).

38. On the ground that ἡγουμενος in all its other occurrences in the New Testament means leader ("chef") *Cothenet* proposes that the term has the same meaning here, and concludes that Judas and Silas may have belonged to the collegium of presbyters in Jerusalem.

39. *Selwyn* (1969:11), followed by *Maly* (1969:78). *Haenchen* thinks it self-evident that Silas cannot have been a notable of Jerusalem, but must have been one of the very few Jews who were open to a law-free Gospel. As Barnabas was once

further on (Acts 15:32) Luke speaks of Judas and Si!vanus as being prophets.

If 1 Thess 2:7 is to be regarded as including the co-senders of the letter, Silvanus and Timothy (1:1), these two missionaries also were considered "Apostles of Christ" by Paul.[40] If this could apply to Silvanus (who was after all a ἡγούμενος from the earliest days in Jerusalem) it is not probable that Timothy really is included, as he had not seen Christ risen nor, as far as we know, had received a commission directly from Him to preach to the Gentiles (or Jews).[41] From the prescripts to the two letters to Thessalonika and from 2 Cor 1:19 it appears that the later highly trusted Timothy stands below Silvanus in rank—a piece of information which agrees with the report in Acts about the second missionary journey (Acts 16—18).[42] It is important to note that Paul's colleague in this enterprise was a man from the church of Jerusalem[43] and that they worked together in harmony— Silvanus is co-sender of 1 (and perhaps also 2) Thess.

After the second missionary journey Silvanus disappears completely from the group of Paul's co-workers mentioned in his letters. This is probably an indication of his independence: he was not a young assistant, converted by and chosen by Paul, but a respected colleague almost the equal of Paul himself, who after having worked for a period together with Paul chose to continue in other areas.

Apollos. Acts 18:24–28 tells us that Apollos was an "eloquent" or learned (λόγιος) Jewish Christian from Alexandria who taught in the synagogue at Ephesus. As his knowledge of Christianity was deficient—he only knew about the baptism of John, v 25b—he was more thoroughly instructed by Priscilla and Aquila about the way of God.[44] When Paul first

---

also one of the notables of Jerusalem, and Peter and James fully condoned the Gentile Mission without circumcision, it is a little difficult to understand why this could not have applied to Silas-Silvanus.

Nickle considers that Acts 15:22 ff is a historical reminiscence of a connection between Judas, Silas-Silvanus and Paul which has been distorted by the Lukan amalgamation of the Apostolic Council with the formulation of the Apostolic Decree, (1966: 21 f). Cf. above, Chapter 1, n. 168.

40. *Weiss* (1917:527), *Rigaux* (1956:156, 418), *Selwyn* (1969:11), *Ellis* (1971: 439: only Silvanus). Selwyn considers that the thorough-going use of the first person plural in 1 Thess indicates "a closer and more continuous joint-authorship than was always the case at other times" (p. 15). For the question of who were regarded as apostles (of Christ), see the discussion in the previous chapter.

41. *Selwyn* (1969:11 n. 3): Timothy is not included. *Roloff* does not even find Silvanus's apostolate probable, (1965:61).

42. *Fascher* (1937a:1343 f).

43. "Es bedeutete wohl eine Art von Rückversicherung Jerusalem gegenüber, dass Paulus ihn mitgenommen hat", *von Harnack* (1923:85). If this is correct Silvanus's presence was not a kind of control over Paul exercised by the Jerusalem church.

44. This has been discussed by *Käsemann* (1952), who sees vv 25b–26 as a redac-

became acquainted with Apollos he had already become a Christian missionary[45] who had worked in Corinth after Paul had left that city and had then returned to Ephesus where Paul met him personally at the time when 1 Cor was written (1 Cor 16:12).

Apollos seems to have been successful in Corinth, but at the same time his presence there was one of the causes of dissent and schism within this church. Some members looked up to Apollos as their own special authority to the degree of opposing his ways to Paul's. One of the main points in Paul's argument against tendencies to schism in 1 Cor 1:10—4:21 is the complete harmony between the teachers whose teachings the Corinthians are quarrelling about. In 1 Cor 3 he takes Apollos and himself as examples of this: they are both God's "servants" (v 5), "fellow workers" (v 9), "servants of Christ and stewards of the mysteries of God" (4:1). They had different tasks within God's work: Paul planted, Apollos watered—but God gave growth.

Still there is a difference in rank between Apollos and Paul which Paul discreetly makes clear by the choice of his next analogy. He is a "skilled master builder" ($\sigma o\phi os$ $\dot{a}\rho\chi\iota\tau\epsilon\kappa\tau\omega\nu$) who lays the foundation, while Apollos is one who continues building on the foundation (i.e. a mere "builder" or "workman", $\tau\epsilon\kappa\tau\omega\nu$).[46] No names are mentioned, but the apostle makes it clear to the church in Corinth that they have cause to carefully scrutinize the quality of the continued work of construction, while the foundation laid by himself is perfect and cannot be relaid (3:11 ff). Apollos is in no way a rival or a threat to Paul, as they have separate functions.[47]

1 Cor 16:12 shows, on the other hand, that Apollos does not stand under Paul's command and that he is not obliged to obey his wishes. Paul

---

tional insertion by Luke, and is followed by *Haenchen* (1971:556). *Schweizer* (1955) criticizes Käsemann's hypothesis, and is followed in this by *Goppelt* (1966:61 f, n. 36). I find Schweizer's interpretation the more probable one, but this does not make any difference to my statements about Apollos here.

45. *Ellis* (1971:439 n. 8) sees 1 Cor 4:9 as evidence for the theory that Paul regarded Apollos as an apostle (he is mentioned in 4:6). But neither Roloff nor Kasting, who exhaustively discuss which persons Paul could have regarded as apostles discuss this possibility (see above, n. 33 and Chapter 1, n. 190).

46. Cf. the conclusion of *Vielhauer*: "Paulus bringt also mit dem Bild vom Fundamentieren für seine apostolische Tätigkeit 1. das zeitlich Primäre, 2. die sachlich entscheidende Bedeutung seiner Arbeit für jede weitere Arbeit und damit 3. seine absolute Überlegenheit, Autorität und Sonderstellung zum Ausdruck", (cited from *Hainz*, 1972:267 n. 4). Cf. *Pfammatter* (1960:22–24).

47. *Chevallier* (1966:22–48). *Haenchen* (1971:555) also notes the contrast and finds here an indirect confirmation of Acts 18:25: the foundational preaching of Christ was lacking in Apollos's proclamation. On the other hand he had what Paul lacked: eloquence and "wisdom". *Hyldahl* considers that Paul criticizes Apollos in 1 Cor, although not openly (1977:27–29).

says that he "strongly urged him (πολλα παρεκαλεσα αὐτον) to visit you with the other brethren, but it was not at all his will (και παντως οὐκ ἦν θελημα) to come now. He will come when he has opportunity". Some commentators suggest we should understand the genitive "God's" (θεου) instead of "his" (αὐτου) behind "will" (θελημα) thus giving the meaning "but it was not at all God's will that he (Apollos) should come now".[48] This does not fit into the context, however, as we get the definite impression that Paul had asked Apollos to go, not that he asked God to let Apollos go, and that the decision to go or not rested with Apollos who is also the one giving the courteous refusal that he will come when the opportunity arises.[49] This refusal to go was probably made, not in protest against Paul's authority, but out of a delicacy of feeling as Apollos knows of and resents the use of his name to provoke dissension in the Corinthian church. He now lets his supporters know through Paul that he has no intention whatsoever of encouraging this by coming to them.[50]

After 1 Cor 16 Apollos disappears from the Pauline letters, and we may take this as an indication that he henceforth worked independently.

2. Paul and the Gentile Mission: Some Conclusions

It is not possible in this context to discuss the history of the primitive Christian mission,[51] but some conclusions about Paul's role can be drawn from what has been said above about his co-workers.

The first conclusion is that Paul was not the only Christian missionary to Jews and Gentiles in the diaspora and not the first. The second and immediately evident conclusion is that a number of Christian missionaries were working in the diaspora partly or entirely independent of Paul. The church in Damascus was in existence before Paul's conversion (as Acts 9:10, 18b–19 testify, indirectly corroborated by Gal 1:16 f and 2 Cor 11:32 f), as was the church in Antioch, which had begun to convert Gentiles even before the arrival of Paul. There are hints of Christian mission in Alexandria in the forties, and Suetonius's famous reference to the edict of the Emperor Claudius expelling the Jews from Rome in A.D. 49 is

---

48. *Barrett* (1973a:391 f), following *Schrenk* (1938:59 n. 24).

49. *Robertson-Plummer* (1911:392 f) point out that "the will of God" does not fit into the context here as it does with the parallels adduced for this interpretation, Ign.Eph 20, Ign.Rom 1 and Ign.Smyrn 1.

50. *Schmiedel* (1899a:262) interprets Apollos's refusal to go as a sign of "delicacy of feeling" in him, and *Robertson-Plummer* think that he did not want to be captured by the Apollos-party (1911:383). Cf. *Allo* (1935:463) and *Spicq* (1952:215 f) for similar interpretations.

51. For the literature, see *Hengel* (1972b:15 nn. 2 and 3).

generally regarded as evidence that the Christian mission had already reached Rome by this time.[52] When Paul arrives in Corinth (Acts 18) he meets two Christians,[53] Priscilla and Aquila, who have been expelled from Rome by the edict of Claudius, and to judge from Acts 18:26 they were zealous in propagating their faith; and in Ephesus Apollos preached before Paul started any real missionary work there[54] (the short stay mentioned in Acts 18:19 ff does not seem to have had anything to do with the founding of a Christian church in Ephesus, even if Priscilla and Aquila may have been commissioned by Paul to prepare the ground).[55]

Dix summarizes

> As historians we must look behind the drama, and remember that by A.D. 50 the "Gospel" was already lodged in the midst of the Gentile world in a scattering of Jewish-Christian groups of "disciples", ready to break out like a fire through the "God-fearing" Gentile fringe of the synagogues all over the Greek world, as soon as it was released to do so by the Council of Jerusalem. It was this immediate many-centred radiation of preaching from within the Greek world which altered the balance of Jew and Gentile in the Church in much less than a decade, as no single missionary thrust into Hellenism from outside could have done.[56]

It is already quite clear from the fragments of information we can gather from Paul's letters and from Acts that the picture of the expansion of the Christian Church as having one point of origin and then spreading systematically into Palestine, Syria, Cyprus, and Asia Minor, then into Greece and lastly "arriving" in Rome (in the person of Paul) is a simplified picture. It has been constructed in retrospect to show the purposefulness of the Spirit in driving the Church forward in a mighty curve from Jerusalem to the centre of the Empire. It should not blind us to the fact that we simply do not know anything about how large and important churches such as

52. *Dix* (1953:30 f), *Goppelt* (1966:41 f), *Ehrhardt* (1969:65).
53. On the probability that they had already been Christians in Rome, see *Ehrhardt* (1969:98) and *Conzelmann* (1969b:80).
54. Even if *Schweizer* is correct in his assumption that Apollos was a non-Christian Jew when he arrived at Ephesus (cf. n. 44 above), he may have known something about Jesus which he wanted to preach, and according to Acts 18:26 he was in any case a Christian preacher in Ephesus before Paul arrived there (Acts 19:1).
55. What is told about them in Acts and in Paul's letters indicates an unusual degree of energy and initiative in working for the Gospel, and I think it is safe to conclude with *Ellis* (1971:439) that Prisca-Priscilla and Aquila "also should be included among those who, though in friendly association with the Apostle, for the most part work in relative independence of him".
56. *Dix* (1953:55). Cf. *Streeter*'s emphasis on the fact that Gentile Christianity spread almost of its own account and that Paul was not its originator or leader—factors which account for the variety evident in the different parts of the Gentile Church (1929:44 ff).

those in Rome and Alexandria came into existence and what their relations with the mother church in Jerusalem were.[57]

Luke's picture of Paul in Acts is part of this simplification: to him Paul is the great Witness and Missionary, while Barnabas and Silvanus (Silas) are reduced to mere helpers in the margin. But as we saw Paul is not in command over Barnabas, and this applies to Silvanus, Apollos, and perhaps Titus as well. It is thus impossible to understand the agreement of Gal 2:7–9 as if Paul was made the one and only leader of the Gentile Mission, not even of the Antiochene Gentile Mission, with the right to organize the mission and direct the work of all the other missionaries. Of course he had personal assistants, maybe a whole staff, but so had Barnabas and possibly others too.

These remarks are not intended to reduce the enormous importance of Paul during his day or since. But historically he is part of a movement which with great speed spread from Jerusalem over the entire Empire. In parts of Asia Minor and Greece he was one of the pioneers, and he was without comparison "the greatest mind among the recognised leaders in the whole spontaneous movement",[58] and contributed in a decisive way to the crucial decision in Jerusalem A.D. 48 (or 49).[59] He never intended to found a new "Gentile Christianity", he extended the one and only "Israel of God".[60] The "Hellenistic" churches never form a unit with Antioch as their metropolis that can in any way be compared with the manner in which the Jewish churches in Palestine were related to the church in Jerusalem. Gal 2:1 and 11 ff provide sufficient evidence that the Christians of Antioch also regarded this church as their superior authority.[61]

As we saw in the previous chapter the church in Jerusalem did not limit its activity to Palestine. This gives us reason to believe that we should regard the content of the Council agreement not only as the mutual recognition of two different spheres of interest and mission, but also as the agreement on a mutual responsibility of these two spheres. This explains the converging two movements of (a) Jerusalem's interest in the Gentile Mission and (b) the wish of Paul, apostle to the Gentiles, to maintain continuity with Jerusalem.[62]

Jerusalem did endeavour to maintain contact with the extra-Palestinian

57. *Ehrhardt* (1969:71, 108). On the Lukan tendency concerning the origin of the Church, see e.g. *Schmithals* (1963:24–28).
58. *Dix* (1953:56).
59. Cf. above, note 32.
60. *Dix* (1953:56). This view is also prominent in *Munck* (1954).
61. See *Goppelt* (1966:45) on Paul's special theological importance for the Gentile Church.
62. *Bultmann* (1953:94), *Goppelt* (1966:46, 119 f).

churches, as is witnessed to by the cases of Barnabas and Silas, who were both sent by Jerusalem and became prominent missionaries to the Gentiles. Paul's own work is intimately connected with theirs: he begins his "career" as an apostle to the Gentiles as the assistant and younger colleague of Barnabas. When he continues his work he is without doubt the leader of his team of missionaries, but Silvanus, the prophet from Jerusalem, is his respected colleague throughout this journey. Only gradually Paul begins to work with assistants he has converted himself or found willing and able in his churches. Paul is consequently from the beginning part of this movement outwards from Jerusalem and he is fully aware of it (cf. Rom 15:19, 1 Cor 14:36).

As we saw in the discussion of Gal 2 in the previous chapter Paul did not only stress his independence in regard to human beings, he also valued the recognition of his apostolate by the Jerusalem notables. It is also a fact that throughout his apostolic career he strove to manifest the communion of the Gentile Churches with their *fons et origo,* the church in Jerusalem, as is proved by his great Collection (2 Cor 8–9, Rom 15:27).[63]

Thus we find that the investigation of the relationship between Paul and his co-workers not only throws light on his authority at the "regional" level, but also serves to confirm the conclusions reached in the previous chapter: Paul and the church of Jerusalem stand in a relation of mutual, but not symmetric, independence and responsibility.

B. PAUL AND HIS LOCAL CHURCHES

1. Paul, the Founder

Paul's founding of a local church implied a profound, life-transforming and permanent influence on a group of people. This influence transformed every aspect of their existence: spiritual, intellectual, ethical and social.[64]

---

63. This view of the relationship between the missions of Paul and of Jerusalem receives some confirmation from (a) *Laub's* analysis of terminology and content in that Gospel Paul preached to the Gentiles in Thessalonika the first time he came there, (1973:26–40), and his later conclusion: "Diese Beobachtungen führen zu dem Schluss, dass Paulus mit seiner Erstverkündigung vor Griechen nach Sprache und Inhalt in einer Reihe zu sehen ist mit dem missionierenden Judenchristentum im hellenistischen Raum vor und neben ihm" (1976:25, cf. 1973:33); and (b) the analogous conclusion formulated by *Dungan* as a result of his detailed analysis of how Paul and the Synoptic Evangelists perserve, select and interpret the words of Jesus: "The alleged contrast between Pauline Christianity and that branch of the early Church which preserved the Palestinian Jesus-tradition that finally ended up in the Synoptic gospels is a figment of the imagination. In fact, they were one and the same branch . . ." (1971:150). On the relation between Paul and the Synoptic tradition, see also *Fjärstedt* (1974).

64. *Theissen* mentions that this conversion is something of a "third birth" (the first is the biological birth, the second is the socialization into a socio-cultural context), (1974c:44 f).

(a) Spiritual influence

There can be no doubt that Paul's act of founding a local church implied an influence on deep layers of the personalities of the converts. In almost every letter the apostle alludes to this type of experience, as something natural and says that the recipients of the letter have received the Holy Spirit.[65] Phenomena such as ecstatic speaking in tongues (glossolalia), visions and prophecies, miracles of healings have accompanied the conversion of the group and manifested the individual and corporate experience of salvation.[66] The converts have experienced the liberating effects of divine powers in their innermost, and these experiences have significantly affected them for the rest of their lives.

(b) Intellectual reconstruction

The most prominent aspect of Paul's work is his preaching of the Gospel of Jesus Christ. He is bound to the Gospel and the Gospel to him.[67] His preaching and instruction effect an intellectual revolution for those who receive and believe in the Gospel and henceforth they share with Paul the Christian world of ideas. The apostle can presuppose their knowledge of God, His creation of the world and His holy will, His Son Jesus Christ and His resurrection from the dead, His Holy Spirit, who is effused over those who believe and are baptized, the continuity of the Church and Israel and the abolition of the Torah as a road to salvation for Gentiles, how the Church was created, and how the Lord Jesus is soon to return in divine glory with all His angels and judge the whole world. All these mighty ideas with their far-reaching consequences now constitute the fund of knowledge of the local church. This massive intellectual influence from the apostle is evidenced on every page of his letters and needs no detailed confirmation here.

(c) Modification of ethical conduct

The last statement in the preceding paragraph also applies to the influence Paul has exerted on his converts' ethical conduct. The new existence also includes a reconstruction of moral precepts and habits, that has connections with Jewish-biblical and popular philosophical patterns, but that nonetheless has a distinctive Christian character.[68] We find paraenesis in

65. Rom 8:23, 1 Cor 1:5–7, 2:12, 3:16, 12:4–13, 2 Cor 5:5, Gal 3:2 ff, 4:6, 1 Thess 1:6, 4:8, 5:19.

66. "St. Paul assumes the common ground of an experience of salvation", *Williams* (1950:12).

67. See e.g. *Roloff* (1965:83–103), *Stuhlmacher* (1968:56–108), *Schütz* (1975: 35–53).

68. See e.g. *Gerhardsson* (1961:303–305, with literature), *Selwyn* (1969:437–439), *Wendland* (1970:57, 61 f, 67–69, etc.), and any textbook on New Testament ethics.

all of Paul's letters and this points to the fact that we here have a continuation of the influence Paul exerted on the norm-system of the new Christians during the founding period.[69]

(d) Establishment of a corporate life

A large part of the apostolic paraenesis deals with conduct in the "church" (ἐκκλησια), into which the Christians were incorporated by their conversion and baptism. Paul presupposes that baptism is initiation into the Church, without explicitly defining its nature (Rom 6:4, 1 Cor 12:13, Gal 3:27). In the same way he has taught his churches to celebrate the eucharist in the same way and with the same words he had learnt himself (1 Cor 11:17 ff). It is simply a fact that the new Christians assemble to worship God, with prayers, hymns, reading and expounding of the Scriptures, prophecy and glossolalia.

To the corporate life of the church belongs also Paul's teaching on which sins exclude a man from the kingdom of God (1 Cor 6:9–11, Gal 5:18–21). It is in the nature of things that church discipline does not come into the picture during the very first weeks or months of the church's existence, but by the time the letters were written we find that the exhortations concerning those who deviate from Christian norms and instructions on how to treat them are a standing topic (1 Thess 5:14, cf. 2 Thess 3:6–15; Rom 16:17, Phil 3:2, cf. Gal 1:8; 1 Cor 5:11 f and—if it is Pauline—2 Cor 6:14 ff).[70]

(e) Incorporation into the "communion" (κοινωνια) of the whole Church

Paul's foundational preaching, such as we find it in the old, probably Jerusalemite tradition in 1 Cor 15:3 ff,[71] told his converts that he was not alone as apostle[72] and that the Church has its origin in the revelations of the Risen Lord Jesus to his disciples in Jerusalem. Through Paul every local church has a direct relation to the whole Church and to salvation-history and is incorporated into a movement with universal dimensions.

This knowledge has been increased by the apostle's journeys between the different communities and the news he has brought with him. And in his

69. That it is a continuation of something that has begun earlier is shown by texts such as 1 Cor 4:17, 11:1, Phil 2:12, 4:9, 1 Thess 4:1.

70. *Forkman* (1972:132–151, 170–172, 179–181, 191–193).

71. *Gerhardsson* (1961:296 f). Cf. *Brown* (1974:81–83).

72. The unintroduced mention of Cephas in 1 Cor 1:12, the brothers of the Lord in 1 Cor 9:5 and Barnabas in 9:6 and Gal 2:1 shows that Paul's local churches knew about the leading persons of the Church before Paul wrote his letters.

letters we see Paul holding up his churches as examples to one another (Rom 1:8, 2 Cor 8:1–5, 9:2, 1 Thess 1:7 f, 2:14, 4:10a) and thus weaving a net of relations between them. The foremost example of this strengthening of the Church's κοινωνια is of course the Great Collection, which has even been called "a sacrament of unity in the primitive Church".[73]

Paul also wants to establish at least the outlines of a common halakic practice in all his churches, and sometimes refers to this as normative: 1 Cor 7:17 (an apostolic halakah[74]), 11:16 and 14:33b–34a. In the two last cases the apostle probably refers to the custom of *all* churches, including the most important one, Jerusalem, as is seen from 1 Cor 14:36.[75] We may conclude that Paul and his co-workers have acted as transmitters of an authoritative tradition even as regards worship, baptism and the eucharist.[76]

This summary description of Paul's founding work serves to remind us that what we see in his letters is only a small part of a very comprehensive relationship, the fundamental and decisive phase of which lies before the time of these letters. Paul and his addressees have a common history behind them when we meet them, and this history has largely been shaped by the apostle. He is the founder of the churches in Galatia, Thessalonika, Philippi and Corinth and as such has initiated their Christian life. He has every reason to describe himself as their "father" (1 Cor 4:15, 1 Thess 2:11) or "mother" (Gal 4:19, 1 Thess 2:7b), who has brought them to life and let "Christ be formed in them" (Gal 4:19). This fact must not be forgotten when we try to get a clear picture of Paul's power in his churches.[77]

"Paul regarded his apostolic presence to his congregations under three different but related aspects at once: the aspect of the letter, the apostolic

73. *Williams* (1950:100).
74. *Gerhardsson* (1961:314).
75. *Idem*, pp. 275 f, 306. Cf. *Cerfaux* (1965:216 f, 219); *von Campenhausen* (1957:54 n. 45): in 11:16 the Palestinian churches are not necessarily referred to. The authenticity of 14:34–35(38) has been increasingly questioned and these verses thought to be an interpolation (a type of solution that is unfortunately again becoming more popular in New Testament scholarship). For a detailed discussion of this see *Dautzenberg* (1975:257–273, 291–298).
76. "From the evidence of the New Testament, it appears that the early Church thought that the authority of Christ Himself lay behind these two sacraments", *Williams* (1950:97). On worship in the Primitive Church see the survey of *Skjevesland* (1976:128–179), and on Paul's relation to tradition, see *Gerhardsson* (1961:288–323) and the literature cited by *Mussner* (1974:36 n. 166).
77. See *von Campenhausen* (1969:44–46), "It is implicit in the nature of such a 'paternal' relationship that primarily it is simply Paul himself who is *the* authority", p. 45.

emissary, and his own personal presence. All of these are media by which Paul makes his apostolic authority effective in the churches."—"The presence of Paul in person will therefore be the primary medium by which he makes his apostolic authority effective . . . Letter and envoy will be substitutes, less effective perhaps, but sometimes necessary."[78]

Our difficulty in ascertaining what kind and amount of power Paul exercised in his churches consists in the fact that we only have access to evidence from the least powerful substitute for the apostle's primary medium of apostolic authority: his letters. Still, we must try to infer from this evidence what kind of power Paul exercised when present himself in a local church and when acting through an emissary.

2. Paul's Power in the Local Church Exercised by His Personal Presence

In the following I shall reckon with three kinds of evidence: material concerning Paul's self-understanding, his actual (pneumatic) powers and concerning what attitudes and actions towards himself and his wishes he expected as natural manifestations from the church. My intention is not to investigate Paul's theology of his own apostolate and the Gospel in relation to the church,[79] but to draw some conclusions from the reciprocal role expectations of apostle and church to the amount of actual power the apostle exercised.

(a) Evidence from Paul's self-understanding

A recurrent theme in Paul's letters is his insistence on the fact that when he preaches it is God who really is the speaker; for example: "when you received the word of God which you heard from us, you accepted it not as the word of men but as what it really is, the word of God", 1 Thess 2:13; cf. 1 Thess 2:3–4, 4:15, 1 Cor 14:37, 2 Cor 5:18–20 "we are ambassadors for Christ God making his appeal through us" ($\dot{v}\pi\epsilon\rho$ $X\rho\iota\sigma\tau\sigma\nu$ $\sigma\dot{v}\nu$ $\pi\rho\epsilon\sigma\beta\epsilon\nu\sigma\mu\epsilon\nu$ $\dot{\omega}s$ $\tau\sigma\nu$ $\theta\epsilon\sigma\nu$ $\pi\alpha\rho\alpha\kappa\alpha\lambda\sigma\nu\nu\tau\sigma s$ $\delta\iota$ $\dot{\eta}\mu\omega\nu$). As 1 Thess 4 shows this does not apply only to the preaching of reconciliation through Christ, but also to Paul's ethical instructions of which he can say (v 3): "this is the will of God". Anybody who repudiates this or preaches another gospel repudiates God Himself (1 Thess 4:8, Gal 1:8). This enormous claim is based on Paul's own assurance of being an apostle of Christ, as he often reminds his readers (1 Thess 2:6, Gal 1:1, 1 Cor 1:1, 9:1–2, Rom 1:1, 11:13). He is

---

78. *Funk* (1967:249 and 258 respectively).
79. For this see e.g. *Roloff* (1965:104–124), *Hainz* (1972:267–294) and *Schütz* (1975, passim).

bound to the service of Christ and His Gospel as a slave to his lord (Gal 1:10, 1 Cor 9:16–23, Rom 1:1). This places him on the same level as the highest authorities in the Church, the other apostles (1 Cor 12:28, 15: 9–11, 2 Cor 11:5), and gives him his authority and responsibility with respect to all Gentiles (Rom 1:5, 11–15, 11:13, 15:14–24, 2 Cor 11: 28).[80] Thus he finds it perfectly natural to compare himself with Isaiah and Jeremiah (Gal 1:15, Rom 1:1),[81] and to describe his work as "the offering of the Gentiles" to God (Rom 15:16; cf. Phil 2:17).

All of this is stated intrepidly; Paul knows it to be true and does not expect anybody to doubt him or call any of his assertions about his own authority to question.

(b) Evidence for Paul's pneumatic endowment

"Our gospel came to you not only in word, but also in power and in the Holy Spirit and with full conviction" (1 Thess 1:5). Paul preached the message in words, but this "gospel" or "word of the cross" does not consist of mere words but is a power of God (Rom 1:16, 1 Cor 1:18). Both the apostle and his readers have experienced the supernatural effectiveness of this simple, unassuming preaching in transforming the lives of those who heard him.[82] But the apostle has transmitted the Gospel, the Spirit and the power of God not only by verbal means but also through acts that were specifically pneumatic. Paul knows he has the gift of tongues (1 Cor 14:18, 2 Cor 5:13), the gift of prophecy (1 Thess 3:4, 1 Cor 15:51, Rom 11: 25 f, Gal 5:21), the gift of performing healing miracles (2 Cor 12:12, Gal 3:5, Rom 15:19),[83] and he knows that he has been "caught up into Paradise" (2 Cor 12:2 ff). Thus he is fully endowed with extraordinary, pneumatic gifts. Paul is a spiritual man (πνευματικος) (1 Cor 2:15, 7:40),[84] endowed with spirit (πνευμα) and able to transmit these spiritual powers (πνευματικα, 1 Cor 2:13), or, as he prefers to call them, spiritual gifts of grace (χαρισματα) to others.[85] And no doubt a person who with the congregation can deliver a Christian brother to Satan to the destruction of his flesh and can threaten to "come with a rod" to test the strength of the church in Corinth (1 Cor 5:5 and 4:21, respectively), really has power.

80. For many others: *Cerfaux* (1965:213–216).
81. Cf. on this "prophetic" self-understanding *Munck* (1947), *Holtz* (1966) and *Cothenet* (1972:1287 f, with literature).
82. "The power of God in the Gospel and the Church is characterized by a certain element of *incognito*", *Williams* (1950:79).
83. *Brockhaus* (1975:192 n. 226).
84. On this term, see *Ellis* (1974).
85. For a detailed treatment of the Spirit in relation to the apostle and his churches see *Hainz* (1972:322–335), and esp. *Chevallier* (1966:65–135).

But does Paul in fact have the power to do this? He admits himself that his bodily presence is weak and that he is unskilled in speaking (2 Cor 10:10 and 11:6), and the contrast between powerful letters and meek personal performance when he is actually present has been obvious. But even more damaging to Paul's image was the conflict we glimpse in 2 Cor 12:21 "I am afraid lest, when I come, my God should humiliate me again in your presence".[86] As *Barrett* comments, "This may well refer to an occasion . . . when he had received, with meekness, injury and insult from a rival apostle, while the Corinthians had stood by and failed to take his part", an insult consisting of disobedience and revolt in a situation face to face with his rival.[87] Must we assume a hiatus between rhetorical assertion and historical fact with reference to Paul's power in his churches?

To answer this question we must grasp the relation between strength and weakness in Paul's person, and acquire a correct understanding of the conflict between Paul and the Corinthian church that we read of in 2 Cor 10—13.

Paul and his readers knew of his pneumatic endowment from repeated personal experience, and nobody in Corinth doubted that the apostle could speak in tongues, prophesy and heal. The offensive fact was, however, that Paul was a visibly sick man and could not heal himself.[88] Both his power and his sickness[89] were conspicuous and the latter tended to throw discredit on the former. This was an unpalatable *contradictio in adjecto,* and we know Paul asked God to be spared from it (2 Cor 12:8). But he did not interpret it as a paradoxical identification of strength and weakness, as if only his weakness were visible, God's power through him being invisible.[90] He regards it as an unusually clear example of the gulf between the divine

86. *Barrett*'s translation (1973b:329f).
87. *Ibidem.* In his discussion of 7:12, which refers to the same incident, *Barrett* does not exclude the possibility of face-to-face "disobedience and revolt" from a rival apostle to Paul, p. 213.
88. *Jervell* (1976), whom I follow here. Cf. also *von Campenhausen*'s discussion of this (1969:39–44).
89. Many attempts have been made to identify Paul's sickness from Gal 4:13 f and 2 Cor 12:7 "a thorn in the flesh" $\sigma\kappa\delta\lambda o\psi$ $\tau\eta$ $\sigma\alpha\rho\kappa\iota$ *Minn* lists the following main alternatives: speech defect, ophtalmia, epilepsy, recurrent malarial fever. J. B. Lightfoot early stated which criteria any serious attempt to identification must meet: $\sigma\kappa\delta\lambda o\psi$ was (1) of physical character, (2) painful, (3) permanent and recurring, (4) signally handicapped Paul's ministry, (5) was manifest to the world around Paul, (6) of a humiliating character, "liable to expose the Apostle to contempt and ridicule", and (7) something that could be accepted not only with resignation on the part of Paul, but also with satisfaction (2 Cor 12:9b), *Minn* (1972:23–37). *Binder*'s (1976) argument that "weakness" ($\dot\alpha\sigma\theta\epsilon\nu\epsilon\iota\alpha$) in 2 Cor 11–12 does not mean a sickness but human frailty is not consistent with Lightfoot's criteria.
90. *von Campenhausen* (1969:42), *Jervell* (1976:197).

and the human, widened to a painful extreme, so that the message was plain to all. In himself Paul is so weak and disease-ridden that nobody can believe that the mighty work he does is due to his own efforts—there is only one other available conclusion, it is God who works through His apostle. Thus, while the gulf between Paul's own person and the God-given work he performs never lessens, it is by no means true that he does not have the divine power with which to build up and, if need be, tear down (2 Cor 13:10).

This interpretation of Paul's power as real and ready to be exercised even for suppressing and punishing disobedience is also the only one that tallies with the expressions of power-consciousness in 2 Cor 1:23, 10:1-6 and 13:10. The "painful visit" Paul alludes to in 2 Cor 2:1-5, 7:12 and 12:21 cannot be understood as if Paul with all his powers had tried to maintain authority in Corinth in the face of a revolt from the church, but failed.[91] The pain consisted in the fact that the Corinthian church did not support their own apostle, Paul, against the rival apostle (or group of apostles). Not until Titus returns for the second time (the first time he came with good news, 2 Cor 7:6 f) from Corinth, does Paul learn that a new group of "apostles" from the Palestinian church has intruded into his ground and been at least partly successful in ousting him from his position of authority. What Paul threatens to do in 2 Cor 10:1-6 and 13:10 is thus something he has never before attempted in Corinth (perhaps the expulsion mentioned in 1 Cor 5:5 is the closest parallel). Otherwise, we should have to accuse the apostle of engaging in a show of rhetoric, which both he himself and the Corinthians knew to be ridiculously without backing. Rom 15:26 ("Achaia") and the general current agreement that Paul wrote his letter to the Romans from Corinth less than a year after writing 2 Cor admits of the conclusion that Paul actually succeeded in regaining his position in the Corinthian church.[92]

(c) Evidence from the attitude Paul expects from his "children"

Paul's power has not been manifested in an authoritarian way, through giving strict orders and demanding prompt obedience. His "style" consists of teaching, exhorting, explaining and appealing. He has shown considera-

---

91. *Barrett* (1973b:7 f, 19 f).

92. 2 Cor was written in the autumn of A.D. 55 or 56, *Kümmel* (1973:255), while Rom was written from Corinth in the following spring, *idem.* p. 272. So also *Barrett* (1973b:10). Cf. "Paul is plainly counting on the collapse of the opposition which has been formed behind his back, once it is confronted with the moral—and perhaps not merely moral—force of his personal presence", *von Campenhausen* (1969:43).

tion and care and consistently acted towards his converts with the affection of a father. And this analogy must have been of some importance to Paul as he uses it so frequently (1 Thess 2:5–12, Gal 4:19, 1 Cor 3:1–3a, 4:14–16, 2 Cor 6:11–13, 12:14).[93] By calling himself the "father" (or "mother") of his churches the apostle expresses the fact that he has begotten them or given them life by the transmission of the Gospel of Christ.[94] But Paul's "fatherhood" does not consist only in this, but includes a continuing educational relationship with three components: teaching, imitation and correction.[95] The call to imitate the apostle is a consequence of the father-child relation and may be indirect evidence that this is considered to exist even where we only meet the exhortation to imitate Paul. This exhortation is given to the churches in Galatia (Gal 4:12), Thessalonika (1 Thess 1:6, indirectly), Philippi (Phil 3:17, 4:9) and Corinth (1 Cor 4:16, 10:33—11:1), i.e. those churches he had founded or brought to life himself. We can reasonably conclude that Paul thought of himself as the "father" of all the churches he had founded.[96]

The image of fatherhood is not used only to characterize Paul's attitude to his own communities, but is also meant as a description of how they should conduct themselves towards their spiritual father, Paul. We can easily make out a list of obligations to him as follows: (a) They are to recognize their debt of gratitude both for what their "father" has given them (1 Thess 2:8 f, 1 Cor 4:15, 2 Cor 12:14, Philem 19) and for how he did this (1 Thess 2:5–7, 10–12, 2 Cor 12:15 read in the light of 1 Thess 2:9) (b) trust and even be proud of their "father" (2 Cor 5:12, 12:11) (c) repay their debt of gratitude by opening their ears and hearts to him (2 Cor 6:11–13, Gal 4:19 f) (d) recognize their "childish" inferiority and inability to judge their "father" (1 Cor 3:1–4, 4:1–4, 2 Cor 3:1–3) (e) aim their actions at pleasing their "father" (Phil 2:2, 16) (f) imitate their "father" and regard him as a concrete example (1 Cor 4:16, 10:33—11:1, 1 Thess 1:6, Phil 3:17, 4:9, Gal 4:12)[97] (g) obey their "father" (1 Cor 4:21, 2 Cor 2:9, 7:15, 10:6, Phil 2:12, Philem 21) and

---

93. Timothy and Onesimus are described as children of Paul, the former in 1 Cor 4:17 and Phil 2:22, the latter in Philem 10; both were probably converted by Paul himself. This may be true of Titus too, cf. Tit 1:4.

94. *Gutierrez* describes how "fatherhood" was regarded in antiquity (1968:15–83), and gives a very detailed analysis of this conception in Paul's letters. It is still a metaphor in 1 Thess, but not in 1—2 Cor (pp. 116 and 168, respectively).

95. *Idem*, p. 172–196.

96. *Stanley* (1959:872).

97. On *imitatio Pauli* see the discussion and literature cited in *Agrell* (1976:118 f), to which can be added *Austgen* (1966:53–58) and *Gutierrez* (1968:178–188). *Agrell* argues that the treatment of this *topos* in 2 Thess 3:7–9 differs significantly from other genuinely Pauline texts. There Paul always says something about himself imi-

(*h*) be intensely aware of the relation and what it entails (2 Cor 7:7b, 11–12, 8:7b).

Paul does not speak explicitly of himself as "father" in all the texts referred to above, but this is a list of the attitudes he expects to find in his churches as natural manifestations of the relation established between them and him by his founding of the church (their "begetting"). In the whole of the Pauline correspondence there is only one instance (2 Cor 10—13) where the apostle does not take it for granted that he will be obeyed.[98] Consequently we may presume that Paul normally had reason to expect the attitudes from (a) to (h) above in all his dealings with his churches. This is not a matter of wishful thinking on the part of Paul, but a fairly accurate description of the relation existing between apostle and church. And then it is of course also indirect evidence of his power in his local churches. He could count on being listened to and obeyed.

Paul's actual power is not strictly formalized, and we cannot make out a catalogue of well-specified apostolic rights with a corresponding list of obligations on the part of the church even if rights and obligations obviously exist. Instead we find in all letters, except Rom, the conception of apostolic fatherhood and imitation ($\mu\iota\mu\eta\sigma\iota\varsigma$), which, as a description of the relation between apostle and local church is milder and at the same time more demanding than a list of rights and obligations. It is milder because it signifies an affectionate relation, but it is also more demanding—when are you free from the obligation of respecting and obeying "father", and when have you repaid the debt of gratitude to the person who has given you life (eternal)?[99]

---

tating Christ and aims at inculcating an attitude of humility, while in 2 Thess "a specific matter of moral conduct" (p. 119) is treated.

This argument overlooks the fact that Phil 3:17 must be read in the light of 4:9, which undoubtedly refers to Paul's concrete way of life as being in all respects exemplary; so also *Austgen* on 2 Thess 3:7–9 (1966:55). And Timothy is probably sent to Corinth, not to bring the Corinthians some more examples of Paul's humility, but to give concrete guidance as regards conduct in a confused situation. 1 Cor 4:17 together with Phil 2:22 points to the intimate connection between fatherhood and imitation: children should learn correct conduct by imitating their "fathers". Cf. *Laub* (1973:83 f), and *Schürmann* (1968:318 n. 60) about the authoritative-juridical element of Paul's example.

98. *Barrett* (1973b:244). Some doubts as to what Paul expects from the churches of Galatia may also be raised, but Gal 5:10 is hardly a mere *captatio benevolentiae*. But even the qualification regarding 2 Cor 10–13 could be questioned in the light of the preceding discussion about what Paul expected when writing this part of the letter. On the significance of beginning a new paragraph with a $\pi\alpha\rho\alpha\kappa\alpha\lambda\omega$-clause (2 Cor 10:1), see *Bjerkelund* (1967:154 f, 188). Cf. below on Paul's terminology of admonition.

99. *Knox* rightly comments on how Paul stresses his "fatherhood" as regards the Corinthians: "more tenderly (sc. said), but perhaps more coercively on that account" (1955:92 f).

3. Paul's Power in the Local Church
   Exercised through Representatives

Two of Paul's assistants have been used as envoys to his churches more
than others, viz. Timothy (who was sent to Thessalonika, Philippi and Corinth) and Titus (who was twice sent to Corinth). Paul recommends them
to the churches by means of letters of introduction (ἐπιστολαι συστατικαι)
incorporated in his epistles, and this fact alone tells us that his position is
above that of those addressed and of his assistants. But the introduction is
not simply an order to receive the person in question. Normally the person
he "sends" is praised for his (or her) merits, especially the merit of having
been of help to the apostle and his work for the Gospel (1 Cor 4:17, 16:
10, Phil 2:20 ff, 2 Cor 7:15a, 8:16; cf. what is said about Euodia and
Syntyche in Phil 4:3, and Phoebe in Rom 16:2). But in the case of Timothy and Titus the apostle makes it clear that he expects not only that they
will be accepted but also that they will be received as representatives of
the apostle, in teaching (1 Cor 4:17 "remind you of my ways", 16:10
"doing the work of the Lord") or taking charge of the collection for Jerusalem (2 Cor 8:6, 23) for which Paul is responsible (cf. 1 Cor 16:3).

We can summarize what Paul demands for his envoys as follows:

(a) recognition as envoys of the apostle, acting on his authority. Cf. the
    succinct declaration of status in 2 Cor 8:23a "As for Titus, he is my
    partner and fellow worker in your service" (εἰτε ὑπερ Τιτου, κοινωνος
    ἐμος και εἰς ὑμας συνεργος).

(b) obedience (1 Cor 4:17, read in its context; 2 Cor 7:15).

(c) financial support of the same kind as the apostle enjoyed: "speeding
    on" (προπεμψις) (1 Cor 16:11).[100]

We find a certain correspondence between what the apostle can expect
from the churches and what his emissaries can expect. As "media" for the
apostolic presence the emissaries participate in the apostle's power, both as
regards what they convey from him (teaching, instruction, leadership) and
as regards what they are entitled to receive from the churches.

4. Paul's Power in the Local Church
   Exercised through Letters

It is a commonplace of the literature on Paul's letters that they are not
private letters but official documents within the apostolic ministry.[101]
Through the letters he builds upon the foundation he laid on his first visit.

---

100. See below on Paul's financial relation to his churches.
101. "Der Brief steht für den Apostel! Sein Brief ist kein blosser 'Gelegenheits-
brief.' auch kein blosser 'Anlassbrief', sondern die Stimme des Apostels selbst",
Mussner (1974:44 f). Cf. *Funk* (1967:265 et passim).

We can even observe this in Paul's earliest extant letter, 1 Thess. In 3:10 he says that it is his earnest prayer that he may meet the Thessalonians face to face and "supply what is lacking in your faith". This wish must for the time being be fulfilled through the letter itself, as we can see from Paul's use of the phrase "concerning . . . you have no need to have any one write to you" (περι . . . οὐ χρειαν ἐχετε γραφειν ὑμιν, 4:9, 5:1). That which the recipients already practice (4:9) or know (5:1) he has no need to teach them, but merely remind them of. Paul probably regards his expositions (4:13–18) and exhortations (4:1–8, 5:12 ff) as such "supplements" to the foundation he had laid. The concluding request in 5:27 (cf. Col 4: 16) shows that Paul himself considers his letter important and wants all the members of the church[102] to have contact with their apostle through the medium of the letter.[103]

This building upon the foundation comprises theoretical and practical instruction; in the Pauline letters we find theological expositions, definitions of problems and answers to them, exhortations to conduct themselves in accordance with Christian norms and concrete advice or instructions in unclear or controversial questions, sometimes also sharp criticism and rebukes. Even a summary reading of these letters shows that the apostle uses them as media for the modification of belief or conduct or, in other words, that he exercises apostolic authority through his letters.[104] But this general impression needs qualification and a more accurate definition. A detailed discussion of each and every exhortation and expression of the apostle's will would lead too far and cannot be undertaken here. But I shall try to establish what degree of normativity Paul's exhortations have, by investigating how much freedom of action he leaves his readers, and by looking more closely at the terminology he uses for manifestations of his own will.

(a) Independent choice of action?

We may presume that Paul wanted his churches to grow up to Christian maturity (1 Cor 3:1 ff), which entails a capacity to make independent decisions. And we notice that sometimes he would have liked to have seen

102. Cf. *Ellis's* hypothesis that "the brothers" (οἰ ἀδελφοι) in this context (and some others) does not refer to all Christians in the local church but to a group of apostolic co-workers (1971:446 ff, esp. 449 f).

103. *Forkman* has shown the role of letters in reproval or admonition. Each occasion, whether established by personal presence or by letter, adds to the number of times a certain admonition or reproval has been delivered, and this is of consequence for the rule of repetition of reprovals (Deut 19:15: two or three witnesses). Paul (and the Damascus Document, CD) interprets Deut 19:15 as if "witnesses" from different occasions can be united in order to make judgment possible, which explains 2 Cor 13:1–2 and some of the repetitions in 1 and 2 Thess (1972:133 f).

104. On this see *von Campenhausen* (1941, 1957, 1969:44–52), *Käseman* (1955: 75–77).

manifestations of this independence, which have however failed to appear (1 Cor 5:2, 6:5). In 2 Cor 2:5-10 we see him counting on the church making the right decision, while 1 Cor 5:3-5 prescribes what the church shall decide and ought already to have decided.[105] But where do we find the apostle giving his churches freedom of action?

There are a number of cases where Paul leaves the choice open, not because he does not know which is the better choice, but because both choices are possible:[106]

(a) 1 Cor 7:3-6; sexual relations are normal in marriage, spouses may abstain for a time, but are not obliged to do so.[107]

(b) 1 Cor 8:8-10, 10:25-28, Rom 14:13-23: the norm is "all food is permitted", but one ought to abstain from meat from sacrifices if one has scruples about it, on one's own or another's behalf.

(c) 1 Cor 7:8 f, 28, 38: those who are unmarried may marry, but would be better off if they abstained from marriage.

(d) 2 Cor 8:8-10 (and the whole of ch. 8—9): the Corinthians ought to give generously to the Collection for Jerusalem, but are not obliged to do so.

(e) Philem 8-10, 17, 21 f: the norm is "treat Onesimus as a brother", Philemon is free to find out for himself what this means, but can count on Paul wanting to know his decision (v 22).[108]

I have deliberately formulated the conclusion from the cited texts so that it will be clear that the alternatives are not equally good in Paul's eyes. Even in those cases where he explicitly qualifies the normative force of what he wishes and does allow different alternatives, freedom of choice is in reality restricted. This is especially true of cases (d) and (e), in spite of Paul's qualification "I say this not as a command" ($o\dot{v}$ $\kappa a\tau$' $\dot{\epsilon}\pi\iota\tau a\gamma\eta\nu$ $\lambda\epsilon\gamma\omega$).[109]

---

105. See *Barrett* (1973a:125), *Hainz* (1972:54–58) and esp. *Forkman* (1972:139–151).

106. *von Campenhausen* (1969:49).

107. Here I follow *Barrett*'s interpretation of Paul's concession (1973a:157 f): you spouses *may* abstain from sexual relations sometimes, but (and this is said against prevalent exaggerated asceticism) this is not a command that you *shall* make pauses. So also *Héring* (1949:52). "Or he may be labelling as a concession his advice against prolongation of continence", *Daube* (1971:232 and 1959:12). *Dungan*'s interpretation "You may marry" (1971:87 f) seems improbable to me, as to *von Campenhausen* (1957:51 n. 38) who however decides that it means, "You may have sexual relations within matrimony", which is even more improbable from the context.

108. Phil 3:15 f which, together with Rom 14:5, is sometimes taken as indication of a certain freedom of opinion in Pauline churches, cf. *Barrett* (1970:383), cannot allow such an interpretation, as *Gnilka* has clearly shown (1968:200–202).

109. On the Philemon case, see *Lohse*: "Es wird also nicht in sein Belieben gestellt, ob er sich zum Handeln in der Liebe bereitfinden will oder nicht, sondern er wird zum Gehorsam gegenüber dem apostolischen Wort verpflichtet" (1968:286 f).

As mentioned above the whole of 2 Cor 8—9 is a campaign of persuasion on the part of the apostle, and it is only by disregarding psychological and sociological realities that one can conclude from 8:8 and 10 that Paul allows the Corinthians "their liberty in any matter that does not concern Christ and his word".[110] This is not to deny what was said at the outset about Paul's wish to see his converts grow up to maturity and his general wish not to burden them unnecessarily (cf. 2 Cor 1:24, 4:5).[111] But the apostle's intentions of fostering independence do not invalidate the power he actually has and exercises, be it ever so modestly. With this in mind we shall now examine the terminology Paul uses when manifesting his will in his letters.

(b) Terminology of admonition

The most frequent term of admonition is "urge" (παρακαλω), which is not severe. *Bjerkelund* has made a thorough investigation of the cases where the verb is used in 1. pers. sing, the παρακαλω-clauses.[112] His conclusion is of interest here:

"In the p.-clauses παρακαλω has neither a sense of commanding (ἐπιτασσω) nor a sense of entreating (δεομαι). παρακαλω is used by Paul when the question of authority is unproblematical and the apostle can addresss the members of the congregation as his brothers knowing that they will acknowledge him as apostle" (my translation).[113]

Admonitions begun in this way are thus not orders or imperatives, but a type of admonition that takes into account the moral judgment and spiritual independence of the church.[114] Still it is interesting to note that the agent of the verb in those cases where it does not mean "comfort" is almost without exception a person who is commissioned to exhort other Christians (the possible exception being 1 Thess 5:11, where it may, however, mean "encourage" (RSV) or "hearten" (NEB) one another). "Urging, exhortation" (παρακλησις) thus seems to presuppose a degree of authority in the

110. *von Campenhausen* (1969:49). Cf. *Austgen* on 2 Cor 8–9, "in which Paul . . . with the professional finesse of a social psychologist attempts to sell the venture to that community" (1966:70 f). A. points out that in these chapters Paul does not rely upon religious motives, but upon a "series of contemporary natural motives, largely derived from the moral standards of Greek social life" (p. 71). From this foundation Paul leads the Corinthians to religious applications and motives (pp. 72–82).
111. A good discussion of this in *von Campenhausen* (1969:49–52). Cf. below, n. 120.
112. *Bjerkelund* (1967:13–19) lists them all.
113. *Idem*, p. 188.
114. *Idem*, p. 190. Cf. *Dahl* (1967:319).

"sender". νουθετειν is a rather mild, fatherly type of admonition (1 Cor 4:14), with the connotation "bringing (children, or unreasonable persons) to reason". It naturally presupposes that some people have more reason than others.

"I want" (θελω) in 1. sing. present tense signifies "a wish that is capable of realization, and ought to be realized . . . , almost a command", [115] at least in most cases (Rom 16:19, 1 Cor 7:32, 10:20, 11:3). I think, however, that in 1 Cor 7:7 and 14:5 the apostle expresses a wish which he knows to be unrealizable.[116]

In most cases the phrase "I say", (ἐγώ) λεγω does not have the connotation "authority". But in three cases its meaning is approximately "I, the Apostle, hereby declare". This is most obvious in 1 Cor 7:12 where, as a number of commentators agree, Paul formulates a commandment with a high degree of normative force.[117] The two other cases of this "halakic" use of λεγω are Gal 5:2 and Rom 12:3, where Paul makes statements of more than usual importance. In Gal 5 it concerns the consequences of circumcision for baptised Gentiles; in Rom 12 it introduces the image of the church as the Body of Christ, a conception Paul knows from experience is fundamental to the life of any church.[118]

In four cases Paul makes a distinction between the normative force of his own admonition and that of the "order" (ἐπιταγη, ἐπιτασσειν). 1 Cor 7:6, 2 Cor 8:8 and 10, Philem 8–10 were discussed above. In the fourth case, 1 Cor 7:25, the apostle explains: "concerning the unmarried, I have no command of the Lord" (as I had concerning divorce, in v 10) "but I give my opinion" (Περι δε των παρθενων ἐπιταγην κυριου οὐκ ἐχω, γνωμην δε διδωμι). This might give the impression that Paul has no authority or right to order (ἐπιτασσειν) or instruct (παραγγελλειν) his fellow Christians, unless he has an explicit command from the Lord to support him. But Philem 8 shows this impression is wrong: Paul could indeed give Philemon orders concerning the slave Onesimus who is Philemon's property.[119] But Paul purposely uses a lesser normative force than that available to him, probably because he wants to preserve the personal, "father-son" character of the

115. *Barrett* (1973a:158).
116. *Schrenk* (1938:45 n. 8) and *Greeven* (1952/53:311).
117. *Gerhardsson* (1961:313), "it is pronounced κατ᾽ ἐπιταγην". Among those who think that this apostolic charge has an authority not significantly less than that of verse 10 are *Barrett* (1973a:163), *Hainz* (1972:61 f), and cf. *Kugelmann* (1970: §39) and *Conzelmann* (1969a:146 n. 25).
118. *Brockhaus* (1975:195 f).
119. "Paulus hätte das volle Recht, Befehle zu erteilen. Und über eine ἐπιταγη, die kraft apostolischen Rechtes ergeht, wäre kein weiteres Wort zu verlieren, sondern ihr ist als bindender Weisung unbedingt zu gehorchen", *Lohse* (1968:276).

relationship with Philemon. This choice is an important indication that Paul may be able to choose between different degrees of normative force when manifesting his will, and that he does not necessarily use the maximally available degree. As a matter of fact there are reasons for making the opposite assumption: Paul usually wants to stress the personal, "fatherly" side of his role vis-à-vis the church in his letters (1 Thess 2:7–9, 2 Cor 12:14). His attitude is well expressed in 2 Cor 1:24 "Not that we lord it over your faith; we work with you for your joy". But in the same letter we find the apostle in a situation of great strain threatening the Corinthians with a manifestation of his power (13:10). It can be concluded from this that Paul has more power than he wishes to use, and that he intentionally refrains from burdening his churches with more rules and heavier demands than is necessary.[120]

The verb "command" (διατασσειν) is not as strong as "order" (ἐπιτασσειν), and we find Paul using it three times in connection with his own instructions: in 1 Cor 7:17, a "proof of the Apostle's own 'legislative' authority",[121] in 1 Cor 11:34 and 16:1. The same term is used in 9:14 about the "command" of the Lord regarding the support of preachers, where "Paul does not however quote a saying of Jesus; he produces a halakah based on such a saying".[122] The use of διατασσειν seems to signify instructions of halakic character, whether they are based on a saying of Jesus or they come from Paul direct.[123]

The use of "give charge" (παραγγελλειν) also indicates that the distinction between the authority of the Lord and that of His apostle does not exclude the fact that the latter's instructions are binding. To judge from 1 Cor 7:10 "I give charge, not I but the Lord" (παραγγελλω, οὐκ ἐγω ἀλλα ὁ κυριος) the term signifies a high degree of normative force (cf. 7:25). But in 1 Thess 4:2 and 11 we find it used about the apostle's own instructions,

120. *Gerhardsson* (1961:314, who considers this to be Paul's heritage from bet Hillel and from Jesus, p. 309 f). On this subject see *Daube* (1971).

121. *Ibidem*, continuing, "He has laid down (διατασσειν) a halakah for *all* his churches, to the effect that each person is to remain in the state he was in when he was called." Cf. *Conzelmann*'s contrary opinion, in the teeth of the evidence here and in 11:16, 14:34, 36, "Paulus vertritt nicht ein Prinzip der Einheit der Kirchenordnung. Er kämpft ja gerade gegen die Schematisierung, welche eine bestimmte Weise der κλησις postuliert" (1969a:151).

122. *Gerhardsson* (1961:318).

123. *Dodd* states (1953:104 n. 1) that the sense of the term is not as strong when Paul uses it of his own instructions. Naturally there is a difference between the Lord's authority and that of the apostle, but halakot can also be given on the latter basis. Cf. "der Gebrauch des Verbums διατασσω hat in 1 Kor (7, 17; 9, 14; 11, 34; 16, 1) durchaus gesetzlichen oder Kirchenordnungscharakter", *Dautzenberg* (1969:216). *Roloff* remarks that Paul sees the will of the Lord in the custom of the churches (1965:130 f).

including that about working with one's own hands. And in 1 Cor 11:17a he characterizes his instructions on women wearing veils during worship (vv 3–16) as a "charge" (παραγγελλων)[124] which, together with the emphasis put on this question, may indicate that Paul regards himself as speaking as normatively in 1 Cor 11:3–16 as in 7:10. In both cases he is the Apostle, commissioned by the Lord, although in 11:3 ff he has no word of Jesus to base his halakah on. This is not to deny that Paul is aware that he must distinguish between speaking by right of his own authority and when he is supported by the word of the Lord.

In the above discussion I have touched on the question of the relation between Paul's authority and that of Christ. But as I am here only presenting evidence for the power Paul actually exercises in his churches there is no need to go fully into this complex question.[125]

The different degrees of apostolic authority cannot always have been easy to distinguish clearly, and this must have been particularly difficult for Paul's audience. This means that when harmonious relations prevail the apostle is presumed to be speaking with a high degree of normative force throughout.

5. Paul's Financial Relations with His Churches

The first thing to be stated here is that financial relations do exist between Paul and his churches and not only in exceptional cases. The issue is touched upon in almost every one of the seven homologoumena.[126]

(a) Προπεμπεσθαι

One kind of financial support the apostle probably received from all churches is that which lies behind the term προπεμπεσθαι. The plain meaning of the verb is "follow on his way, accompany", as in Acts 20:38 and 21:5. In the Primitive Church it became part of a fixed missionary terminology[127] and acquired a richer content: "to equip somebody for the continuation of a journey" by providing food, money, guides, travelling company and making arrangement for travelling by boat, etc.[128]

The remarkable thing is that we find an expectation of this kind of ma-

124. See Barrett's discussion of the textual criticism of this verse (1973a:258 n. 1, 260). The Greek New Testament, 3d ed., 1975 (=Nestle, 26th ed.) gives the text I have chosen, without any alternatives.
125. See, e.g. Schütz (1975:205–232) or the works of von Campenhausen in the bibliography.
126. Or in every one of them if Strelan (1975) is right; see below.
127. "ein fester Ausdruck der Missionssprache", Michel (1966:369 n. 3).
128. Bauer (1958:1407), and Michel (see preceding note), who adds "Empfehlungsbriefe", and Schlier (1977:435).

terial support in Paul's letters to Corinth (although Paul had told them that he would never accept any support from them, 1 Cor 9:15b, 2 Cor 11:9b f) and to Rome (a church that Paul had neither founded nor visited before). From 1 Cor 16:6 we gather that this expectation of being equipped for the continuation of a journey is not restricted to one particular journey ("wherever I go"), nor does it apply to short journeys only as we learn from 2 Cor 1:16 ("to Judea") and from Rom 15:24 ("to Spain"!). 1 Cor 16:11b tells us that this expectation also applied to Paul's assistants.[129]

Here we have an obligation to support missionaries so fundamental and indisputable, that it does not even enter the discussion of the delicate question of why Paul did not avail himself of his apostolic rights (1 Cor 9, 2 Cor 11—12). And nonetheless this must have been a considerable cost for the churches.

(b) The rights of apostleship

Paul's most detailed exposition of his apostolic right to material support is found in 1 Cor 9 where he attaches great importance to the fact that he has not availed himself of this right (ἐξουσια). As he, the apostle, has abstained from exercising this right "rather than put an obstacle in the way of the gospel of Christ" (1 Cor 9:12b) so the "strong ones" in Corinth ought to abstain from their freedom and "right" to eat all kinds of meat rather than become a stumbling block to the weak ones (8:9).[130]

To an apostle's rights (ἐξουσιαι) can be counted: 1) "eat and drink" (φαγειν και πειν),[131] 2) "to be accompanied by a wife" (ἀδελφην γυναικα περιαγειν),[132] and 3) "refrain from working for a living" (μη ἐργαζεσθαι) (9:4-6). These rights do not apply to Jewish Christian apostles only, including Cephas and James, but also to the apostles of the Gentile Church here represented by the leading pair, Paul and Barnabas. This is said not with the aim of producing this kind of support from the church in Corinth, but rather the opposite—with the aim of explaining why Paul has in fact

129. This custom applied not only to the Palestinian missionaries who opposed Paul in Corinth, as it appears in *Theissen* (1975a:203). In passing it may be mentioned that this observation applies also to letters of introduction: we find such letters incorporated in Paul's letters, as was shown above.

130. *Dungan* stresses the fact that Chapters 8 and 9 must be seen as connected (1971:5). For the whole of the following see *Agrell's* detailed discussion (1976:106–115).

131. According to *Barrett* (1973a:202) this means freedom to eat any kind of food and to do this at the church's expense.

132. This means only that an apostle's wife is provided for by the churches, not that she accompanies him on his travels, *Dungan* (1971:6 f, n. 1).

not exercised his rights. Even in Paul's way of referring to the tradition or "word" from Jesus[133] it is obvious that this word could be understood as a command, a duty for any missionary ("the Lord commanded ($\delta\iota\epsilon\tau\alpha\xi\epsilon\nu$) that those who proclaim the gospel should get their living by the gospel", 9:14). *Theissen* has argued that this tradition was interpreted, at least in the Palestinian church, as being a command to the wandering missionaries to live in charismatic poverty or, in other words, as prohibiting them to procure or even plan any form of sustenance for themselves. The missionary ("apostle" or "prophet") is to know that he belongs to Christ and stands under His protection; the Lord will provide for him through the spontaneous giving of others, so that he should not even ask to be provided for.[134] The Palestinian missionaries who have visited Corinth (perhaps Cephas was among them, see above) may have asked critical questions when they heard that Paul had not followed this clear command of the Lord, but had worked for his own living. And this is why Paul re-interprets this *duty* to live without making plans, totally dependent on others, to a *privilege* that he has not availed himself of.[135] He does not deny the right of others to receive support (9:12a), only places himself in a unique position which is determined by his apostolic calling and the necessity of working for the Gospel (9:15b–18). But nobody in Corinth can be any longer in doubt as to his right to material support or fail to know that their church actually is indebted to the apostle in this regard.

The church in Thessalonika could also rightly have been made to feel the "weight" of Paul and his company, ($\delta\upsilon\nu\alpha\mu\epsilon\nu\omicron\iota$ $\dot{\epsilon}\nu$ $\beta\alpha\rho\epsilon\iota$ $\epsilon\dot{\iota}\nu\alpha\iota$ $\dot{\omega}\varsigma$ $X\rho\iota\sigma\tau\omicron\upsilon$ $\dot{\alpha}\pi\omicron\sigma\tau\omicron\lambda\omicron\iota$, 1 Thess 2:6), i.e. "we could have made use of the rights and privileges belonging to us as apostles of Christ."[136] But instead "we worked

133. Matth. 10:9 f, Luke 10:7. Cf. *Dungan's* description of the complex process of development from Jesus's original saying to what we read in the Gospels and Paul's letters (1971:3–80).

134. *Theissen* (1975a, esp. p. 199, 206 f, 210 f).

135. *Idem,* p. 207. This aspect-displacement has been observed by many commentators but is most clearly expressed in *Gerhardsson's* distinction, "Paul classified Jesus' commandment as a permission ($\dot{\epsilon}\xi\omicron\upsilon\sigma\iota\alpha$ *reshut*) for the Apostles, not as an obligation ($\dot{\omicron}\phi\epsilon\iota\lambda\eta\mu\alpha$, *chobah*)" (1961:319). The same distinction is found e.g. in 1 Cor 7:6, although expressed in the terms of $\sigma\upsilon\gamma\gamma\nu\omega\mu\eta$—$\dot{\epsilon}\pi\iota\tau\alpha\gamma\eta$, *Daube* (1971:232). *Agrell* aptly speaks of the "two-sidedness" of this regulation: it could easily be misused as a pretext for living on others' money instead of working (1976:110).

136. My paraphrase, cf. *Gerhardsson* (1961:309). *Laub* controverts the opinion that $\beta\alpha\rho\omicron\varsigma$ here means financial charge (with v 5 in mind), and considers that it refers to v 6 and means moral weight, "Wichtigkeit, Ansehen" (1973: 78–80). So also *Rigaux* (1956:417). The verse then means that Paul has refrained from using his full apostolic authority, exemplified by his capacity to give binding "instructions" ($\pi\alpha\rho\alpha\gamma\gamma\epsilon\lambda\iota\alpha\iota$) (4:2). *Laub* seems to overlook the fact that 4:2 does not refer to hypothetical authority, which has not been exercised. And to be "father" of the church does not entail having a lesser amount of power in it, or a voluntary abstention from

night and day, that we might not burden (ἐπιβαρῆσαι) any of you while we preached to you the gospel of God" (2:9). *Strelan* has collected linguistic material to show that the word-group βαρ- with cognates is used in Greek papyri with the meaning "financial charge", and that texts such as 1 Thess 2:5–9, 2 Cor 11:10, 12:16, 1 Tim 5:16, 2 Thess 3:8 f probably have this connotation.[137] The similarity between 1 Thess 2:9 and 2 Cor 11:9 is especially enlightening in this respect.

In his letter to the church in Philippi Paul does not use the term "right" (ἐξουσια) when commenting on the financial support he has received, but nonetheless makes it clear that it is the duty of the church to support him. Epaphroditus is described as "your messenger (ἀποστολος) and minister (λειτουργος) to my need" (2:25), who on behalf of the apostle's needs (= the work of Christ, v 30) has risked his life "to complete your service to me", v 30. What lies behind this expression is of course the fact that the church is obliged to furnish the apostle with his needs as he works for Christ, and that Epaphroditus acts for the Philippian church when he serves Paul (for a close parallel see Philem 13). *Hainz* rightly speaks of a "geschuldete κοινωνια", and understands this κοινωνια to be the necessary basic relation between the apostle and any of his churches, even if Paul is cautious in using this claim in concrete paraenesis.[138]

(c) Paul's abstention from financial support

But if all of Paul's churches are in principle obliged to support their apostle, why does he not receive support from them? Why only from the church in Philippi?

We get no clear answer to this by examining Paul's explanations, as these vary considerably from place to place:[139]

(a) In 1 Thess 2:7 ff as in 2 Cor 12:14 f (cf. 11:11) the reason is Paul's affectionate parental love for his converts,

(b) in 2 Thess 3:7–9[140] the reason is that he wants to be an example to the Thessalonians by working with his own hands.

---

giving παραγγελιαι. The only reasonable interpretation is the one Laub mentions in a note, that the two possible interpretations do not exclude one another, "da mit dem Anspruch auf Lebensunterhalt zugleich die ‚autoritative Sonderstellung als Apostel Jesu Christi unterstrichen wäre", (p. 79 n. 134).

137. *Strelan* (1975:267–270). S. argues that Gal 6:2–10 treats financial obligations, in 2–5 probably towards the apostle and his continuing work.

138. *Hainz* (1972:287–290), the quotation from p. 287.

139. *von Campenhausen* (1957:38 f n. 15).

140. 2 Thess is considered authentic by many scholars, e.g. *Kümmel* (1973:228–232), *Ellis* (1971) and *Robinson* (1976), and in the context of all different interpretations the one given here is not so singular.

(c) in 1 Cor 9:12 the reason is that Paul does not want to put any obstacle in the way of the Gospel. This probably means that he did not
want to be (mis)understood as a sophist, who peddles his teaching
and miracles, cf. 1 Thess 2:5 and 2 Cor 2:17 ("peddlers of God's
word"), 11:20, 12:14b, 17,[141] and perhaps also that he did not want
to deter poor people from becoming Christians.[142]

(d) in 1 Cor 9:17, however, the reason is Paul's unique connection with
the Gospel, he is its slave, and a slave cannot lay claim to being paid
for working.[143]

"One cannot help getting the impression that we do not learn the real reasons for Paul's attitude"

is the conclusion that *Betz*[144] comes to and indeed it is not easy to see all
these different reasons forming a logically consistent whole.[145] They are
rather to be understood as a group of *ad hoc* reasons given in the argument
and not inconsistent with Paul's general conception of himself and his
apostolate, although not constituting the real reasons for his practice.

When Paul and Barnabas started their first missionary enterprise in a
distinctly non-Jewish world they entered a cultural and social environment
that necessitated a missionary strategy differing in certain respects from
what had been previously used. To start one's mission with a demand to be
supported by one's audience would in this society, with its ingrained ironical mistrust of sophists who lived at the expense of others, have been a

141. On the criticism against sophists and "imposters", see *Betz* (1972:104–115),
who considers that Paul uses this anti-sophistic topos against his rivals in Corinth, pp.
115–117.

142. *Dungan* (1971:15 f), *Odeberg* (1953:10 f, 136). *Theissen* calls this Paul's
"functional legitimation" of his abstention (1975a:214). *Agrell* lists three more possible hindrances (1976:110 f): (c) he may have wished to avoid becoming dependent
on those who supported him, cf. *von Campenhausen* (1969:46 n. 127), (d) the collection for Jerusalem might be misinterpreted if Paul did not provide for himself and
(e) "it would be incongruous with a gospel of Jesus' sacrificial love if the preachers
of this gospel insisted on their rights and accepted payment for their preaching"
(1976:205 n. 70). It can be said that (c) did not prevent Paul from accepting support,
once a full κοινωνια had been established between him and a church, and that (d) can
hardly be regarded as a fundamental principle governing the practice of all the missionaries to the Gentiles (cf. below). And (e) sounds too anachronistic: we know
that the Palestinian church, which was poorer than the church in Greece, (cf. n. 151
below), had no qualms about demanding this from their adherents and probably did
not have to "insist" on it.

143. *Theissen* (1975a:211 f): the "charismatic legitimation" of the apostle.

144. *Betz* (1972:104).

145. *Dautzenberg* (1969) tries to do this by defining the Gospel and apostolic self-
understanding as the common point of reference. In this way the picture becomes a
little too uniform, and the important social realities that D. begins with (p. 217 f) are
more or less forgotten in the end.

measure that would decisively have diminished the reliability of the message, and the conclusion was natural: missionaries had to work for their own living.[146] This was common practice for the "top levels of the entire Gentile mission":[147] Barnabas (1 Cor 9:6), Silvanus and Timothy (1 Thess 2:7–9), Titus (2 Cor 12:18) and Paul himself. Paul's practice is not his own invention, and not a *novum* which he has introduced and must now defend. The apology in 1 Cor 9 and 2 Cor 11—12 is caused by the collision between two different types of apostolic practice in this respect.[148]

On the other hand Paul's abstention from financial support is not based on the principle never to accept anything from his churches, but is rather more pragmatic. It is a fact that at the same time as he abstains from accepting support in Corinth for fundamental, high-sounding reasons (1 Cor 9), he is receiving money from Macedonia, as with a measure of embarrassment he admits in 2 Cor 11:7 ff. Paul supports himself by the work of his hands, but only when this is necessary.[149] But why did he accept money from Philippi, and not from Thessalonika and Corinth if no principle prevented him from doing so? One answer to this question is that people in the two last-mentioned churches were too poor to be asked to support Paul.[150] But this is not very probable as the Mediterranean cities flourished at this time,[151] the Macedonians if anything being poorer than the Christians in Corinth (cf. 2 Cor 8:1–5),[152] and Phil 4:10 rather suggests that the church of Philippi was so poor that they had not been able to send Paul permanent support.[153] I submit two other reasons: (a) Only when Paul has left a church he has founded does he accept any money from it,[154] in order to stress the fact that it has the character of support in his continued missionary work.[155] (b) Only when (and if) the relation between the apostle and the church has developed into a full, trusting κοινωνια does Paul accept any money from the church.[156]

"In the beginning of the gospel" (Phil 4:15) the church in Philippi was

146. *Theissen* (1975a:200–205).
147. *Dungan* (1971:8).
148. *Theissen* (1975a, passim).
149. *Maly* (1969:79 f).
150. *Dungan* (1971:15, 30 f). Cf. *Agrell* (1976:204 n. 67).
151. "Während Palestina im 1. Jahrhundert unter erhöhtem ökonomischen Druck stand, erlebte die städtische Mittelmeerwelt damals eine wirtschaftliche Blütezeit. Man musste nicht zur allerobersten Schicht gehören, um einen gewissen Wohlstand zu erringen", *Theissen* (1975a: 201).
152. Cf. *Betz* (1972:101).
153. So *Gnilka* (1968:174).
154. Noted by many, e.g. *Odeberg* (1953:136), *Dungan* (1971:32).
155. *Georgi* (1964:236).
156. Cf. *Nickle* (1966:103 f).

the only one to stand in such a relation to the apostle. The expression indicates that at the time of writing the number of such churches has increased—an indication confirmed by the plural in 2 Cor 11:8.[157] It is not
impossible that the "brothers coming from Macedonia" in 2 Cor 11:9 are
Silas and Timothy coming from Macedonia with the support that enables
Paul to occupy himself wholly with the word (Acts 18:5).[158] Then it is not
the church in Philippi that proves the exception to Paul's rule of not accepting money from his churches;[159] on the contrary, it is the church in
Corinth that is the exception to Paul's custom of permitting and gladly
accepting financial support from his churches after full κοινωνια has been
established and he has left them to continue his apostolic work in some
other place.

The reason for this is probably the lack of mutual trust between apostle
and church, which is more than hinted at in 1 and 2 Cor (cf. 1 Cor 1:12,
4:3, 8–13, 9:2–3; 2 Cor 6:11–13, 10:6a, 13:3). Unfortunately Paul's re-
luctance to ask for or accept financial support from this church led to a
growing distrust, which eventually broke into open conflict. Paul's abstention thus had the opposite effect to what he had intended, "not to put any
obstacle in the way of the gospel of Christ" (1 Cor 9:12).[160] The church
could not lightly accept the fact that their apostle received money from
Macedonia while staying there and explaining to them that it was on principle impossible for him to accept support from Corinth, as he was a slave
of the Gospel. Once the facts are clear it is difficult for the Corinthians
not to draw the conclusion that they are less respected and less loved by
the apostle than other churches (2 Cor 11:11, 12:13, 15).[161] And from
there it was not far to an even less favourable interpretation of this reluc-
tance to accept Corinthian money: perhaps Paul had not given them their
full share of spiritual gifts either (2 Cor 12:13a),[162] or maybe this is tacit
acknowledgment of the fact that he is inferior to other apostles who do not
hesitate one moment to accept support (2 Cor 11:5 ff, 20, 12:11 ff). Eventually this came to throw suspicion on the Jerusalem collection as well:
could this be Paul's indirect, clandestine way of claiming acknowledgment
as an apostle,[163] or might it even be a sly trick to acquire money through
an intermediary (2 Cor 12:16 ff)?

157. *Gnilka* (1968:178 n. 141), *Dungan* (1971:38).
158. *Maly* (1969:79 f).
159. So *Gnilka* (1968:174) who however admits that the exception was a temporary one, p. 178 n. 141.
160. *Dungan* (1971:36 ff).
161. *Idem*, p. 39, *Georgi* (1964:237). Against this interpretation: *Betz* (1972:117).
162. *Georgi* (1964:237 n. 6, 240 with n. 2).
163. *Idem*, p. 241.

It cost Paul much anxiety, work and intense argument to put this unhappy development of his relationship with the Corinthian church right again. Although we cannot exclude other factors the question of money looms large in this conflict, and it can be taken as evidence of the close connection between financial relations and authority relations. An unclear, unbalanced and eventually doubtful financial relation inevitably causes any authority relation between the parties to deteriorate. And because authority is so often expressed by a financial obligation, the absence of any financial obligation where this could be expected effects adversely even an authority or power relation built on quite another basis. But Corinth was an exception; we may presume that Paul's relation to his churches came with time to include an indisputed element of financial obligation on the part of the churches.

CHAPTER 3

The Distribution of Power
within the Local Pauline Churches

My aim in this chapter is that of the preceding chapters: to establish and describe the phenomena that constitute the distribution of power, but now at the level of the local church. What follows is therefore not a study of Paul's thought about the ministry in the local church or how he planned (or did not plan) a church order or conceived of χαρισμα. The source-material consists of Paul's letters and they contain only scanty information on the internal functioning of his churches, and what information there is does not consist of unbiased descriptions of plain facts.[1] It is thus important to distinguish observable historical facts from more or less subjective interpretations of these (theologies, moral views, paraenetic conceptions, etc.)[2] although interpretations of course are facts in their own right. But here they will primarily be used as evidence of what was going on in the Pauline churches in regard to the two opposite streams: authoritative words, and support and obedience.

I will attempt to arrive at conclusions about the distribution of power by the following brief analysis of the intra-church differentiation of functions (or "ministries") in Pauline churches. This touches on the question of the development of ministries and of ecclesiastical authority in the New Testament, which is a complex subject and is not treated here.[3]

---

1. *Brockhaus* (1975:95).
2. "Kirche ist Versammlung, Versammlung der Berufenen und Erwählten als eine Einheit. *Damit ist etwas Gemeinschaftliches gegeben,* und zwar etwas Gemeinschaftliches, welches sich schon hier *auf Erden* verwirklicht;—Das Genossenschaftliche, Korporative, kann auch vom sublimsten Begriff der Kirche nicht getrennt werden", *von Harnack* (1910:149, 150) in his criticism of Rudolf Sohm's conception of the Church, pp. 121–186.
3. In this chapter I depend to a great extent on the secondary literature on ministries in the New Testament, especially *Greeven* (1952/53), *Schürmann* (1970), *Lemaire* (1971), *Martin* (1972), *Brockhaus* (1975) who gives a detailed history of

A. FUNCTIONAL DIFFERENTIATION IN LOCAL PAULINE CHURCHES

The natural starting-point for investigating which functions were performed by the Christians in a local church is the list of spiritual gifts
($\chi\alpha\rho\iota\sigma\mu\alpha\tau\alpha$) in 1 Cor 12:28 "God has appointed in the church first apostles,
second prophets, third teachers, then workers of miracles, then healers,
helpers, administrators, speakers in various kinds of tongues". I shall begin
with the first three functions.[4]

1. Apostles

The work of apostles is obviously not a function *within* the local church,
in the meaning that we find one or more apostles as resident leaders of
every local church. The "apostles" of local churches mentioned in Phil
2:25 and 2 Cor 8:23 are envoys acting outside their own church. This is
also conceded by those who otherwise maintain that Paul always refers to
the local church when using the term $\grave{\epsilon}\kappa\kappa\lambda\eta\sigma\iota\alpha$.[5]

2. Prophets

Paul presupposes the existence of prophets in Corinth (1 Cor 12:28, 14:
1-5, 27-33), Thessalonika (1 Thess 5:20) and Rome (Rom 12:6), and
the testimony of Acts, Matthew (10:41), Didache and the Revelation of
John shows that prophecy was a universal phenomenon in the nascent
Christian Church.[6] There is no indication in Paul's letters that they were
wandering prophets, rather we must think of them as having an important
and permanent function in worship in the local church.[7] From Paul's treatment of this function (placing it next to that of the apostle) it is evident
that he regarded it as the most important function within any local church.

---

research, pp. 7–94, *Rohde* (1976:11–56). A very full account of Protestant and
Catholic exegetical research in this field is given by *Schütte* (1974:86–135, 236–249),
and a well informed survey which also includes Scandinavian research is found in
Skjevesland (1976:109–127). A number of important essays are now collected in
Kertelge (1977), where the reader also finds a good bibliography, pp. 565–574. Cf.
also *Mühlsteiger* (1977).

    4. "Die Unterscheidung 'Apostel, Propheten und Lehrer' ist eine uralte und in der
ältesten Zeit der Kirche allgemeine gewesen", *von Harnack* (1924:348). See also
Brockhaus (1975:95).

    5. *Hainz* (1972:250–255), following *Cerfaux* (1965); Hainz's concession on p.
254. Among critics of Hainz's one-sided emphasis on the local church as $\grave{\epsilon}\kappa\kappa\lambda\eta\sigma\iota\alpha$
can be named *Kieffer* (1977:169 n. 177).

    6. *Schürmann* (1970:389 and 1977:18 f n. 80), *Brockhaus* (1975:97 n. 11), and
above all the full description of *Cothenet* (1972:1264 ff).

    7. The wandering of prophets was a hypothesis of von Harnack based on Didache,
which has by now lost general approval, see *Greeven* (1952/53:316), *Conzelmann*
(1969a:253 n. 43), *Brockhaus* (1975:97).

But what was that function? The traditional answer is that it consisted of a form of preaching and exhortation of unusual depth and effectivity as is manifested by its fruits: upbuilding, encouragement, consolation (οἰκοδομη, παρακλησις, παραμυθια, 1 Cor 14:3), conviction (ἐλεγξις) and disclosure (φανερωσις, 14:24).[8]

Dautzenberg has, however, shown that the historical context of primitive Christian prophecy is the contemporary Jewish apocalyptic tradition, and that the fundamental principles of apocalyptic prophecy are also to be found in Corinth: it is the revelation of divine secrets, often given in a form (dreams, visions, oracles) that makes an inspired interpretation necessary, as the Word of God in the Torah or in Old Testament prophecy.[9] Prophecy and its interpretation (distinguishing of spirits, διακρισις πνευματων, 1 Cor 12:10) had a place in the common worship of the congregation and was regarded as being the equivalent of what the Torah and its interpretation was in Jewish worship: participation in divine knowledge.[10] This explains why Paul valued prophecy so highly and why the prophets were (later) thought to be almost comparable to the apostles as constituting the "foundation" of the Church (1 Cor 14:4b, Eph 2:20, 3:5); the church-founding divine revelation was seen as flowing into the Church through the Gospel as preached by the apostles and the revelations of the prophets.[11] 1 Cor 14:3 thus describes the consequence of prophecy, not its content.

A much-discussed question is whether prophecy was limited to a permanent group of prophets or was exercised by any Christian on whom the gift of prophecy might fall. Those who advocate the latter view find evidence in texts such as 1 Cor 14:1, 24, 29, 31 and the indication of 1 Thess 5:19 ff that the whole church exercised control over prophecy.[12] *Greeven* has made a thorough analysis of all texts relevant to this question[13] and finds that, with one exception (1 Cor 11:5) they all point to the existence

8. Examples of this could be multiplied, see *Brockhaus,* ibidem, *Cothenet* (1972: 1297 ff) and the examples given by Dautzenberg in his research survey of New Testament prophecy (1975:18–40).

9. *Dautzenberg* (1975:147 f); cf. *Bourke* (1968:500), *Brockhaus* (1975:98, 155 n. 67, 206 f) and *Ridderbos* (1975:451).

10. *Dautzenberg* (1975:289, 299).

11. This is emphasized by *Schürmann* (1970:389 ff, 392), who also points to the fact that Paul wishes to connect disclosure, wisdom and gnosis (1 Cor 12:7 f) with prophecy, cf. 1 Cor 13:2.

Paul's view of his own apostolate is marked by its prophetic traits, especially the motif of divine revelation. See *Stuhlmacher* (1968:69–73, 76–82) and *Holtz* (1966). *Dautzenberg* finds "Auswirkungen von Prophetie" in texts where Paul speaks about revealed divine secrets as in 1 Cor 2:6–16, 15:51–58, Rom 11:25–36, (1975:225), *Ridderbos* (1975:451).

12. So e.g. *Cothenet* (1972:1296).

13. *Greeven* (1952/53:309–315).

of a closed group of prophets who alone were responsible for prophecy.[14] Originally any Christian could receive the gift of prophecy during the worship, but this is a state that has almost ceased to exist when 1 Cor was written, and 11:5 is merely a survival of the earlier state.[15] That Paul ranked prophecy as being more up-building and valuable than glossolalia (1 Cor 14) seems to have been in opposition to opinion in Corinth, and may be more of an exhortatory measure than an accurate description of its actual standing in this church. 1 Thess 5:19 ff also appears to be a defence for prophecy.[16]

3. Teachers[17]

As noted above the term διδασκαλος is probably traditional and as such taken over by Paul from Palestine[18] (or Antioch)[19] where the triad "apostles-prophets-teachers" originated. The fact that he uses it in 1 Cor 12:28, albeit in a list which may not primarily be intended as an accurate description of the situation in Corinth,[20] testifies to the fact that this category of persons was known there. Rom 12:7 ("he who teaches", ὁ διδασκων) and Gal 6:6 ("he who teaches" ὁ κατηχων) confirm this point that Paul refers to a function performed by persons known to the readers, persons whom he acknowledges and (Gal) wants the church to accord concrete recognition.

Greeven has shown convincingly that the "teachers" formed a closed group of recognized and authoritative teachers, neither less well-defined nor less "charismatic" than the group of prophets.[21] Their functions have

---

14. With *Kretschmar* (1964:37) *Roloff* argues against Greeven that Paul wanted to support a development of prophecy which loosened this gift from the prophets and transferred it to the whole of the church (1977:521). This interpretation has not convinced me.

15. *Greeven* (1952/53:315). The same conclusion is reached by *Roloff* (1965: 126), *Goppelt* (1966:125) and *Schnackenburg* (1971:355). Cf. also *Theissen* (1974b:183 n. 1) and *Laub* (1976:37 n. 35).
The well-known discrepancy between 1 Cor 11:5 and 14:34 has been explained in many different ways, which cannot be surveyed here. See the survey of *Dautzenberg* (1975:265–270).

16. *Schürmann* (1970:390 f), *Dautzenberg* (1975:299 f), who points out that primitive Christian prophecy had strong ties with apocalyptic Jewish Christianity and did not find a favourable cultural and religious context in the more Hellenistic societies such as Corinth.

17. See primarily *Greeven* (1952/53:325–344), and cf. *Schürmann* (1970:396–398) and *Brockhaus* (1975:101–103). On teaching in the Primitive Church see *Gerhardsson* (1961, Part 2 passim) and *Schürmann* (1977).

18. *Brockhaus* (1975:124).

19. *Lemaire* (1971:182).

20. *Schürmann* (1970:390 f, 398 and 1977:21) and *Ellis* (1974:129 n. 4).

21. *Greeven* (1952/53:325 f), *Ridderbos* (1975:453). *Kraft* calls this group a "Schriftgelehrtenstand" (1975:93).

much in common with the functions of Jewish scribes and rabbis:[22] they gave instruction and delivered exhortations on seemly conduct, they received, preserved and transmitted the body of tradition in the church (words and narratives from the Jesus-tradition, kerygmatic formulas, etc.) and occupied themselves with interpreting the Holy Scriptures.

> "Man wird also die Tätigkeit der Lehrer im allgemeinen in der *Bewahrung, Weitergabe und Fruchtbarmachung der Tradition* erblicken dürfen, sowohl der alttestamentlichen als der entstehenden christlichen."[23]

4. "Leaders, Administrators"

Under this heading I shall present a group of persons, probably distinct from those mentioned above, who appear under more than one designation.

In 1 Thess 5:12 and Rom 12:8 we read about "those who are over you"; ($\pi\rho o\ddot{\iota}\sigma\tau\alpha\mu\epsilon\nu o\iota$), in 1 Cor 12:28 about "administrations" ($\kappa\upsilon\beta\epsilon\rho\nu\eta\sigma\epsilon\iota\varsigma$), in 1 Cor 16:16 about subordination under Stephanas's house and all who toil ($\kappa o\pi\iota\alpha\nu$) in the same way as this group, and in Phil 1:1 we find "bishops and deacons" ($\dot{\epsilon}\pi\iota\sigma\kappa o\pi o\iota\ \kappa\alpha\iota\ \delta\iota\alpha\kappa o\nu o\iota$), this last category also being mentioned in Rom 16:1–2.

With the exception of 1 Cor 12:28 and Rom 12:8 (which nonetheless presuppose the readers' knowledge of the category mentioned), it is clear from all these texts that the apostle is thinking of particular persons or groups known to him and to his readers and who perform functions specific enough to single them out for mention.[24]

Their functions seem to be of roughly the same kind:
(1) The group mentioned in 1 Thess 5:12 "labour" ($\kappa o\pi\iota\omega\nu\tau\alpha\varsigma$—a verb Paul uses about work for the Lord and the Church, his own and that of others),[25] and they "are over you in the Lord" ($\pi\rho o\ddot{\iota}\sigma\tau\alpha\mu\epsilon\nu o\upsilon\varsigma$, meaning both "to care for" and "to lead"),[26] and they "admonish you" ($\nu o\upsilon\theta\epsilon\tau o\upsilon\nu\tau\alpha\varsigma$).

---

22. *Lemaire* thinks that the title $\delta\iota\delta\alpha\sigma\kappa\alpha\lambda o\varsigma$ was used only of persons who had been Jewish rabbis before their conversion to Christianity, e.g. Apollos. This may account for the rapid disappearance of the title (1971:182).

23. *Greeven* (1952/53:342). Cf. *Schürmann* (1977:5–16) on their functions.

24. It has been discussed whether 1 Thess 5:12 signifies a fixed group or a number of functions that could be exercised by anyone. *Laub* proposes the latter interpretation (1973:91), while the majority of scholars conclude from the grammatical construction that Paul refers to one definite group of persons, *Greeven* (1952/53:348), *Schürmann* (1970:399 n. 132) and *Brockhaus* (1975:107 f).

25. *Greeven* (1952/53:347 f) and *Agrell* (1976:120), who both refer to von Harnack's much-cited article in ZNW 27, 1928, 1–10.

26. *Reicke* (1959) shows that $\pi\rho o\ddot{\iota}\sigma\tau\alpha\sigma\theta\alpha\iota$ includes the two meanings "to lead" and "to care for". *Brockhaus* concludes with e.g. Greeven, Sohm, *Goppelt* (1965:6) and *von Campenhausen* (1969:65) that the verb signifies "eine fürsorgende Autorität oder eine autoritative Fürsorge" (1975:107).

(2) The function of Stephanas and his "house" is described as being "service of the saints" (διακονιαν τοις ἁγιοις) and "labour" (κοπιαν, 1 Cor 16:15 f).

(3) Both in 1 Cor 12 and Rom 12 the function of leading is mentioned after the function of giving material help: ἀντιλημψεις—κυβερνησεις[27] in 1 Cor 12:28, ὁ μεταδιδους—ὁ προϊσταμενος in Rom 12:8 (cf. the double meaning of προϊστασθαι).

(4) It is tempting to see these two functions behind the titles of διακονοι and ἐπισκοποι in Phil 1:1, but we have no indication of what their functions were, except what can be inferred from the meaning of the titles themselves. Much work has been done to investigate the background, origin and content of these titles, but this has not resulted in any consensus.[28] The two titles probably designate two different groups of persons which consequently cannot have identical functions.[29] From the Hellenistic and Jewish backgrounds we can infer that διακονοι had a subordinate position (as the name implies), if not subordinate to the ἐπισκοποι then subordinate to the church. To judge from the designations διακονοι had something to do with "services" (presumably of a practical kind)[30] while the ἐπισκοποι were concerned with supervision. We do not know if this applies to functions in the act of worship or in the practical management of church affairs (taking care of poor members, guests, etc.) or both.[31]

---

27. *Bauer* (1958:902): "Leitung". *Brockhaus* (1975:109 nn. 76 and 78).

28. *Dibelius* (1937) gives some of the Hellenistic material and has been followed by e.g. Lietzmann, Bultmann and *Gnilka* (1969:103) in seeing this as the formative background of the Christian use, while others have thought to find this in the Jewish milieu, the synagogue, the temple, Qumran, etc. For the literature see *Braun* (1966/ II:326–334, esp. on parallels in Qumran), *Lemaire* (1971:27–35), *Brockhaus* (1975: 99 n. 19) and *Hainz* (1976a:97–101).

29. That they were two separate groups is maintained against e.g. *Georgi* (1964: 34f) and *Lemaire* (1971:99, 186) by *Dibelius* (1937:415 f), *Goppelt* (1965:5 f), *Gnilka* (1969:101), *Schürmann* (1970:399 n. 132), *Hainz* (1976a: 102–107).

30. The term διακονος is used in two different senses: Paul uses it about himself, Apollos, and other co-workers who were active in preaching and teaching, *Gnilka* (1969:103), *Ellis* (1971:442), *Lemaire* (1971:185 f; 1974:62), *Rohde* (1976:54), and it is used in Phil 1:1 and Rom 16:1 f (cf. 12:7) as these churches' own designation of a group of persons serving the local church. Gnilka and Ellis combine these two series of texts and consider that the local, sedentary διακονοι also were teachers, which is not very probable, cf. *Roloff* (1977:522). As is well known, in the generation after Paul the function of the local teacher merged, not with the function of the διακονος, but with that of the πρεσβυτερος-ἐπισκοπος; this may be an indication that διακονος never was a teaching function. Cf. *Colson* (1962:14–19) and *Käsemann* (1974:330), who interprets Rom 12:7 to signify an "office" of the same distinct type as that in Philippi and Cenchreae.

31. *Brockhaus* gives a list of the different functions ἐπισκοποι και διακονοι have been thought to fill (1975:99 n. 20). Cf. the "summary" of *Hainz* (1976a:106 f).

As the similarity between these ministries and the title-less functions previously mentioned is obvious, many scholars draw the conclusion that all these designations refer to the same kind of leaders who are responsible for and serve the local churches by helping, organizing, caring for, leading where these services are needed.[32]

The feature of "serving" is characteristic of these functions but does not exclude the fact that the persons performing them are at the same time leaders of the congregations (and become increasingly so). Our earliest witness (1 Thess 5:12) gives a picture of care concerned with concrete needs exercised by people capable of leading, helping and exhorting (this last function implies that they take responsibility for the conduct of others).[33] *von Dobschütz* has listed ten types of actions, which it can be presumed the προῖσταμενοι undertook on behalf of the church:

> (1) Hergeben des Lokals für die Gemeindeversammlung, (2) vielleicht auch Herstellung der nötigen Ordnung dabei, (3) Vorbeten, (4) Vorlesen, (5) Vorsingen, (6) Gewährung von Unterkunft und Unterhalt für zureisende Brüder, (7) von Unterstützung für Arme, (8) Stellung von Kaution (vgl. Jason Apg 17:9), (9) Vertretung vor Gericht (Patronisieren!), (10) gelegentlich vielleicht eine Reise im Interesse der Gemeinde, kurz alle Pflichten, die später dem Vorsteher, dem Bischof zufielen, aber alles als freiwillige Leistung, ohne rechtlichen Auftrag, ohne gehaltsmässige Vergütung . . .".[34]

With the exception of (3)–(5) it is not difficult to recognize these functions in Paul's letters and in Acts, for instance in what we know about Stephanas (he owns a house, i.e. (1) and (2), makes a journey on behalf of the church, i.e. (10), and generally devotes himself to serving the church i.e. (6) and (7)). All the functions listed except (3)–(5) presuppose a certain degree of wealth and social standing: owning a house which can accommodate (part of) the church for worship, time and leisure to take

32. *Greeven* (1952/53:354), *Goppelt* (1966:125), *Gnilka* (1969:96 ff), *Grelot* (1971:455, citing Küng), *Laub* (1973:72 and 1976:33), *Martin* (1972:26), *Hainz* (1976a:92) and *Roloff* (1977:522). This is also reflected in Eph 4:11, on which see *Schweizer* (1959:181 f), *Roloff* (1965:134 f) and *Rohde* (1976:50–54).

33. As shown by *Greeven* (1952/53:346), Reicke (1959) and *Brockhaus* (1975: 107 f) the verb "be over", προῖστασθαι, is used about the protective, authoritative care of superiors and therefore includes an element of leadership.

1 Thess is a letter written only a short time after the founding of the church in Thessalonika and is not coloured by any intra-church conflicts. It may therefore be presumed to give a picture of universal application of Paul's relation to one of his churches and of the beginnings of a church order in a newly founded Pauline church, *Laub* (1976:17, 32).

34. *von Dobschütz* (1909:215 f); the numbers are added by me.

care of the needs of others and the financial means to do so, civil rights in one's city. This is an important observation which will be discussed below.

5. Other Functions

In 1 Cor 14:6 we observe that Paul knows of different kinds of inspired speech in Corinth:[35] speaking in tongues, in revelation, in knowledge, in prophecy, in teaching (λαλειν γλωσσαις, ἐν ἀποκαλυψει ἢ ἐν γνωσει ἢ ἐν προφητεια ἢ [ἐν] διδαχῃ). All these are closely allied to the gift of prophecy, as they are regarded as coming from the Spirit.[36] They are probably not bound to special persons, if not to some of the prophets.[37] Of all these kinds of inspired speech the ecstatic, incomprehensible speaking in tongues was valued most highly by the Christians in Corinth, while Paul resolutely places this gift last whenever it is mentioned together with other spiritual gifts.[38]

The πιστις of 1 Cor 12:9 is probably the faith that can work miracles, the faith that removes mountains (1 Cor 13:2) and thus closely related to healings (χαρισματα ἰαματων) and to (exorcistic) miracles (ἐνεργηματα δυναμεων, δυναμεις).[39] We do not hear of any professional, full-time healers in the Primitive Church so these gifts probably appeared sporadically. Paul and other missionaries are often mentioned as being endowed with these χαρισματα (cf. Acts and 2 Cor 12:12, Rom 15:19), while we do not hear from any other church than the Corinthian church that the local Christians perform miracles. This may be another indication that this church was untypically endowed with pneumatic gifts.

Probably neither the different forms of inspired speech nor miracle-working faith were reserved each for a particular, permanent circle distinct from those mentioned above. These charismata were not sufficiently exclusive or permanent to give rise to groups with a practice and a title of their own even if they were of importance for the internal functioning of the church in which they appeared.[40]

---

35. *Käsemann* points to the difference here between the churches of Corinth and Rome: in the latter we hear nothing of any pneumatic (=ecstatic) gifts, "Dafür treten die kerygmatischen und die weitgefasste Diakonie in den Vordergrund" (1974:327).
36. *Schürmann* describes the different kinds of speech (1970:392–394).
37. *Idem*, p. 389, 392, and cf. *Brockhaus* (1975:104 f) on the relation between prophets and the gift of tongues. *Chevallier* (1966:169, 206) thinks that these functions belong to the teachers; cf. *Brockhaus* (1975:206 n. 10), and his warning against an exaggerated systematization of the different gifts.
38. " . . . wird von Paulus vielmehr mit Nachdruck in die private Sphäre verwiesen", *Greeven* (1952/53:344). Cf. *Ridderbos* (1975:464–467).
39. *Ridderbos* (1975:463 f).
40. "Aufs Ganze gesehen haben aber diese Gaben (sc. Zungenrede, Krafttaten und Heilungen) kein 'Amt' hervorgebracht, und zwar eindeutig deshalb, weil sie nicht οἰκοδομη sind", *Greeven* (1952/53:344). Cf. *Brockhaus* (1975:155 n. 67) and *Ridderbos* (1975:459).

B. ORIGINS OF THIS FUNCTIONAL DIFFERENTIATION

1. Pneumatic Differences

The first and obvious origin of the functional differentiation we observe in the Pauline churches is the difference in pneumatical endowment. Not everyone has received the gift of prophesying, healing the sick or speaking in tongues, 1 Cor 12:29. And as some of the functions Paul mentions result from super-human endowment which cannot be acquired through training, part of the functional differentiation occurs quite independently of human effort or will.

The most important of these gifts is prophecy (at least in Paul's eyes), which is regarded by the apostle as having a fundamental, up-building function in the church. The ministry of the teacher is to a greater extent one that can be achieved by a person with a talent for study, but nevertheless has an affinity with prophecy and is by no means a private matter.[41] Naturally, inspired speech and healing cannot be practised by anyone who has not received the gift.

2. Social Differences

But not all functions in the church are based on a supernatural pneumatic gift. Some of them are based upon common differences in human ability (intelligence, initiative, capacity for work) and upon social and cultural differences. *Theissen* has given a comprehensive and concrete description of social stratification in the church of Corinth which he considers typical of the structure of the Hellenistic churches in general.[42] As this description is highly relevant to my investigation I shall retail it below.

> 1 Cor 1:26–29 tells us that there were some who were "wise, powerful, and of noble birth" in the Corinthian church and *Theissen* finds four criteria useful to find out who these persons with high social status were: (1) civil or religious office in the city of Corinth, (2) to have a "house", (3) to have been of service to the church or Paul or both, (4) making journeys (the last two criteria are not in themselves sufficient to indicate high social status).[43]

Ad (1): Crispus was "ruler of the synagogue" (Acts 18:8) i.e. he held a respected office whose incumbents normally were rich men. Erastus was probably "city treasurer" (*quaestor*), later *aedilis* of the city (Rom 16:23).

Ad (2): Crispus and Stephanas (1 Cor 1:14–16, 16:15 ff, cf. Acts 18:8) were baptized by Paul with the whole "house," which included wife, children

---

41. *Greeven* (1952/53:342 f).
42. *Theissen* (1974a:232).
43. *Idem*, "Soziale Schichtung in der korinthischen Gemeinde", ZNW 65, 1974, 232–272 = 1974a.

and servants. Acts mentions three other conversions of moderately wealthy people and their households: the centurion Cornelius (10:1 f, 11:14), Lydia the seller of purple fabric (16:15), and the jailer in Philippi (16:31–33).

Ad (3): Stephanas with his house has devoted himself to "the service of the saints" (1 Cor 16:15 f), and it is not improbable that he has supported Paul in his material needs, as Phoebe, διακονος in Cenchreae did (Rom 16:2). Paul stayed with three different families in Corinth: with that of Gaius (Rom 16:23), Prisca (Priscilla) and Aquila (1 Cor 16:19, Rom 16:3, cf. Acts 18:2 f) and Titius Justus (Acts 18:7).

Ad (4): We find several Corinthians travelling: Aquila and his wife (see above and Acts 18:18), Erastus (Acts 19:22), Stephanas with Fortunatus and Achaicus (1 Cor 16:15–18), Chloe's people (1 Cor 1:11), perhaps also Sosthenes (if the man in Acts 18:17 is identical with the co-sender of 1 Cor).

Thus we see that a large part of the most active and most important church members probably belong to the small group of Corinthian Christians with high social status.

This picture of the social stratification of this church is verified by *Theissen*'s analysis of the conflict concerning the Lord's supper (1 Cor 11:17–34).[44] From 11:21 f we learn that two groups confront each other in this conflict, viz. those who have no food of their own with them (μη ἐχοντες) and those who bring their own food (ἰδιον δειπνον) in addition to the Lord's supper (κυριακον δειπνον). The rich Christians probably invited all Christians to their own homes to a supper consisting of bread and wine, which through the reading of the words of institution (1 Cor 11:23 ff) became the Lord's supper and the church's supper. But in addition to this common supper the hosts invited their own equals who were offered better food (meat, etc.) and began eating before the poor people and the slaves had arrived from the day's work. This practice destroyed the unity of "the Body" by sharply manifesting the social differences within it.[45] Paul seems to view this conflict from the aspect of the poor members, which may indicate that his information comes from these quarters (cf. 1 Cor 1:11 and 11:18),[46] but he proposes a compromise which does not abolish the stratum-specific differences. At the Lord's supper the unity of the church must have precedence, which means that all shall partake of the same food and begin eating at the same time; but on other occasions the rich may eat as is their custom (11:33 f). This solution of the problem of the social integration within a heterogeneous church is marked by "patriarchalism of love".[47] This means that social differences are accepted, and rich and poor are bound to one another by demanding respect and caring for the needs of the poor on the part of the rich and trusting submission under the wealthy and leading from the poor.

In a third essay *Theissen* analyses stratum-specific characteristics concerning eating habits, forms of social intercourse, and of legitimation and communica-

---

44. *Idem*, "Soziale Integration und sakramentales Handeln", NT 24, 1974, 179–206 = 1974b.

45. The same reconstruction by *Bornkamm* (1956:141–145).

46. It may also be thought to come from Stephanas, who is visiting Paul, *Grelot* (1971:458).

47. The term "Liebespatriarkalismus" has its roots in *Troeltsch* (1912:67 f, 93) and is an important one for *Theissen* (1974a:269 f), (1974b:201) and (1975a:171).

tion.[48] His analysis of the question of eating sacrificial meat shows that "the strong ones" are in fact more or less identical with the wealthy and cultured members of the congregation and that their legitimation of their conduct shows signs of a typical transformation of the Christian belief as it ascends into higher strata.[49]

When analysed from this point of view 1 Cor is also seen to have been predominantly addressed to the rich members, and treats their deficiencies and problems (divisions in factions, read: "houses",[50] lawsuits concerning βιωτικα (6:3), i.e. material assets,[51] puffed-up spiritual self-confidence because of superior "gnosis", meat-eating, opposition to the apostle). The conclusion must reasonably be that the "weak" ones (the poor) had a minor role in the church, but that the "strong" ones (the rich and the educated) dominate its interior life, acting as its hosts, as creators of public opinion and as heads of the different factions.

The function of being host to the congregation is thus not so unimportant as may first seem.[52] It probably meant that the host presided at the meal and at the act of worship closely connected with it and that he was responsible for order (such as it was). And within a generation this function had developed conspicuously.

The host of such a group was almost inevitably a man of some education, with a fairly broad background and at least some administrative ability. Moreover, many of these hosts in the earliest years of the Gentile church came from the "God-fearers," who had shown independence enough to leave their ancestral or native faith and establish contact with the synagogues.[53] They had thus shown themselves to be men of initiative and decision. In a mission movement which required resourcefulness and courage, they were likely candidates for leadership.[54]

48. *Idem,* "Die Starken und Schwachen in Korinth", EvTh 35, 1975, 155–172 = 1975a.
49. (1975a:166).
50. *Idem* (1974a:258), *Filson* (1939:110).
51. *Theissen* (1974a:259).
52. *Filson* (1939) is a much-needed reminder of the vital importance of the house-churches, which has not received its due attention in subsequent research.
53. The 'God-fearers' were Gentiles rich enough to suffer great loss of social standing and possibility to communicate with their equals if they became proselytes, so proselytes were generally women, cf. *Daube* (1971:241 n. 4), or poor people, *Theissen* (1974a:265).
54. *Filson* (1939:111 f), cf. *Lemaire* (1974:65 f). *Greeven* argues against this hypothesis that (1) we can discern no special leaders of worship at all in Corinth, instead order was kept voluntarily, in submission to the presence of the Holy Ghost, (2) if the hosts had had anything to do with leading the church Paul would surely have demanded of them to right the unsatisfactory state of things, (1952/53:356 n. 93). Against Greeven it must be maintained that Paul's "command" (διαταξις) in 1 Cor 11:33 f is after all directed towards the hosts, as they and nobody else provided the fare and decided when to begin eating! Besides, *Filson* only states that "after the loss of 'apostolic' guidance . . . everything . . . favored the emergence of the host as the most prominent and influential member of the group" (1939:112).

We may presume that Paul realized the importance of energetic and influential persons for his mission and the growth of the local church. We
have indirect evidence of this in 1 Cor 1:14–16 where Paul enumerates
the people he has baptized in Corinth. There prove to be only three of
them, but these were all the most important: Crispus, the ruler of the synagogue, Gaius (who had a house large enough to accommodate the whole
church in Corinth, Rom 16:23) and "the first-fruit of Achaia" Stephanas
with his household. It may not be unreasonable to find here a piece of conscious missionary strategy: the first thing Paul needs in a new city is a place
to serve as a centre for his work and for the life of the congregation. This
he finds by early converting the head of a family who has appropriate
means (house, wealth, initiative); in Corinth we know his name as he
turned out to be exactly what Paul had hoped for.[55] These kind of men he
could expect to meet in the synagogue among his own compatriots or the
group of "God-fearers" attached to the synagogues all over the Greek
world. It was such men that he wanted for building a local church, and he
himself came with a gospel of incorporation into the full salvation of Israel
without circumcision, which was exactly what the "God-fearers" wanted.
No wonder that within a few years a number of churches had sprung into
existence in the cities of Asia Minor and Greece, that Paul had visited!

3. Human Initiative

The concluding lines of the last paragraph open up the question of whether
the functional differentiation within the Pauline churches may have yet another origin, viz. human initiative, especially that of the apostle.

If we disregard Acts 14:23 and 20:17, 28 as Lukan fictions,[56] we have
no indication that Paul instituted a ministry or ordained any office-holders
in his churches. This is generally interpreted to mean that no apostolic institution of offices existed.[57] As Paul normally wants to strengthen the authority of the leaders in his churches (1 Thess 5:12, 1 Cor 16:15), his most

---

55. *Idem*, p. 111. *Austgen* (1966:53). *Rohde* considers that the individual leaders
of housechurches in a town formed "ein Leitungsgremium der Gesamtgemeinde",
(1976:45). Cf. *Schürmann* (1977:31 n. 121).

56. See however *Ehrhardt* (1969:85) and *Grelot* (1971:466) who maintain that
14:23 may contain a historical truth: this is after all the very first missionary journey,
Barnabas is its leader, and both he and Paul are influenced by the structure of the
Jewish-Christian church (Acts 13:1 prophets and teachers, imposition of hands).
Ehrhardt considers that Barnabas expressly wanted πρεσβύτεροι as this was the Jerusalemite pattern (Acts 11:30) while Paul, when he is free to decide for himself,
chooses to introduce the Antiochene pattern in his churches, i.e. prophets and teachers,
see 1 Cor 12:28. Cf. *von Campenhausen* (1969:70).

57. *Roloff* (1965:134), *Pesch* (1971:444), *Martin* (1972:30), *Barrett* (1973a:394)
"they appointed themselves", and *Brockhaus* (1975:108), cf. *Vögtle* (1977:162).

effective argument would have been to refer to the fact that he had instituted them himself. But as we do not hear anything in this way we can conclude that nothing of the sort had occurred.[58] Consequently the emergence of these functions of leadership is often pictured as having been voluntary and spontaneous. We can observe the natural tendency in any permanent group for a leading stratum to emerge to fill the group's need of leadership also at work in these churches, and the resulting church order of the Pauline churches is a thing that has grown "from below" from the church itself and its internal interaction over time.[59]

This statement needs to be qualified. First, we need to keep in mind that the words "voluntary" and "spontaneous" are not identical. The functions exercised by prophets, glossolalists and healers may be spontaneous, but the element of "holy compulsion" (from the Spirit) may yet be considerable. And some functions, such as prophecy or inspired insight, must be discerned and recognized as genuine by the congregation before they can be said to exist. Lastly, we must take into account that at least some of the functions mentioned in 1 Cor 12 probably emerged during Paul's first visit to Corinth, which lasted eighteen months. It cannot be taken for granted that the profusion of gifts described here began emerging only after the apostle had left Corinth and only then was confirmed by him through his letter.

Here historical reconstruction is hindered by postulating alternatives of the type "all-or-nothing" and then choosing between them (e.g.: Did Paul designate and ordain men into the ministry or did he regard these matters as unimportant and leave them untouched?).[60] We must instead use a number of different criteria (such as: degree of interest, positive—negative interest, passive—active, kinds of activity if any, etc.) in order to determine the nature of Paul's participation in the emergence of ministerial functions or offices in his churches.[61] In the same way the degree of voluntariness and initiative in the persons who perform the different functions may vary, as may the participation of the church.

---

58. So e.g. *Laub* (1973:85).

59. "Bei dieser sich anbahnenden 'Gemeindeordnung' scheinen zunächst einfach soziologische Gesetzmässigkeiten und Notwendigkeiten bestimmend gewesen zu sein", *ibidem.* Cf. *Knox* (1955:91).

60. *Pesch* rightly warns against operating only with the alternatives "ordination ministérielle" and "l'émanation d'une spontanéité enthousiaste", (1971:446). *Budillon*'s history of research is instructive in this regard, (1971:471–478).

61. "Il nous paraît désirable d'éviter le terme trop rigide d'institution (par l'Apôtre), par contre il est difficile de ne pas admettre une action organisatrice de Paul dans les communautés qu'il a fondées et de ne pas reconnaître l'importance qu'avaient pour lui des modèles judéo-chretiens", *Jaubert* (1974:18 n. 3).

It seems reasonable to assume that in most cases we can presume that there was co-operation between all three parties: the founder and "father" Paul, the local church as a body, and the person concerned.[62] The main initiative may come from any one of the parties, but all of them must eventually agree that the function in question is authentic and beneficial or, in Paul's words, a χαρισμα from God to his church.

This co-operation is not manifested in a uniform, standardized way. While Timothy and Titus are sent by Paul to the church, vouched for by Paul, who asks the church to receive them, it seems to be rather different in the case of Epaphroditus who was sent by the church to Paul who then gave his approval. In the case of Stephanas the initiative seems to come from himself. Paul estimates his service as valuable (in his terminology it is a χαρισμα;[63] consisting of κυβερνησις and ἀντιλημψις), and requests the church as a whole to acknowledge this by subordinating themselves to this "house" (and to men like them). Stephanas may have already taken the first step while Paul was still in Corinth,[64] and with Paul's strategy as regards capable men in mind it is not impossible that the apostle himself influenced Stephanas's decision to labour (κοπιαν) for the church.[65]

Still, this is perhaps not the usual course of events; in most cases a function-bearer has to give proof of his χαρισμα before he is acknowledged by the church, and normally it is the affair of the local church to recognize and give formal recognition to its own function-bearers without first asking the approval of the apostle.[66]

Both when he is present and in his absence Paul counts on the emergence and development of what he liked to call χαρισματα, including the charismata of leadership in the church. He interprets these functions as being gifts from the Holy Spirit acting in the church, and wishes the churches in Corinth and Rome to do the same.[67] This view evolves in a situation where the apostle cannot simply authorize what has occurred in the field of functional differentiation as he usually did (1 Thess 5, Gal 6,

62. This important insight is clearly formulated by *Lemaire* (1974:67 f). The French Catholic discussion after 1970 of the question about offices contains a methodological consciousness and an originality in formulating insights and hypotheses, which make it an indispensable counterpart of the contemporary German discussion.

63. *Grelot* (1971:459).

64. *Idem*, p. 458.

65. The letter to Philemon proves that Paul can be extremely charming when he wants to, and 2 Cor 8—9 is proof enough of his ability to entreat and persuade.

66. *Lemaire* (1974:68), referring to 1 Cor 16:15 f and 1 Thess 5:12; cf. Did 15:1, Acts 6:3.

67. *Budillon* (1971:480–483), and below, n. 121.

Rom 12, Phil 1). 1 Cor 12—14 permit us to see Paul's role more clearly than usual and recognize the truth in *Grelot's* conclusion:[68]

"The real access to ministerial functions" (or rather: The emergence of real offices) "seems to be situated at the point *where the upsurge of individual charisma . . . meets the action of the apostle,* who has recognized the authenticity of these charisms and joined their incumbents to himself as co-workers in the preaching of the Gospel and the building up of the Church."[69]

C. THE FUNCTIONS IN RELATION TO THE CHURCH AND TO ONE ANOTHER

1. Can These Functions Be Termed "Offices"?

Before this question can be answered it is necessary to define what is meant by "office". The term has no equivalent in the New Testament,[70] it is a modern term and not Paul's. "Office" is an analytical concept used to summarize a cluster of functions which exhibit certain characteristics in common.

Brockhaus has instructively summed up what the majority of scholars consider to be the formal characteristics of "office":

Regarded as constitutive for "office" are
1. the element of permanency,
2. the element of recognition in the church (an indication of permanency and recognition is the established title of office),
3. the position apart ("Sonderstellung") of individuals in regard to the church (position of authority or dignity),
4. the regular commission (imposition of hands),
5. the legal element, the legal securing of the function in question.[71]

---

68. *Grelot* (1971:459). The "action of the apostle" can take the form of formulating and carefully explaining a principle such as "building up of the church" (οἰκοδομή τῆς ἐκκλησίας), by which the local church can subsequently judge internal "charismatic" developments and make "offices" of them, if they meet the requirements of οἰκοδομή. See further *Hainz* (1972:210–214, 349–351 and 1976a and b) and *Vögtle* (1977:161–163, 177).

69. There are both Catholic and Protestant scholars today who hold that Paul appointed his co-workers *in* the churches as well as his co-workers *to* the churches, cf. *Hainz* (1972:46) and *Ellis* (1971:441 n. 4 with v. Harnack, 444 n. 3, 451 f). "Appointment" need not mean "ordination by imposition of hands", but in the light of Paul's surprising dependence on Jewish-Christian customs in matters of worship (1 Cor 11:3–16, 23 ff, 14:34 ff) *Grelot* finds it not improbable that the form of appointment may also have been borrowed from this context, (1971:461 f), so also *Jaubert* (1974:18 n. 3). Cf. note 56 above, and the fact that Paul himself received the imposition of hands in Antioch (Acts 13:3). On ordination in contemporary Judaism, see *Westerholm* (1978:31–39).

70. See *Schweizer* (1959:154–164), *Stuhlmacher* (1971:30 f), *Pesch* (1971:439 f), *Delorme* (1974:317, with n. 26).

71. *Brockhaus* (1975:24 f n. 106), my translation.

After having listed the characteristics of what is considered as "charisma" in a corresponding manner, *Brockhaus* continues:

> The consecutive numbering corresponds to the continuing consolidation of the concept. 1. is the core of the constitutive elements, 5. is the periphery. Most scholars do not advance as far as including 5. (sc. in the definition of "office").[71]

Later on in his book *Brockhaus* adds two criteria of "office", viz. legitimation ("Legitimierung") by letters of recommendation, and payment ("Bezahlung").[72]

It is not difficult to see that the functions discussed above exhibit the first three criteria listed by *Brockhaus*. In Thessalonika about A.D. 50, only a few months after the local church had been founded (a process Paul was not given time to finish, according to Acts), we find a circle of persons with the function of leaders who are distinct from the rest of the church—something presupposing a certain permanence of this differentiation.[73] Paul acknowledges their work without reserve and requests the church to "respect", recognize (εἰδέναι) them and hold them in high esteem because of their work (1 Thess 5:13). In Rome and Corinth the situation is analogous, and we note that the church in Corinth is even exhorted to subordinate (ὑποτάσσεσθαι) themselves to Stephanas and his house.[74] In Philippi and Cenchreae there are function-bearers with established titles of office.[75] The mere existence of titles is in itself an indication of the permanency and general acknowledgement of a function, and its position apart in relation to the church. But we do not hear anything about the subordination of the church to men exercising these functions.[76]

In addition to these "working authorities"[77] we find function-bearers sufficiently established to be accorded titles, which go back to the primitive Christianity of Jerusalem and Antioch: prophets and teachers. In this case the elements 1.-3. are exhibited, and we may even notice that the function of the teacher is once explicitly said to entitle the one who performs this function to payment (otherwise an apostolic right), Gal 6:6.

---

71. *Brockhaus* (1975:24 f n. 106), my translation.
72. *Idem*, p. 123.
73. *Greeven* (1952/53:345 f, 350), *Goppelt* (1966:125), *von Campenhausen* (1969:68), *Gnilka* (1969:96), *Martin* (1972:26 f) and *Brockhaus* (1975:108) all emphasize the fact that this text refers to permanent functions performed by a fixed group of persons.
74. On the meaning of "first-fruit" (ἀπαρχή), see *Brockhaus* (1975:111, 124).
75. These are not designations of functions, but established titles of offices, *Bultmann* (1953:448), *von Campenhausen* (1969:68), *Gnilka* (1969:101) and *Brockhaus* (1975:98).
76. *Gnilka* emphasizes this (1969:96, 104).
77. *Brockhaus* (1975:124), cf. *Greeven* (1952/53:349).

Payment of local teachers is indicated in Gal 6:6, 2 Thess 3:6–12 and 1 Tim 5:17.[78] I am not prepared to take this last text as evidence of practice in Paul's days, and there may be some doubt about the authenticity of 2 Thess[79] and whether or not 3:6–12 is a reference to a teaching ministry.[80] This leaves us with Gal 6:6 as the only text where payment to local officers of the church is mentioned by Paul, but this is entirely unambiguous. *Brockhaus* has convincingly shown that this text concerns material support of persons who perform a permanent teaching function. The request indicates that this is more or less a full-time occupation.[81]

In the generation after Paul we have several witnesses that πρεσβυτεροι-ἐπισκοποι, who were by now attracting to themselves the function of teaching, are said to receive payment for their work (e.g. 1 Tim 5:17) and are warned from aspiring to the office out of greed (1 Tim 3:3, Tit 1:7, 1 Petr 5:2, cf. Acts 20:33–35).

We have now seen which elements of office characteristics already existed in Paul's days:[82] permanent acknowledged functions in local churches filled by stable groups of persons who lead and serve and take responsibility for their congregations in different ways, in some cases even having a designation or title and some form of material support. The conclusion must be

---

78. This question has recently been discussed by *Ellis* (1971:443 f), *Kirk* (1972/ 73) and *Brockhaus* (1975:101–103). *Kirk* rightly points out (p. 105) that we must distinguish between itinerant ministers (apostles, etc.) and local (full-time) leaders, and it is because *Ellis* does not observe this distinction that he arrives a little too easily at a "class of paid teachers" (the expression from *Burton* 1921:335) in local churches; cf. n. 30 above.

79. Both *Forkman* (1972:132–139) and *Agrell* (1976:116–126) treat this text fully; only the former regards it as having been written by Paul.

80. *Kirk* maintains that it does not (1972/73:106), *Forkman* doubts it (1972: 137), *Agrell* mentions the possibility in passing (1976:122), citing *de Boer,* who considers that the "disorderly" may have been "grasping for positions of superiority" (1962:126–138, quotation on p. 133).

81. "Paulus kennt und anerkennt also eine feste, dauernde und mehr oder weniger vollzeitliche Lehrerfunktion in den christlichen Gemeinden, und er befürwortet die materielle Unterstützung dieser Lehrer", *Brockhaus* (1975:102 f), cf. *Lemaire* (1974: 71). *Kirk* is of course right in pointing out that this does not mean a regular, formal stipend or salary (1972/73:108), but nonetheless the principle of rewarding spiritual help with material gifts is undoubtedly at work here.

82. Some authors want to conclude from an alleged late dating of Phil (after A.D. 58) that a certain development concerning the consolidation of offices may have taken place since 1 Cor was written (A.D. 54?); so e.g. Küng, according to *Grelot* (1971: 455), *Goppelt* (1966:125) and *Pesch* (1971:445), *Roloff* (1977:522). Against this it is pointed out by *Grelot* (1971:445 f) and *Brockhaus* (1975:126) that Phil *may* have been written at the same time as (or even before) 1 Cor, cf. *Bornkamm* (1971:130 n. 31), and that it cannot be postulated that all churches have to go through the same development, from (Corinth's) pneumatic "chaos" to a more solid structure. In Philippi the church may have had a harmonious solidification of functions, and the independence resulting from this (cf. *Gnilka* 1969:99 f, 104), from the very beginning.

that we can rightly speak of offices in Paul's churches, even if they are not yet fully developed[83] or legally authorized.[84]

2. To What Extent Had the Local Leadership of the Church Developed?

The general impression we get when reading Paul's letters is that the local offices were rather unimportant. They are seldom mentioned, even if the apostle seems to appreciate them, and there are a number of functions they could be expected to have performed, but which we do not find them doing:[85] (a) They do not represent the church to outside authorities. (b) They are not responsible for any central church fund (cf. 1 Cor 16:2 παρ' ἑαυτῳ). (c) They are not in charge of church discipline (1 Cor 5) nor do they act as arbitrators between Christian brothers (1 Cor 6). (d) They do not lead worship or keep order during it. (e) When serious conflicts arise within the church Paul does not ask the local leaders to settle them nor does he give them any responsibility at all. Must we not conclude that the local church leaders had no authority of their own, or in other words that their function of leading was so rudimentary as to be almost non-existent?[86]

Before we come to this conclusion some circumstances must be considered. First, it is evident that even a general exhortation such as "Admonish the idle (or: disorderly)" or "Help the weak" (1 Thess 5:14) presupposes the fact that some people in the church are more orderly, are stronger, and more capable of admonishing and helping than others are. And this actual difference seems from the few hints we have to partly coincide with the existence of leaders who admonish when necessary (1 Thess 5:12), care for the weak, serve the local church (cf. Stephanas, whom Paul explicitly authorizes).[87] But more important than these observations is the fact that our picture of the interior life of a Pauline church is to so great an extent determined by 1 Cor. All the examples of ministerial insignificance above are taken from the church in Corinth, and may not apply to the other Pauline churches. Concerning (a) we can simply note that the need did not arise in Corinth, where both Crispus and Erastus had high social standing and social influence. But in Thessalonika Jason, the house-owner, seems to

83. Concerning element 4. (ordered appointment, imposition of hands), see notes 56 and 69 above. Generally speaking, this belongs to the generation after Paul, *Brockhaus* (1975:214 n. 53).

84. *Idem*, p. 126.

85. *Greeven* (1952/53:350–360).

86. *Brockhaus* (1975:126 f, 213). Cf. *Greeven* (see previous note), *Schweizer* (1959:91) and *Käsemann* (1960:128).

87. *Dahl* (1967:324 f): Stephanas was opposed in Corinth, and Paul wants to back him up (16:15 is the third παρακαλω-clause of the letter).

represent the congregation (Acts 17:9) as did Alexander in Ephesus (Acts 19:33). The remark (b) is correct, but tells us more about the character of communal life in Hellenistic congregations which was not identical with that of Jerusalem. In the former type of community charity may have depended more on the charity of wealthy houses than on centralized funds. As regards (c) it can be said that the case of 1 Cor 5 was a case of "sinning" with good conscience and that not only the sinner alone could have thought his liaison theoretically justified.[88] And in the case of Christians sueing one another, it may not have been possible to ask the local leaders to settle this as it might well have been they themselves who were the guilty ones.[89] If the problem in Corinth consisted of lack of unity, self-discipline, love and wisdom, primarily situated in the leading stratum it is no wonder that Paul cannot appeal to them to set all this aright except by a letter addressed to *all* Christians in Corinth, where he impresses on them that they are one body and must act as such.

This is not to deny, however, that local leadership was only rudimentary when Paul wrote his letters. We are only seeing the beginning of what was later to mature into a fully-developed office structure. And the question is why this is so.

Greeven considered this an indication that there were no leaders in Corinth apart from the prophets and teachers. The leading of worship, the enforcing of church discipline together with functions of responsibility that were needed from time to time were functions that were performed (or were expected to be performed) by these pneumatically endowed men. Paul did not wish any kind of presbyterium to lead the church and dissociates himself from this practice in the Jewish Christian churches on fundamental theological grounds: only if the pneumatics lead can the Spirit lead the church as directly as possible.[90]

---

88. *Daube* (1971:224).
89. See above n. 51.
90. *Greeven* (1952/53:352, 356–359), *Rohde* (1976:44) on 1 Thess 5:12 "noch mit einer Personalunion des Charismas der Lehre und Gemeindeleitung zu rechnen", *Roloff* (1977:521).

Greeven's statement on Paul's fundamental opposition to the presbyterate (p. 357 ff) is seconded by *Schweizer* (1959:90) and *von Campenhausen* (1969:76 f); the latter restricts this to a theological opposition and considers that the non-existence of presbyters in the Pauline churches is not necessarily deliberately polemical against Jewish Christianity, p. 70. *Goppelt* criticizes these attempts at making a (too) sharp distinction between an allegedly non-charismatic, legal-institutional presbyterate and the προϊσταμενοι (and ἐπισκοποι και διακονοι) of Paul (1965 and 1966:127 f), cf. *Bourke* (1968:502), and *Martin* has effectively criticized von Campenhausen's assumption of the fundamental theological opposition between the offices in Pauline and Jewish churches (1972:44–47).

In this context *Käsemann's* influential essay in "Sätze des heiligen Rechtes im NT"

This conception of a pneumatic leadership and a "charismatic" church order has had its proponents both before and after *Greeven,*[91] but its value as a historical reconstruction is open to question. As *Greeven* himself points out[92] the teachers of the church represent the tradition, while the prophets alone receive direct communication from the Spirit. The prominence of teachers does not square with a fundamental repudiation of the Jewish Christian principle of tradition.[93] Further, it seems almost certain that behind the abstract nouns of 1 Cor 12:28 stand persons which cannot simply be identified with the prophets and teachers.[94] We do not know if the latter were particularly concerned with church discipline, caring for the poor, presiding at the common act of worship. As seen above these functions seem to have been performed by persons whose endowments were not necessarily pneumatic, but rather material, practical and social. We need not postulate a well-defined boundary between the two groups of functions in order to state that teaching and prophecy in the context of worship and authoritative care and service in everyday situations probably engaged the services of different people. The fact that both prophets and teachers had a distinctly Jewish background also served to delimit the range of their leadership in Hellenistic churches.[95]

Still, the situation in Corinth was apparently so fluid that *Greeven* is correct in saying that *nobody* exercised the functions of leadership that Paul had expected the church to cope with. Thus it can rightly be said to lack stability and independence, as it lacks an integrated body of leaders, acknowledged by all its members. And it is this immaturity that forces Paul to intervene with rebukes, orders, admonitions, explanations and detailed rules to an extent that is unique in his letters. These kinds of disturbances

---

(1955) should be mentioned as it presents much the same view on the leadership of prophets in the early Pauline communities as *Greeven* (1955:79 f). *von Campenhausen* has characterized this hypothesis as "etwas willkürliche Hypostasierung eines philologischen Phänomens ins Historische", (1957:70 n. 82). Lately it has been subjected to devastating criticism by Klaus *Berger* (1970), who rejects the hypothesis on form-critical grounds, and by *Dautzenberg* (1975:24–27), who finds it historically unfounded. Cf. also *Cothenet*'s criticism (1972:1285).

91. *Greeven* himself points to a certain similarity between his results on the one hand and views in the "consensus" of the 1880's and in Sohm's works on the other, (1952/53:306 and 360).

92. *Greeven* (1952/53:343).

93. *Idem,* p. 358.

94. *Brockhaus* (1975:207).

95. *Dautzenberg* (1975:299). Cf. "wissen wir für die Frühzeit, wenn ich recht sehe, von keinem christlichen Propheten, der nicht mit Palästina-Syrien im Zusammenhang stand", *Kretschmar* (1964:38 n. 26). Kretschmar makes an exception to this statement for Pauline churches referring to 1 Cor 14: 31, which exception in the light of Dautzenberg's investigation (cf. n. 107 below) need not be made. Cf. also *Theissen* (1977:107).

and shortcomings are however not the normal thing in the Pauline churches and should not be permitted to colour our interpretation of the whole situation.[96]

Phil 1:1, 1 Thess 5:12 and Rom 12:6-8, 16:1-2 are evidence that in other Pauline churches (Cenchreae was the seaport of Corinth)[97] the functions of leadership developed more harmoniously. As early as the middle of the fifties (within some five or ten years from the founding of the church) we encounter persons who have fixed office titles;[98] this is also an indirect witness to the consolidation of the church.[99]

Even if the explanation that is based on the assumption of a "charismatic", specially Pauline church order is unsatisfactory, we should not exclude theological reasons for the visible insignificance of local offices. One such reason is the Pauline view of the church: Paul always addresses his letters and their contents to the *whole* of a particular church, treating it as a unity. And this he does in order to create and maintain that unity. What he has to say concerns all Christians, even if it is only a part of the church that has the responsibility of realizing it. And then his theology of χαρισματα works in the same direction. The developing offices, which Paul observes and supports, the χαρισματα beside other gifts, parts of a whole with their specific functions. This is why he can on the one hand fully acknowledge and authorize them and on the other cannot rank this kind of χαρισμα higher than any other. One member cannot be made responsible for the life of the

---

96. *Karrer* (1955:78–84), *Roloff* (1965:134 and 1977:521), *Goppelt* (1966:128), *Bourke* (1968:509 f), *Gnilka* (1969:95, 99 f), *Budillon* (1971:478 f, 483 f) and *Rohde* (1976:56).

97. *Schlier* points out that Rom 16:1 f is a confirmation of Corinth's exceptional character (1977:441 n. 7).

98. *Brockhaus* (1975:100).

99. Even if these leaders are not called πρεσβυτεροι one should remember that ἐπισκοποι = προϊσταμενοι do not differ functionally from the Christian πρεσβυτεροι, *Bultmann* (1953:448), *Goppelt* (1966:128), *Lemaire* (1971:192). We can also see from Acts 20:17, 28, Past and 1 Clem that Pauline churches had presbyters as early as the nineties (*Roloff* 1977:523, in the eighties). On this see *von Campenhausen* (1969: 91), *Stuhlmacher* (1971:39 f), *Budillon* (1971:484), *Martin* (1972:33, 50 ff) and esp. *Schürmann* (1968). On the question of the identity of πρεσβυτεροι and ἐπισκοποι in Past, see *Ridderbos* (1975:457 f), and on presbyters in general *Bornkamm* (1959).

Schürmann has put the question whether churches within the missionary district of Antioch and even Pauline churches, cf. Phil 1:1, may not have had presbyteries of their own (1970:397 n. 124), ditto *Bourke* (1958:502). To begin with they were not very active in the government of the church which lay more in the hands of the pneumatically gifted. After a time they emerged as the responsible, reliable element, appropriating to themselves a teaching responsibility when pneumatic teachers ran wild or ceased to appear. This serves to explain the emergence of presbyters who are προεστωτες πρεσβυτεροι (1 Tim 5:17), and makes the leaders mentioned in 1 Thess 5:12, 1 Cor 12:28, 16:15 f, Rom 12:8 and Phil 1:1 something of a "pre-structure" of the subsequent presbyterate in these same churches, *idem*, p. 396 f. Cf. *idem* (1977:39–43).

whole body, because that function or responsibility belongs to the Spirit Himself alone.[100]

But there are sociological reasons for the relative insignificance of local offices, too. One of them is the fact that this "office structure" has developed before the eyes of all concerned. It goes without saying that this type of authority ("working authority") is less normative than that exercised by the apostle himself, or instituted by him as a natural and necessary part of Christian life from its inception.[101]

The decisive reason is, however, the personage of Paul himself. The founder has not left the scene, but is fully and energetically active in his churches (especially in Corinth). His letters show that he had full control over the life and development of his churches and regarded himself as having a permanent responsibility for them. Even if he aimed at fostering maturity and independence in his churches the letters do not give the impression that he gave them the reins. And it is just this "potential accessibility" of the apostle, the fact that he is still actively present and his authority fully accessible, that prevents the full (social, legal and theological) development of those beginnings of an office structure we observe in the Pauline letters.[102] This aspect of local church life does not really start to develop until after the apostle's death.[103]

As a cautious summary of this discussion I conclude that in most of Paul's churches we have a group of persons who teach, guide, transmit divine revelations, expound the Scriptures and formulate God's will in concrete, everyday life, and here we find the prophets and teachers. Presumably this type of function was of an unusually pneumatic (ecstatic) brand in the church of Corinth, not found in other churches. Beside this group we find another, not so clearly defined, consisting of people with sufficient initiative, wealth and compassion to care for the sick and poor, to receive travelling missionaries and other Christians, to be able to accommodate the worshippers and the communal meals of the church in their own houses, sometimes travelling on behalf of the church and generally taking administrative responsibility.

---

100. *Brockhaus* (1975:237). Cf. *Käsemann* (1960:124).

101. With Phil as a possible exception, all Paul's letters to his own churches are written to congregations that have been founded from without and are in the very first years of their existence. No mission church begins with self-governing congregations, *Skjevesland* (1976:123).

102. "Da Paulus die Gemeindedienste durch seine Autorität stützte, Normen für die Verkündigung setzte und schliesslich Anweisungen für das Gemeindeleben gab, bestand keine dringende Notwendigkeit, die Entscheidungskompetenzen in den paulinischen Gemeinden genau zu regeln", *Martin* (1972:32 f), who also coined the term "potentielle Verfügbarkeit", *ibidem*.

103. See above, n. 99.

3. What Kind of Authority Did These Offices Exercise?

In describing the relation between ministry and church some modern scholars tend to emphasize the fundamental equality of the church and the "office-holders", and argue that no function (except the apostolate) was strictly reserved for the latter.[104] We see, for instance in 1 Thess 4:18, 5:11 and 14, that the church can "comfort" (παρακαλειν), "build up" (οἰκοδομειν), "admonish" (νουθετειν) and "encourage" (παραμυθεισθαι), functions that are similar to or identical with those of the leaders (5:12). And from 5:19–21 we learn that the whole church is expected to be able to test prophecy and "hold fast what is good"; and we find no limitation on who may prophecy.[105] 1 Cor 12:10 and 14:29 have sometimes been interpreted as saying the same[106] which is, however, incorrect: these texts refer to the inspired interpretation of prophecies by the prophets themselves, not to any general control or authority to judge divine inspirations on the part of the church.[107] (This may indicate how prophecy was tested also in Thessalonika.)

Naturally every Christian is thought to a free, responsible and spiritually gifted person (1 Cor 8:9, 12:11–13, etc.), and Paul always addresses himself to the whole local church as to a responsible and active entity. But this does not exclude a differentiation of functions and responsibility within the church, even entailing a certain amount of subordination. Even *Laub,* who considers that the boundary between the church in general and a special group with a responsibility of their own is so fluid as to hardly exist,[108] speaks of a superordination and subordination ("Über- und Unterordnung") that grows "from below" out of mutual service.[109]

This superordination and subordination is characterized by *Jaubert,* with

---

104. Strongly emphasized by *Schweizer* (1959:185), who is criticized by *Greeven* (1952/53:344 n. 69). The same tendency is found both in Catholic authors, such as *Laub* (1973, 1976), *Küng* (1967) and *Pesch* (1971), and Protestant ones, such as *von Campenhausen* (1957, 1969) and *Käsemann* (e.g. 1960:121 ff).

105. *Laub* (1973:93 f and 1976:37 n. 35).

106. E.g. by *Bultmann* (1953:445), *Schürmann* (1970:405), *Martin* (1972:27) and *Ridderbos* (1975:451).

107. "Der Gedanke einer Bedrohung der christlichen Freiheit einer Gemeinde durch Propheten und Ämter, welcher durch eine 'Beurteilung' gesteuert werden müsste, ist erst aus späteren kirchengeschichtlichen Erfahrungen geboren und darf nicht in 1 Kor 12–14 eingetragen werden. Die *diakrisis pneumaton* ist kein Super-Charisma, sie ist der Prophetie nicht über-, sondern ihr zugeordnet. Sie meint einge-gebenes Verstehen und Deuten, aber nicht eingegebenes Richten und Beurteilen", *Dautzenberg* (1975:147). *Greeven* also argued that the διακρισις is carried out by the prophetic spirit in other prophets, not by the church in general (1952/53:319–323); the same opinion is found in *von Campenhausen* (1969:62), *Chevallier* (1966:190 f), and *Ellis* (1974:129 n. 7).

108. *Laub* (1973:91 and 1976:34).

109. *Idem* (1973:85, 1976:35). *Linton's* remarks on the structure of the Primitive Church as "beschliessende, ungleichmässige Versammlung" (1932:189–195) are still pertinent in this discussion to broaden the sometimes too "Western" and modern

a felicitous term, as dialectical authority.[110] By this she means that the opposites of equality and subordination are not a very fit category with which to describe the relation between the church in general and its functions or offices. It cannot be denied, for instance, that οἰκοδομή is a task for every Christian (1 Cor 8:1, 14:17, and cf. 1 Thess 5:11), for the prophets (1 Cor 14:3) and for the apostle (1 Cor 3:9–11).[111] The task of the leaders does thus not differ qualitatively from that of those they lead (cf. Rom 15:14 f), and yet there exists a subtle dialectic between the responsibility of all and the responsibility of some. Both parties are dependent upon each other, but not in the same way. Both parties are to serve the other, but not in the same way, as we see from the dialectic between τασσειν ἑαυτον εἰς διακονιαν τοις ἁγιοις and ὑποτασσεσθαι τοις τοιουτοις in 1 Cor 16:15 f. The one party, the house of Stephanas, serves the others and toils for them, the church, which in its turn is requested to willingly subject themselves to the first party (i.e. obey). The leaders and the congregation are related to each other in a context of love and co-operation, and stand in a relation of mutual, but not symmetric, dependence on each other.[112]

4. Was There Any Difference of Rank between the Offices (Functions)?

As our information on offices in 1 Thess, Gal, Phil, Philem is very meagre and hardly tells us anything about any differences between various offices,[113] we must find the answer to the question from what is said in Rom 12 and 1 Cor 12—14.

Most scholars conclude from the sequence of the charisma lists and from what Paul says on the value of prophecy contra speaking in tongues in 1 Cor 14 that the apostle makes a clear difference in rank between different gifts (functions, offices).[114] That "apostle" ranks above every other func-

---

frames of reference of commentators. Linton's view on Acts 15 has been followed up by *Reicke* (1957), *Gerhardsson* (1961:245–254), who adduces extensive parallels from Qumran and rabbinical literature, and by *Larsson* (1976:7–13).

110. *Jaubert* (1974:23–28, 33). The concept has also been used by *Sesboué* (1974: 369 f).

111. Cf. *Hainz* (1972:42–47), and his conclusion on the role of the leaders: "Ihre Aufgabe ist grundsätzlich keine andere als die der Gemeinde, nämlich Dienst an ihrer οἰκοδομή, allerdings ist ihr Dienst ein besonders qualifizierter" (p. 47). See also *Chevallier* (1966:64) and *Ridderbos*'s remarks on the church as both subject and object of the authority from God (1975:473–475).

112. *Jaubert* (1974:26 f). Jaubert's view is a needed complement to and a correction of the one-sidedness of e.g. *Käsemann* (1960:123 f) and *Laub* (see n. 108).

113. *Schweizer* assumes that the διακονοι were servants to the ἐπισκοποι (1959:181), and *Hainz* thinks that the former were in a more subordinate position in relation to the church than the latter (1976:104).

114. *Greeven* (1952/53:343 f), *Käsemann* (1960:120): "Gleichheit ist für Paulus kein Prinzip der kirchlichen Ordnung", *Chevallier* (1966:167, 169 f), *Nickle* (1966:

tion does not need any discussion (1 Cor 12:28 just confirms what is evident to any reader). Number two are the prophets, and number three the teachers (1 Cor 12:28 f, Rom 12:6 f, where however διακονια is inserted between them), while glossolalia is studiously placed last on the list of gifts (in 1 Cor 12:8 ff and 28 f). The criterion of rank is οἰκοδομη, the value or objective benefit a gift has in building up the church. With the help of this criterion one could attempt a hypothetical ranking of the gifts mentioned between the highest (prophecy) and the lowest (speaking in tongues).

The capacity to work miracles and to exorcise is, like glossolalia, important as a manifestation of the power and the presence of the Spirit in the congregation. But as these capacities have no constitutive, "upbuilding" function, making them vitally necessary to the existence of the church in the long run, they are accorded lower rank than the Corinthians would wish to believe. On the other hand, prosaic, everyday functions such as caring for prisoners and poor brothers, receiving Christian travellers in one's home, being the host of the church at worship (and other similar services) are in the long run of vital importance to the church, in spite of their lack of visible pneumatic character. That is why Paul (probably to the surprise of the Corinthians)[115] included this type of function in his lists of gifts of the Spirit. And Phil 1:1 is evidence that this cluster of functions soon became regarded as distinctive and important enough to acquire office titles.

But this ranking is so far only an extrapolation of Paul's theological and pastoral assessment of the different functions, an interpretation of them made with a paraenetic purpose (see below). And this did not correspond with the actual order of rank between functions in the church of Corinth, which exalted glossolalia and γνωσις above every other gift or service. In reality there hardly existed any *hierarchical* differentiation between the various functions or, in other words, no function at the time of Paul's letter-writing was legally subordinated to any other ("I as a prophet order you, a mere ἐπισκοπος, to do so and so").[116] We know for certain that Paul's purpose in 1 Cor 12 is explicitly anti-hierarchical (cf. especially 12:21–26), even if we can read between the lines that all functions do not have the same value.[117]

117 n. 158), *Gnilka* (1969:97), *Schürmann* (1970:384 ff), *Pesch* (1971:445 f), *Martin* (1972:27), *Brockhaus* (1975:215) and *Ridderbos* (1975:443).

115. *Bultmann* (1953:153, 333), *Schweizer* (1959:92), *Schürmann* (1970:384), *Brockhaus* (1975:208).

116. Cf. however *Schweizer*: "der Dienst der Propheten (ist) . . . noch bestimmender geworden als der des Vorstehers oder Bischofs" (1959:171).

117. *von Campenhausen* (1969:64), *Stuhlmacher* (1971:35 f), *Martin* (1972:27). *Brockhaus* rightly criticizes (1975:203–210) *Schürmann*'s exaggeratedly hierarchical

But there may have existed a less strictly formalized difference in status between the functions, based on conspicuous pneumatic endowment (cf. Corinthian overestimation of speaking in tongues and "wisdom") or on socio-cultural superiority (the rich, educated and socially influential probably were the leaders of opinion in the congregation and could get their own way more easily than others).[118] In Corinth this difference in status was so marked that it became a real problem for the unity of the congregation and has to be countered by Paul by his theological conception of the different functions as χαρισματα from the same Spirit.

5. "Charismatic" and "Institutional" Offices

It is important to keep in mind that the lists of χαρισματα and Paul's exposition in 1 Cor 12–14 is not primarily a description of reality in Corinth but an attempt to transform this reality.[119] The primary problem was the Corinthian overestimation of glossolalia (τα πνευματικα), and the concomitant belief that some Christians had a special endowment of Spirit, manifesting itself "pneumatically".[120] Paul's purpose is antienthusiastic and paraenetic: he wants *all* Christians to realize that they all have gifts from God, that every one of them has his unique task and talent with which he should contribute to the upbuilding of the whole church.[121] Χαρισματα are thus *not* identical with πνευματικα,[122] as we find various kinds of non-"pneumatic" or non-ecstatic functions and activities numbered among the χαρισματα.[123]

Paul lists those gifts that come to mind as he writes: some pneumatic-enthusiastic phenomena, some authoritative functions that already had tra-

---

interpretation of the order of sequence of the gifts in the different lists (1970:384 ff). Brockhaus and *Chevallier* (1966:167–170) have clearly shown how different the charisma-lists are in content and purpose, and that they exclude any strict hierarchical understanding of the gifts.

118. *Theissen* (1975a:170).

119. *Brockhaus* (1975:80 n. 70, 207–209), and *Gnilka* (1969:97).

120. *Brockhaus* (1975:150–156).

121. This perspective on Paul's theology of χαρισμα has been fully worked out by *Chevallier* (1966:139–170) and, independent of him, by *Brockhaus* (1975:128–239), but it can be found also in other authors' works: *Budillon* (1971:480–483), *Ridderbos* (1975:442 f), *Schulz* (1976:446, 454 f), *Herten* (1976). For further literature on χαρισμα see *Schürmann's* postscript in *Kertelge* (1977:412). I have not seen R. Giesriegl's dissertation "Amt und Charisma nach dem ersten Korintherbrief des Apostels Paulus", Salzburg 1970/71.

122. This confusion is found in e.g. *Bultmann* (1953:151–162 passim), *Conzelmann* (1969a:245, 275 n. 13), but thoroughly refuted by the analyses of Chevallier and Brockhaus, cf. also *Hainz* (1972:362) and *Ellis* (1974:129).

123. See *Schütz's* remarks on χαρισμα as a Pauline "ordering principle" (1975:256–259). His treatment is somewhat marred by an unclear distinction between χαρισματα and πνευματικα, cf. especially p. 255.

ditional Jewish-Christian titles (apostles, teachers, prophets), other functions of leadership without any titles (κυβερνήσεις), different kinds of teaching and interpretation (utterance of wisdom, of knowledge, interpretation
of inspired speech) and different aspects of practical help (service, exercise of charity, ἀντιλήμψις); and from all these elements he creates before
the eyes of the Corinthian (and later the Roman) Christians "a unitary,
living cosmos of free spiritual gifts which serve and complement one another".[124] But this is not a naturalistic portrait of the Corinthian church but
a paragon and an ideal, with which the apostle wants to transform reality.[125] His list and his theology of χαρισμα is a theological-paraenetical
creation, a utopian model for Christian life in any congregation.[126]

This fact makes it impossible to speak of "charismatic" function, office
or church order in contrast to non-charismatic ones.[127] The term is Pauline,
and in Paul's mind there exists no opposition between χαρισμα and office,[128]
or χαρισμα and institution,[129] as the term signifies any gift, task, or service
of benefit to the whole church that a Christian has been enabled by God
to practise. *Brockhaus* has convincingly shown[130] that Paul's theology of
χαρισμα is in reality neither a criticism of[131] nor a plea for[132] offices in his
churches, and that it cannot even be used as (or was ever intended as) a
draft for a possible or ideal church order.[133]

124. *von Campenhausen* (1969:64).
125. *Brockhaus* (1975:209), partly admitted by *von Campenhausen*, ibidem.
126. "Das Wort Charisma wird zum Signal einer utopischen, aber wahrhaft christlichen Brüdergemeinde", *Herten* (1976:84).
127. *Bultmann* (1953:449 f), *Schweizer* (1959:164–171), *Roloff* (1965:126),
Käsemann (1974:329), *Ridderbos* (1975:442) and *Rohde* (1976:46) refute this distinction. *Kraft* makes a distinction between "offices, whose incumbents are appointed
directly by God" and "offices whose incumbents are appointed through men" and
names the former "charismatic" and the latter "institutional" (1975:82). This terminology is inappropriate, and the criterion is disputable. See *Delorme's* balanced discussion of the "mandate", "competence" and "investiture" of different offices (1974:
328–343). Cf. also *Ridderbos* (1975:474–478).
128. It could be said that a "charismatic ministry" is simply the same as a "Christian ministry", cf. *Bultmann* (1953:450). This is the element of truth in *Käsemann's*
otherwise excessive extension of the concept (1960:109–121), in which he is followed
by *Schulz* (1976:456–460). *Brockhaus's* convincing criticism (pp. 220–226 of Käsemann's ethicization of χαρισμα was first published in 1972, and was thus known to
Schulz, who however does not try to refute it. Käsemann is also criticized on this
point by *Ridderbos* (1975:441 f n. 40).
129. On this point *Ridderbos* criticizes Käsemann, Schweizer and von Campenhausen (1975:443–446).
130. *Brockhaus* (1975:210–218).
131. So e.g. von Campenhausen, Käsemann.
132. So e.g. Goppelt, Grau, Schlier, Schnackenburg.
133. *Brockhaus* (1975:218–220), cf. also *Roloff* (1965.126) and *Cothenet* (1972:
1301–1303). This refutes *Hasenhüttl's* conception (1973:71 ff) of a special "charismatic fundamental structure" ("charismatische Grundstruktur") in the Pauline
churches.

PART TWO

The Structure of Authority in the Primitive Church

The description given in Part I is not "pure" history, but it is only in Part II that I try to analyse historical reality with the help of sociological analytical concepts, to form a clearer picture of authority in the Primitive Church, especially in its Pauline region. I have thus postponed a discussion of these analytical concepts until this point.

In the next chapter a number of fundamental distinctions and definitions must be made before turning to the analysis proper of the material presented in Part I.

CHAPTER 4
Power and Authority

A. SOME FUNDAMENTAL DISTINCTIONS

A study of what the sociological literature has to say on concepts such as "power", "authority", "violence", "legitimacy", etc. shows that there is no uniform nomenclature. It seems necessary for every author working in this field to make his own definitions, or at least inform the reader of which definitions will be used. The following discussion is the result of a series of choice and combination where the German sociologist *Max Weber*'s classical work forms the basis.[1] My primary intention, however, has not been to give only a correct interpretation of *Weber,* but to find and formulate useful analytical perspectives.

1. Power—Domination—Authority

In the first, concept-defining part of his monumental "Wirtschaft und Gesellschaft" *Weber* gives definitions of "power" ("Macht") and "domination" ("Herrschaft")[2] which have had a great influence on sociological tradition:

---

1. Of *Weber*'s main work "Wirtschaft und Gesellschaft" I use the latest German edition, published by Johannes *Winckelmann* in Tübingen 1976, and the first complete English translation: "Economy and Society", vol. 1–3, eds. Günther *Roth* and Claus *Wittich,* New York 1968. For a bibliography of secondary literature on Max Weber see the work of *Seyfarth* and *Schmidt* (1977).
2. No uniformity exists in the translation of "Herrschaft". *Parsons* used the phrase "imperative control"; *Friedrich* proposed "rule" as being the linguistically and objectively best equivalent (1961:9 n. 10); *Bendix*'s translation "domination" (1960:296 n. 16) has been taken over by *Roth-Wittich,* cf. *Weber* (1968:61 f n. 31, 299 n. 1). However, in those parts where Weber treats predominantly "legitime Herrschaft", *Roth-Wittich* translate "Herrschaft" by "authority", *ibidem.* Cf. the discussion in *Cohen-Hazelrigg-Pope* (1975:237 ff).

'Power' is the probability that one actor within a social relationship will be in a position to carry out his own will despite resistance, regardless of the basis on which this probability rests.[3]

This abstract definition covers a great variety of phenomena, e.g. relationships based on coercion or based on a utilitarian constellation of interests of both parties, and is therefore of less value as an analytical tool. So *Weber* introduces a subcategory of power, namely "domination" ("Herrschaft"):

'Domination' is the probability that a command with a given specific content will be obeyed by a given group of persons.[4]

It thus does not include every mode of exercising 'power' or 'influence' over other persons. Domination ('authority') in this sense may be based on the most diverse motives of compliance: all the way from simple habituation to the most purely rational calculation of advantage. Hence every genuine form of domination implies a minimum of voluntary compliance, that is, an *interest* (based on ulterior motives or genuine acceptance) in obedience.[5]

The last quotation explains why "authority" has been included in the heading of this section; in Weber's terminology "Autorität" is roughly synonymous with "Herrschaft", although the term "Autorität" can have a more restricted sense.[6] From the context of these quotations it appears that domination is normally connected with the existence of a permanent organized group ("Verband") with a leader and often also an administrative staff, and that those who obey do so on the basis of voluntary compliance. Among the different motives for obeying the most important is belief in the leader's legitimacy and this is what *Weber* later uses as a criterion in his typology of domination. "Domination" thus signifies a power relation that is legitimate and institutionalized.[7]

---

3. *Weber* (1968:53 = 1976:28). "Chance/probability" is deliberately chosen by Weber to exclude the necessity of treating the psychological element in the relation, *Hartmann* (1964:6 f). On deficiencies in Weber's concept of power, see *Martin* (1971:241 ff).
4. Continuation of the quotation in preceding note.
5. *Weber* (1968:212 = 1976:122).
6. *Hartmann* (1964:6 f), *Schütz* (1975:17,268). The quotation in note 5 is an example of a synonymous use of the two concepts; but they are also used separately, for example, in *Weber* (1976:822 f).
7. *Schelsky* (1975:20 ff). *Cohen-Hazelrigg-Pope* criticize the (Parsonian) overemphasis on the normative element of belief in legitimacy and point out that Weber himself saw other kinds of motivations beside this belief as upholding a legitimate order (1975:239). Weber has been criticized for not being consistent in his use of "Herrschaft", see *Blau* (1963:306 n. 10), *Hennen-Prigge* (1977:6) and cf. *Bendix* (1960:294 and 302).

2. Domination—Authority

"Authority" in *Weber's* terminology can, though need not, signify a form of power, and this is how the concept is defined by some authors.[8] To avoid confusion,[9] however, the concepts of power and authority should be kept apart, and this has to be done by making a conceptual distinction between "domination" and "authority", although they are closely connected in reality. In doing this I shall follow *Hennen-Prigge* (1977) in the distinction they make between these two concepts:[10]

Domination is a quality pertaining to a social system, while authority is a quality pertaining to a person or a group of persons. The bearer of authority is always (in the last resort) a human being.[11] He exercises an active influence on somebody else who submits to this influence. The visible part of the relation is the empirical fact that one person gives an "order" and another "obeys" it (to use *Weber's* terms). But the "invisible" and specific characteristic of an authority relation is that the ruler and the subordinate both consider it the duty of the latter to obey. The subordinate gives his assent to the order and obeys without questioning it on the principle that an order from a legitimate ruler must be obeyed. Social organization consists of such latent principles structuring the manifest relations of social life, and the latent structural principle of an authority relation is termed "domination". Authority is the manifestation of the latent domination.[12]

The relation between ruler and subordinate at the manifest level corresponds at the latent level with the relation between legitimation and validity. This means that the authority-holder's claim to be entitled to give orders is justified by reference to a legitimation that is valid to the one who submits to authority. The influence in question is justified in both quarters by reference to an existing social order, the rightness of which needs no justification.

8. *Lasswell-Kaplan*: "formal power" (1950:133); *Bierstedt*: "institutionalized power" (1954:79 f). Cf. *Blau*, who sees authority as a form of social control (1963: 307, 313) and *Bochenski* who even includes the hold-up in this concept (1974:81 f).

9. A number of scholars argue that authority cannot be identified with power, *Friedrich* (1958:29,37), (1960:2,8), (1964), and (1972:46), *Sternberger* (1959:11 f, 17 f), *Arendt* (1970:42 ff), *Bachrach-Baratz* (1972:41 f).

10. *Hennen-Prigge* (1977:9–32). It must be observed that "Herrschaft" in their terminology only covers what Weber termed "legitime Herrschaft".

11. *Bochenski* shows (1974:32–36) that this mode of expression presupposes the choice of an Aristotelian rather than a Hegelian ontology. A sociologist would perhaps call it a choosing between a Weberian and a Durkheimian way of looking at society, cf. *Berger* (1963b: 145 f, 149).

12. See *Hennen-Prigge's* diagram (1977:22).

But authority does not function by means of a conscious process of deliberation on questions of legitimacy taking place every time the subordinate receives influence from the ruler. All participants in a society have so many opinions in common about what is right, obvious and natural, that social organization (which consists of such opinions) is simply an objective fact of social life, comparable in objectivity to the facts of geography of the community in which they live. What is legitimate and valid is determined socially, and this means that it is generally absorbed into the minds of the actors through the ordinary socialization process (i.e. by learning the language, growing familiar with the prevailing culture, knowledge and norm system).[13]

Relations where one person submits to the influence of another on other grounds than belief in legitimacy must be classified as differing from the authority relation.

Orders may be based on the threat of physical sanctions. *Hennen-Prigge* term this structural principle "violence" and its manifestation at the personal level "power", and see this as a border-line case or pathological form of the domination/authority relation.[14]

Orders may also be based on some kind of proof ("Bewährung") that it is to the advantage of the subordinate to obey.[15] In this situation the latter has a positive, if only material, interest in obeying the ruler. This kind of relation is an intermediate between coercive power and legitimate domination and I shall call it "contractual" domination. Here the motives of the actors are predominantly calculative and the relation between them is an exchange relation and is the only means of getting what they want from each other.[16]

3. Authority—Legitimacy—Legality

In the terminology used above "authority" is an empirical fact, while "legitimacy" is a quality pertaining to an invisible structure, viz. domina-

13. See *Berger-Luckmann* (1967:129 ff).
14. *Hennen-Prigge* (1977:27–29). The diagram on p. 29 and the lower half of that on p. 31 depict the same state; the latter represents the mental state prevailing when violence is the structuring principle of society. "Anomie" can hardly be said to be a structuring principle at all.
15. *Idem,* p. 31 f.
16. *Widengren* treats "contract power" in a thorough discussion (1977, Chap. 12), and gives a typology of exchange relations (p. 120 f) in which the relation I have described above would be termed "symmetrical contractual exchange". This type of relation may be transformed into an authority relation through the development of an internalized group norm among the subordinates that one ought to obey the ruler, cf. *Blau* (1963:312 f and 1964:205 ff). On exchange and power see *Cartwright* (1965) and *Dahlström* (1966). *Ekeh* (1974) gives an interesting criticism of usual exchange theories.

tion. The two concepts thus belong to different "systems" or spheres of reality. Legitimacy is the quality of being in accordance with the norm of "rightness".

Legitimacy should be distinguished from "legality", which is the quality of being in accordance with a positive law.[17] If the positive law in a society does not accurately reflect the society's sense of fitness and rightness, a certain social order may be acknowledged to have legality but not legitimacy. The difference between legality and legitimacy thus may, but must not, lie in the realm of material content. Legality presupposes a higher degree of formalization than legitimacy does (law, not mere custom), but formalization is a generic feature of legitimacy too: it emerges where a pattern of roles, status and deference has developed.[18]

4. Authority—Leadership—Competence

Leadership has sometimes been equated with authority, not the least by *Weber* who under the category "charismatic authority" included a number of different types of inspirational leadership relations (among his examples are Jesus, Napoleon, berserks, political demagogues, prophets).[19] In general leadership is a small-group, situation-based, temporary phenomenon, while larger groups are generally structured according to the principles described above (power, domination or contractual domination).[20] But the real difference between an authority relation and a leadership relation is that while the latter is voluntary, the former is not: the internalized and socially upheld group norm that it is a duty to obey the legitimate ruler constrains the subordinate to obey him.[21]

Still less can authority be equated with competence. Anybody who knows his trade exerts an influence in it, i.e. is listened to (and even "obeyed") by those who need his expertise. But this obedience is of course voluntary and not unconditional as in the authority relation.[22] Using an-

17. This distinction is made by many authors, e.g. *Friedrich* (1963:234 and 1972: 92 f), *Schelsky* (1975:23) and *Schütz* (1975:15).
18. *Schütz* (1975:16). "This development, or formalization, is itself an attempt to express the authority behind it, an authority implicitly lodged in the social aggregate", continues *Schütz*, and concludes: "Thus *legitimacy* is *an interpretation of authority, i.e. an attempt to communicate authority and make it accessible*". This way of describing the relation between the two terms presupposes that authority is the less visible of them. Cf. *Luhmann* (1964:152).
19. *Weber* (1968:242, 1111–114 = 1976:140, 654–656). The confusion resulting from this has been criticized by *Bierstedt* (1954:70 ff), *Worsley* (1957:272), *Bendix* (1960:301 and 1971:173 n. 7), and *Friedrich* (1961:12), etc.
20. See e.g. *Bernsdorf* (1969:76), *Hartmann* (1964:82–84) and the literature cited there.
21. Cf. *Blau* (1963:313).
22. *Bierstedt* (1954:69 f), *Schütz* (1975:9).

other terminology *Bochenski* has brought out the difference clearly: competence, he says, is a binary relation (between a person and a field of science, for instance), while authority is always at least a ternary relation, consisting of three elements: the authority-holder, the field in which he is competent, and the subordinate who submits to authority.[23]

B. AUTHORITY AS SUCH

As I have now made a number of distinctions between authority and related concepts I shall try to give a more detailed description of authority as such. The first problem to discuss is as follows:

1. What Type of Phenomenon Is Authority?

The suggestion that authority should be considered a form of power has rightly been criticized as blurring the distinction between the two concepts. But there are other ways of characterizing it:

    (a) authority is a social relation (*Bochenski*),[24]

    (b) authority is a quality pertaining to persons (*Hennen-Prigge*),[25]

    (c) authority is a quality pertaining to communications (*Friedrich*),[26]

    (d) authority is a quality pertaining to social systems (*Bierstedt*).[27]

Now the difference between these descriptions is not so great as it might seem. *Bochenski* concludes that the bearer of authority is always a person (= b)[28]; *Friedrich* cites with approval *de Jouvenel*'s definition that authority is a man's faculty or capacity of gaining another man's assent (= b)[29], and he also defines authority as a relationship (= a)[30]; *Hennen-Prigge* also state that the basis of authority is always a social organization (= d)[31], and so on.

23. *Bochenski* (1974:60). B. terms the latter relation "epistemic authority" and defines this on p. 57. I find Bochenski's terminology too inclusive. My concept of authority agrees rather with what he terms "deontic solidarity authority" (pp. 101–106).

24. "Die Autorität ist eine Relation", *Bochenski* (1974:21). B. defines "T ist eine Autorität für S im Gebiet G genau dann, wenn S prinzipiell alles, was ihm von T mit Behauptung mitgeteilt wird und zum Gebiet G gehört, anerkennt" (p. 25).

25. "Wir gehen davon aus, dass Autorität die Eigenschaft einer Person oder Gruppe von Personen ist, während Herrschaft die Eigenschaft eines sozialen Systems heissen soll," *Hennen-Prigge* (1977:10).

26. "Authority is a quality of communications, rather than of persons" *Friedrich* (1958:36). Cf. *Luhmann* (1964:151) and *Bachrach-Baratz* (1972:41 f).

27. "Authority is always a property of social organization" *Bierstedt* (1954:72). This definition is partly endorsed by *Schütz* (1975:11 f). Cf. also *Blau* (1963:307), *Sternberger* (1959: 20 f) and *Bernsdorf* (1969:74).

28. *Bochenski* (1974:35).

29. *Friedrich* (1964:42).

30. *Idem* (1958:34).

31. *Hennen-Prigge* (1977:10,13).

Most of these different aspects of the phenomenon can be arranged as in *Bendix's* analysis of Weberian "Herrschaft" (domination). This, he says, has five components: (1) the ruler, (2) the ruled, (3) an expression of the ruler's will to influence the behaviour of the ruled (even if this is only anticipated or even imagined by the ruled), (4) the actual compliance of the ruled and (5) the subjective acceptance of this by the ruled.[32] As the first four components are present in any power relation, component (5) must be the one that distinguishes domination from power. And as I (with *Hennen-Prigge*) have confined the term "domination" to the sense legitimate domination, "subjective acceptance" must be further specified, too. This five-component pattern is thus only an outline of the context of authority, not a definition of it. When we say that a person "exercises" authority, it is tacitly implied that all five components are necessary to form the authority relation, and that this relation is part of a larger social order which has given the actors their places. But the really interesting and distinctive quality of the relation is latent which is what we shall study next.

2. The Element of Rationality in Authority

In an authority relation there is something in the ruler's person or behaviour that effects willing compliance on the part of the subordinate. He is constrained to submit to the other, not by any external means, but out of the conviction that it is right to do so, that it is indeed his duty. The authority relation may be said to be a relation that is determined by a certain type of rationality or, to put it briefly, the belief in legitimacy.

An investigation of the origin of the term authority in ancient Roman history[33] and an analysis of everyday authority relations show that the fact that authority is related to reason (*ratio*) is its distinctive characteristic.[34] *Friedrich* has shown that the question for authority is not: Why should I obey? but: Why should I agree with this communication?[35] This can be demonstrated by looking at parental authority: A newly born baby is totally dependent on its parents and is in their power. As it grows up the

32. *Bendix* (1960:295); cf. *Bochenski* (1974) and *Hennen-Prigge* (1977) for the same "componental" description of authority.
   The differences between this Weberian concept ("domination") and my concept of authority are: (a) authority is not, as in Weber, a subcategory of power, (b) I do not equate authority with domination, as they are here seen as belonging to different systems—the personal and the social/structural, and (c) authority is a manifestation of legitimate domination only, not of contractual domination.
33. This is discussed thoroughly by *Lütcke* (1968:14–50). Short summaries can be found in *Friedrich* (1972:47 f) and G. *Friedrich* (1970:12–15).
34. See all Carl *Friedrich's* works cited in the bibliography, especially (1958) and (1972:45–56).
35. *Friedrich* (1960:5).

parents appeal more and more to the child's understanding and its assent by explaining their admonitions and giving reasons why the child should obey. In this way the child is taught to participate in the grown-up world of knowledge, belief, and norm systems, and thus gradually "discipline is transformed into self-discipline".[36]

Authority rests upon the ability to issue communications capable of reasoned elaboration; and "by reasoning I do not mean the absolute rationality alleged to be possessed by mathematics and logic,[37] . . . but rather the reasoning which relates actions to opinions and beliefs, and opinions and beliefs to values".[38] Reasoning of this kind argues not only in terms of (ultimate) ends but also in terms of means and external conditions, in other words, reasoning is both instrumental and valuational.[39]

Normally authority is not demonstrated by instant appeal to a body of "reason". Instead the authority-bearer is credited with having the capacity of reasoned elaboration of his communications.[40] This sometimes arises out of earlier demonstrations of the capacity in question, but often in other ways too; for example by the internalization of group-norms concerning which people "have" authority. Ideally authority is based upon the insight of the actors into the common "knowledge" or *ratio,* but in practice it is based upon the trust the subordinate places in the ruler. This is why an established authority relation is often permanent, especially when the basic *ratio* (the socially valid body of "knowledge", beliefs, values, and norms) is of a religious nature (meta-rational opinions are less easily shaken than rational ones).[41] Confidence in the ruler's access to *ratio* is greater than confidence in one's own insight, and in some cases can even cause one to abandon what one knows to be true.[42]

To accept authority does not mean that the subordinate examines every single manifestation of authority in regard to its intelligibility and appro-

---

36. *Idem* (1958:34).

37. The type of authority that is based on absolute or highly objective rationality is a specifically modern phenomenon. It has been described by *Hartmann* as "funktionale Autorität" in his book with this title (1964).

38. *Friedrich* (1958:35). Cf. the discussion in *Winch* (1958:227–230).

39. This "reason" or *ratio* is closely related to "knowledge" as defined by the sociologists of knowledge *Berger-Luckmann* (1967), and may include knowledge of many different kinds: cosmogony, hunting tricks, kinship taxonomies, etiquette, cooking, sacred lore, etc. *Friedrich* also stresses that the "reason" in question is the reason prevailing in a given group or society (1960:9), and this need of course not appear reasonable to us.

40. *Friedrich* (1958:38), *Bachrach-Baratz* (1972:42).

41. Cf. *Hartmann* (1964:60 f).

42. *Bochenski*'s example, taken from the field of aviation (1974:65 f), shows that this may well apply to non-religious, everyday authority relations as well.

priateness—rather it is the opposite that occurs. But the confidence and trust that supports the relation do not emerge by pure chance. The ruler's capacity for reasoned elaboration must really exist and somehow, sometimes be perceived to exist. Neither insight nor trust can be excluded from the authority relation, they stand in a dialectical relation to each other. In other words, the specific character of the authority relation demands that both element (3), the ruler's expression of will, and (5), the subordinate's subjective acceptance, have some reference to the common *ratio*. This reference is seldom explicitly expressed; authority characteristically functions through a real but *indirect* relation to the underlying *ratio*. An authority relation building exclusively on insight permanently satisfied, would have to be characterized as a border-line case of modern, "functional" (and unstable) authority,[43] while an authority relation founded exclusively on trust would in reality be a strictly personal relation based on affective motives which relation would also of necessity be unstable.[44]

This dialectical relation between insight and trust can be described as demanding a certain "transparency" of authority.[45] It must be transparent in regard to the norm it represents or, to use my previous terminology, the authority relation must somehow, sometimes allow the actors to perceive that the underlying domination is in fact legitimate. And to be legitimate it must be in accordance with a generally valid, "objective" reason. If this demand is not met authority will cease to exist—either the relation will be dissolved or else it will be transformed into another type of relation.

If the subordinate believes the ruler has the capacity for reasoned elaboration though this is not so, we apply the term "false authority" which as long as the true conditions remain hidden, will pass for and function socially as genuine authority. When the subordinate discovers, suddenly or gradually, that the opinions, beliefs and values to which the ruler appeals have no social validity the ruler's authority ceases to exist.[46]

---

43. See above, note 38.
44. *von Heyl* (1963:130) gave me the idea of complementing Friedrich's somewhat too rationalistic understanding of authority by an elaboration of the dialectic relation between insight and trust. A broad discussion on this subject can be found in *Thielicke* (1958:220–235).
45. *Fries* (1970:60), based on Thielicke.
46. *Bochenski* (1974:83 f). *Friedrich* argues that the capacity to give a reasoned elaboration is the sole decisive factor for the existence of authority, not "psychological concomitants" such as the belief of the would-be subordinates (1958:37 and 1960:5 ff). This curious statement overlooks the fact that if authority has a rational component, it also has a psychological one: the capacity for reasoned elaboration that is not known to any other human being or is laughed out of town can hardly be said to constitute authority. Otherwise Friedrich is not insensitive to the fact that someone who enjoys authority can lose it (1958:38, 45, 47 and 1960:8 f).

NOTE ON THE SOURCE OF AUTHORITY

Schütz attempts to describe authority by analysing its source.[47] He begins by accepting the definition of authority as formal or institutionalized power located in a social aggregate, but does not consider it an adequate explanation to say that people submit to authority because it is a part of the social organization whose goals they share. We must first ask what rationale underlines the organization, and that means going beyond it. *Schütz* adopts de *Jouvenel*'s view that a community or organization is created by a call from an *auctor,* a creator or instigator, who gives the impulse through his own example and guarantees the rightness of the action. This he does by augmenting his will or elaborating it "in such a way that the will seems appropriate and beneficial, perhaps even dangerous if disregarded".[48] This can be done in at least two ways: he elaborates his will through reasoning in the way *Friedrich* has described, or he makes power itself available to the members of the group. The former source is said to be proximate, the latter being the ultimate source of authority. "Power is always the ultimate source of authority, though there may be more proximate sources and implicit causes".[49]

It is obvious that the sense in which the term "power" is used here is not that we find in the Weberian tradition. Power is to *Schütz* something that permeates the whole social aggregate and is present in different forms. It is some sort of transpersonal or perhaps transhuman energy (*Schütz* equates it with "charisma"[50]), the flow of which can be stabilized or solidified into certain channels by specially gifted human beings. "Authority" is said to be an "interpretation", a kind of solidification of the first order of (fluid) power, just as then legitimacy is seen as an "interpretation" of authority (a solidification of power of the second order).[51]

My criticism of *Schütz* is that we never get a clear picture of what power is (for instance if it is an empirical phenomenon), and that he

47. *Schütz* (1975:11–21).
48. *Idem,* p. 13. The attempt to understand "authority" from its etymology (*augere*) is criticized by *Lütcke* (1968:23). Cf. *Friedrich* (1972:47 n. 5).
49. *Schütz* (1975:14).
50. *Idem,* p. 18 ff. I doubt that the last case (an authority relation based on that the subordinates are given access to that power on which the association is built) can be generalized to describe authority relations other than distinctly religious ones as for instance between Jesus and his disciples. If so, it appears methodologically unsound to make this special case the basis of an analysis of religious authority. Besides, it is hard to tell whether the category of "ultimate source of authority" is anything more than a sociologized idealism.
51. This idea faintly resembles what is said about the relation between authority and domination in *Hennen-Prigge* (1977:10 f).

imperceptibly passes from a description of what authority *is* to a description of what it *does* with power. This results in a lack of distinctness between those two concepts, in spite of the author's declared intention of keeping them apart.[52]

To sum up: "Authority" signifies a type of social relation between at least two persons where one is the ruler. The relation is based on a latent structural principle termed "domination" which places the actors in their respective positions. An authority relation is distinguished from a power relation by the fact that the subordinate is caused to assent to the ruler's order, not by external constraint or out of sheer calculative interest, but out of conviction. This conviction is part of a socially valid and thus objective body of reason (*ratio*), which says, both to the ruler and to the subordinate, that the ruler is entitled to give orders and that it is the moral duty of the subordinate to obey and recognize the legitimacy of the ruler's position and orders. The ruler's communications, within the sphere where he is ruler, are credited with being capable of reasoned elaboration. This is upheld, not by a permanent and explicit rational demonstration of this capacity, but mostly by indirect means that inspire the subordinate's trust in the ruler's legitimacy.

---

52. Cf. the expression that authority "is a *version* of power" (my italics). *Schütz* (1975:21).

CHAPTER 5
Charismatic Authority

A. CHARISMATIC AUTHORITY ACCORDING TO WEBER

1. Weber's Typology of Authority

Max *Weber* formulated a typology of legitimate domination ("legitime Herrschaft"), based on different grounds of validity, that has been of great influence. He distinguished between three types:

(1) Rational or legal domination, the legitimation of which rests "on a belief in the legality of enacted rules and the right of those elevated to authority under such rules to issue commands".[1]

(2) Traditional domination, the legitimation of which rests "on an established belief in the sanctity of immemorial traditions and the legitimacy of those exercising authority under them".[1]

(3) Charismatic domination, the legitimation of which rests "on devotion to the exceptional sanctity, heroism or exemplary character of an individual person, and of the normative patterns or order revealed or ordained by him".[1]

This typology is in reality a typology of legitimate domination only (contractual domination is based on a constellation of interests and not on legitimacy), of which authority relations are a manifestation. Therefore we can rightly speak of rational-legal, traditional and charismatic authority.

Naturally this typology is not the only possible one,[2] but it is still something of a commonplace of sociology. It has been shown to have certain short-comings (it does not cover some modern forms of legitimate domination[3]), but the most serious criticism against it is that the three types are not logically distinct. Some critics argue that they all presuppose the idea of

1. *Weber* (1968:215 = 1976:124).
2. Cf. *Blau* (1963:313 f.).
3. *Hartmann* (1964:4), *Sternberger* (1968:247).

tradition,[4] others that all authority is ultimately charismatic to some degree, i.e. in contact with society's centre of values and the roots of social order.[5] To some extent this kind of criticism is countered by *Weber*'s open acknowledgement of the fact that the historical existence of pure types is exceptional and that his typology is an analytical classification.[6] But this shows the difficulty of constructing complex "ideal types", where the elements of one type may prove to vary independently of one another and have roots in common with elements of another type, which were not perceived in the original examples chosen to illustrate the different types.[7] Still it cannot be denied that *Weber*'s classification is of analytical value, especially in non-modern historical situations.[8] As the terminology is much used by other scholars, my employment of it will also ensure the continuity of scholarly discussion.

From reasons which will be obvious when we come to the description of charismatic authority, I have chosen to analyse this type of authority in order to achieve a clearer understanding of the exercise of authority in the Primitive Church.

2. *Weber's* Description of Charismatic Authority[9]

The term 'charisma' will be applied to a certain quality of an individual personality by virtue of which he is considered extraordinary and treated as endowed with supernatural, superhuman, or at least specifically exceptional powers or qualities. These are such as are not accessible to the ordinary person, but are regarded as of divine origin or as exemplary, and on the basis of them the individual concerned is treated as a 'leader'.[10]

This is *Weber*'s definition of charisma and charismatic authority, and he points out that it is a completely value-free ("wertfrei") one, as sociology does not examine the reality of the leader's magical or superhuman powers,

4. See *Winch* (1958:238), *Friedrich* (1963:235) and *Sternberger* (1968:247).
5. *Shils* (1965), *Eisenstadt* (1968a); cf. below.
6. *Weber* (1968:262–264 = 1976:153–155).
7. This part of Weber's methodology has been much discussed, cf. *Blau* (1963:309–311).
8. Much of the criticism of the typology concerns its applicability to modern situations, *Loewenstein* (1965:80–88) and *Sternberger* (1968:247).
9. *Weber* described charismatic authority primarily in two different contexts: the earliest version, written 1913 (cf. 1968:1133), is found as part 5 in his book-length chapter on "Soziologie der Herrschaft" (=1976:654–687; 1968:1111–1157). The second version, written during 1918–1920 (cf. 1968:XCIV), is found in his "Soziologische Kategorienlehre", chapter 3 (1976:124, 140–148 = 1968:215–216, 241–255). Not a few remarks can also be found in his Sociology of Religion (1976:245–381 = 1968:399–634), especially in Section 4 on the prophet, and 5 on the community around the prophet. This was written during the time between the two above-mentioned texts. In the following account only direct quotations will be supplied with foot-notes.
10. *Weber* (1968:241 = 1976:140).

but starts from the fact that he is *considered* to have them. This explains why his first four examples of charismatic authority differ so widely. They are: berserk, shaman, Joseph Smith (the founder of Mormonism) and Kurt Eisner (a social democratic littérateur who proclaimed the "Bavarian republic" in November 1918 and was murdered in February 1919[11]), all these leaders having followers who regard them as leaders endowed with "specifically exceptional powers or qualities".[12]

Charisma is not an individual psychological trait but a strictly *social* phenomenon; without acknowledgement from a group of believers charisma simply does not exist. Thus it is a quality characterizing some authority relations thereby distinguishing them from other types of authority relations.

But the basis of genuine charisma is not constituted by its social validation ("I must be sent by God because people think so"), but quite the opposite ("I am/he is sent by God, so they/we must obey me/him unconditionally"). In primitive and religion-permeated societies it is normally a display of magical powers of some sort that initiates this kind of authority relation and draws a group of devoted adherents to form a charismatic community ("Gemeinde") around the leader. This group normally becomes differentiated into a "staff" of disciples in close association with him and a wider circle of supporting members who believe in him. This staff is in all respects dependent on the charismatic leader: they are summoned by him into his service on the basis of the charismatic qualification he has perceived in them, they are assigned their tasks by him, they have no definite rank or sphere of competence independent of him, and live in a communistic relationship with him on means provided by "voluntary" gifts from the larger circle of group members.

There are no established administrative organs in the group and no system of formal rules, abstract legal principles or judicial precedents. Judgements are created afresh from case to case, and are regarded as divine judgements and revelations. Charismatic authority is thus "extra-ordinary"

11. *Idem* (1968:300 n. 6).
12. In his Sociology of Religion *Weber* equates charisma with magical powers producing effects in meteorology, healing, divination and telepathy. Then he continues: "Charisma may be either of two types. Where this appellation is fully merited, charisma is a gift that inheres in an object or person simply by virtue of natural endowment. Such primary charisma cannot be acquired by any means. But charisma of the other type may be produced artificially in an object or person through some extraordinary means. Even then, it is assumed that charismatic powers can be developed only in people or objects in which the germ already existed but would have remained dormant unless evoked by some ascetic or other regimen", (1968:400 = 1976:245 f). *Hill* remarks that for Weber the archetypal form of charismatic authority is the Hebrew prophet (1973:263).

("ausser-alltäglich") to an extreme degree and consequently sharply opposed to rational and traditional authority which are everyday forms of authority. In the charismatic group the hitherto prevailing everyday rationality and tradition in economic conduct, regular work, family life, religious custom is despised and repudiated and replaced by a totally new way of life.

Charisma is a great revolutionary force in changing society, especially during traditionalist periods. It does not work from *without,* but "may effect a subjective or *internal* reorientation born out of suffering, conflicts, or enthusiasm. It may then result in a radical alteration of the central attitudes and directions of action with a completely new orientation of all attitudes toward the different problems of the 'world'."[13]

Charismatic authority is specifically foreign to everyday routine structures, it is anti-economic, anti-organizational and highly personal. And that is why charisma in its pure form is an unstable, short-lived type of authority which very soon becomes either traditionalized or rationalized or both. The hot flowing lava of the charismatic eruption soon cools and hardens into structures of normal solidity. (This process will be described more closely in the next chapter.)

We must bear in mind, however, the fact that Weber saw charisma as residing not only in persons but also in objects and institutional roles. He speaks of hereditary charisma (as that of royal families) and of office charisma (e.g. the Christian non-hereditary priesthood). This "impersonal" or "routinized" charisma is sharply opposed to the pure, revolutionary kind, but is nonetheless a type of charisma because of its quality of extraordinariness.[14]

B. CHARISMATIC AUTHORITY AFTER WEBER

The dialectical and multifocused approach makes Weber's analysis rich and full of fascinating insights, but it also makes his theories somewhat unsystematic and open to diverse criticisms.[15]

This remark is to the point; *Weber's* account of charismatic authority has had great influence on subsequent sociology, but it has also been criticized on a number of points. Some authors find the concept totally unusable and even detrimental to sound analysis,[16] while the majority of critics content

13. (1968:245). The German original is clearer: ". . . *kann* Charisma eine Umformung von innen her sein, die, aus Not oder Begeisterung geboren, eine Wandlung der zentralen Gesinnungs- und Tatenrichtung unter völliger Neuorientierung aller Einstellungen zu allen einzelnen Lebensformen und zur 'Welt' überhaupt bedeutet", (1976:142).

14. *Idem* (1968:1135 = 1976:671).

15. *Blau* (1963:306).

16. E.g. *Worsley* (1957:272), *Ratnam* (1964) and *Wolpe* (1968).

themselves with pointing out its contradictions and restricted applicability.[17] In the following I shall make use of this critical discussion in trying to develop a modified and complemented version or interpretation of Weber's conception.

1. Charisma Defined Psychologically and/or Sociologically

To begin my reconstructive criticism of *Weber* with two less important points, it must be said that *Weber* oscillated between a psychological and a sociological definition of the charismatic phenomenon. It is sometimes defined as a personal quality in the leader (originally always the quality of having magical powers) which arouses devotion among followers and causes their obedience to become a duty. Sometimes, however, it is said that charisma without social validation does not exist but has to be proved time and again to the followers who may refuse to recognize any charismatic endowment. In the former case charisma is something that can be tested empirically and that exists objectively in the leader,[18] but in the latter it is located in the faith of the group. The question of the psychology of charismatic leadership is important in itself but must be separated from the question of how charismatic authority functions.[19]

2. The Charismatic Group in the Centre of Interest

Several critics propose that, instead of *Weber*'s predominant connection between charisma and the leader's personal equipment, the charismatic group should be placed in the centre of a sociological analysis.[20] This entails focusing on the conditions required for the genesis of this type of social movement. It appears from some passages in *Weber*'s work that charismatic authority emerges as an answer to situations of social distress and crisis, but he does not develop this side of the question.[21] In later sociological discussions of charisma this has become a major point of interest.[22]

17. *Friedrich* (1961:15–19), *Loewenstein* (1965:78 f, 82), *Cohen* (1972:304 f), *Bensman-Givant* (1975:600–602, 610).

18. Cf. the quotation in n. 12 above, and Weber's remarks on Jesus's charisma as building on his consciousness of having magical powers (1968:440 = 1976:269). Critical of this oscillation are *Friedland* (1964:20), *Ratnam* (1964:342), *Wolpe* (1968:311 f), *Cohen* (1972:300). Cf. *Willner* (1968:3).

19. Among authors who treat the personal psychological aspects of charisma are *Mühlmann* (1962:45–49), *Emmet* (1972:223–229) and, focusing on modern political charismatic leadership, *Tucker* (1968:748 f) and *Willner* (1968, Chap. 4 and 5).

20. *Eisenstadt* (1968a:XX), *Tucker* (1968:737), *Deltgen* (1969:422), *Stark* (1969:4 f), *Eisenstadt* (1973:123). *Stark* maintains that historically the "collective" charisma belonging to a certain qualified group is an older phenomenon than the crystallization of this into one person, *ibidem*.

21. See *Weber* (1968:1111 f, 1121 = 1976:654, 661).

22. See especially *Tucker* (1968:742–748). Cf. also *Shils* (1968:389), *Deltgen* (1969:425 f), *Bensman-Givant* (1975:573).

The group around the charismatic leader consists of persons whose distress and need have not been satisfied by existing society and its institutions. This "charisma-hunger"[23] is intensified and articulated by the charismatic leader when he defines their situation as intolerable and proclaims a new set of values, a new way of life, a new and true view of the world, a new social or religious order or both and directly or indirectly promises to deliver them from their predicaments. By those who believe in him he is regarded as their "saviour" in whom their hope of deliverance from their acutely felt distress is embodied. Thus charisma may be viewed as the historical product of the interaction between a leader with special qualities and a situation of acute social distress.[24] But logically the conditions for the genesis of charismatic authority do not belong to its defining characteristics,[25] especially not as the variety of distress and need situations is so great as to permit charisma to emerge at almost any place or time.[26]

3. Charismatic Leadership and Charismatic Authority

A more serious criticism of *Weber* is that his concept of charisma is too unspecific. He does not distinguish clearly between charismatic leadership and charismatic authority.[27] Charismatic leadership in its "pure" or "intense" form can be defined as a relation between a leader and his followers characterized by a high degree of emotional and cognitive identification of the followers with the leader and his mission. The emotional attitudes that may characterize other types of leadership are here raised to a pitch of absolute intensity: affection becomes devotion, admiration becomes awe, respect turns into reverence, and the feeling of trust approaches blind faith. The leader can do nothing wrong, everything he says, wishes or prescribes is absolutely true and right as he is considered to be a source of goodness, truth and strength in himself. It is not unusual for a charismatic leader to be opposed as vehemently as he is supported; to his opponents he may appear a veritable devil, to his followers a demigod.[28]

When discussing charismatic authority it is necessary to disregard purely

---

23. This term was coined by Erik H. Ericksson, who distinguished between three components in this kind of distress: fear for one's life, anxiety about one's identity and existential dread because of the break-down of the rituals of existence; cited from *Tucker* (1968:745).

24. *Tucker* (1968:744), *Willner* (1968, Chap. 3), *Spencer* (1973:352).

25. *Willner* (1968:9 f).

26. See *Eisenstadt* (1968a:XXVI-XXXII and 1973:124–126).

27. *Bendix* (1960:301), building on *Bierstedt* (1954), *Friedrich* (1961:12 f, 22 f), *Bendix* (1971:173 n. 7), *Cohen* (1972:300), *Schütz* (1974:52, 1975:10). Cf. *Worsley* (1957:272) and *Emmet* (1972:233).

28. *Willner* (1968:7), *Tucker* (1968:746).

transitory phenomena of the type described (berserks, for instance, can hardly be said to exercise charismatic authority) and concentrate on the group of "disciples" and "followers" that is the typical result of the charismatic eruption. What makes this group's willing, unconditional compliance with the leader's wishes an authority relation is the fact that it is not the result of purely emotional rapture or of any real or imaginary threat from the leader's extraordinary powers. It rests upon the group's shared belief that it is *legitimate* for the superior to impose his will upon them and that it is illegitimate for them to refuse obedience.[29] In a religious context the inevitable conceptualization of this attitude to the leader is the belief that he is more than an ordinary human being, that he has a divine gift and calling and is consequently closer to God than the rest of mankind. This belief originates, of course, in the charismatic's own view of himself.

On the other hand not all charismatic authority exhibits the revolutionary type of inspirational leadership that *Weber* has in mind. A leader who has charismatic authority, i.e. is considered to have been divinely called and to be divinely equipped for his task (to take an example from a religious context), may be an innovator and founder but also a leader whose function it is to preserve and maintain existing order or to protect his followers.[30] Charismatic authority can have very different aims and function in very different contexts, a fact which is sometimes felt to necessitate some differentiation between types of charisma, the most usual being the distinction between religious and secular (or political) charisma.[31]

4. Charisma and the World of Ideas, Norms and Beliefs

It is evident that a certain charismatic leader is not a social phenomenon that fits into any context. His charisma must fit into a specific historical situation and fill a specific need, which is another way of saying that his

29. Cf. *Blau*'s definition of authority (1963:307).
30. *Friedrich* (1961:20–23). Cf. *Willner* (1968:10–17) and *Stark* (1969:74–77).
31. *Loewenstein* (1965:78), *McIntosh* (1970:909 f), *Emmet* (1972:233–236), *Spencer* (1973). *Stark* points out that Weber himself (in the essay "Politik als Beruf") distinguished between Machiavelli's "Erfolgsethik" and Jesus's "Gesinnungsethik" and makes their attitude to power the distinguishing criterion (1969:32). *Friedrich* (1961: 19, 23) and *Loewenstein* find charisma closely connected with religion and consider its use in political science should be restricted to pre-Cartesian cultures, i.e. Europe before A.D. 1600 and some African and Asian "new" states in our own time (Loewenstein).
This distinction and restriction is criticized by *Willner* (1968:15–17) and especially by *Tucker* (who points out that the secularization of the West has not meant that religion as such has disappeared, only that its appearances have changed, and that the motives of religious and political leaders cannot be neatly divided into pro-power and anti-power motives) (1968:732 f).

message must be relevant. *Weber* expressly excludes the question of the content of the charisma from his investigation of it, and this may be the reason why he could never explain why a charismatic leader has such a strong fascination for his followers.

But in his sociology of religion *Weber* has given the beginning of a description of the relation between charisma and the world of ideas, values, norms and beliefs.

> We shall understand 'prophet' to mean a purely individual bearer of charisma, who by virtue of his mission proclaims a religious doctrine or divine commandment.[32]

> . . . prophetic revelation involves for both the prophet himself and for his followers . . . a unified view of the world derived from a consciously integrated meaningful attitude toward life. To the prophet, both the life of man and the world, both social and cosmic events, have a certain systematic and coherent meaning, to which man's conduct must be oriented if it is to bring salvation.[33]

The prophet is certainly important as a "medium" (according to *Weber* he is considered to have magical powers), but his "message" is also "extraordinary" as it is a mediation of direct communication with the sacred (God). The characteristic property of this "new" message is that it is radical, and literally so: it penetrates to the very roots, to the deep, fundamental level of beliefs and values. By virtue of his "supernatural" endowment the charismatic leader can by-pass existing institutions, traditions and intervening media for contact with his society's vital stratum of central beliefs and values (which in older cultures had an expressly religious character). The fascination exercised by a religious charismatic leader lies in his closer and more intense contact with the sacred: his "new" message is a renewed contact with the primordial basis of the religious tradition.[34] Jesus and the canonical Hebrew prophets are examples of this.[35]

Thus the content of a charismatic leader's message must be specific and culturally determined, in close contact with what is believed and felt to be

32. *Weber* (1968:439 = 1976:268).
33. *Idem* (1968:450 = 1976:275).
34. See the important work of *Shils* (1965, esp. pp. 200–203, 1968), followed by *Eisenstadt* (1968a, 1973), *Spencer* (1973), *Schütz* (1975). Cf. *Bendix* (1960:303), *Ratnam* (1964:345), *San Juan Jr* (1967), *Deltgen* (1969), *Stark* (1969:36 f), and *Tucker* (1968:742–748, 751) who with *Cohen* (1972) and *Hill* (1973:263) stresses that charismatic authority is *not* a case of "the medium is the message".
35. On the relation between the prophets and the Torah, see e.g. *von Rad* (1965: 421–428). *Winch* points, against Weber, to Jesus as an example of a radical break with a traditional Law, which nonetheless presupposes this tradition (1958:238), cf. *von Rad* (1965:433–435). *Schütz's* counter-criticism of Winch only serves to validate the latter's argument, (1975:269 f n. 1).

central, vital and "sacred" to the people he addresses.[36] Only this accounts
for the effect of charismatic authority on the way of thinking of the followers, which *Weber* describes as a revolution "from within, from a central *metanoia* of the followers' attitudes".[37] *Weber's* own proposal that this
transformation "rests upon a belief in revelation and heroes ('Offenbarungs-
und Heroenglauben')", which he characterizes as an "emotional conviction",[38] or as "surrender to heroism of any kind", or surrender to "the
extraordinary and unheard of, to what is alien to all regulation and tradition and therefore is viewed as divine"[39] is rather a feeble explanation. His
determination not to discuss the content or validity of charisma forces him
to emphasize the element of emotion and irrationality to such a degree that
he equates it with an unthinking, frenzied flight from reason and custom.
And this crude psychologizing (explaining A's belief that B is a hero by
calling it emotional, irrational hero-worship) simply leaves the phenomenon of charismatic authority unexplained as a mere process.[40]

Charisma may be defined concisely as contact with "the sacred", which
is clearly observable in the figure of a prophet. But the manifestation of
contact with "the sacred" may occur, not only in individual persons, but
also in roles, institutions, belief systems, families or strata of society. Naturally it is more diffuse in these manifestations, but is nonetheless effective. This aspect is found in *Weber's* own concepts hereditary and office
charisma, which concepts

> . . . constitute the first step in the replacement of the classification which
> defines purely charismatic and purely routine actions or structures as pure
> and incompatible by a classification which sees charismatic activities and
> orientations as analytical elements which are inherent, even if in varying
> degrees, in all social relations and organizations.[41]

Seen in this light charisma exists not only in that extreme case of intense
and concentrated manifestation that *Weber* called "pure charisma" viz.
where contact with "the sacred" is focused on one individual, but also in
the other types of authority relation. It cannot be denied that this development of *Weber's* concept by *Shils* and *Eisenstadt* involves a certain amount

---

36. *Shils* (1965:201 and 1968:386). *Tucker* specifies this by saying that "charismatic leadership is specifically salvationist or messianic in nature" (1968:743), and
Deltgen argues that the expectation of imminent salvation (be it religious and meta-
physical or inner-worldly) is a necessary pre-condition for the existence of a charismatic group, (1969:425).
37. *Weber* (1968:1117), cf. n. 13 above.
38. *Idem* (1976:657, partly my translation).
39. *Idem* (1968:1121 and 1115 = 1976:661, 657).
40. See the criticism by *Schütz* (1975:268–271) and, indirectly, *Wolpe* (1968).
41. *Eisenstadt* (1968a:XXII).

of "conceptual stretching",[42] i.e. extends the original meaning (a radical, personal phenomenon of discontinuity) and makes charisma more or less synonymous with legitimacy.[43] But in this investigation I need not take a stand on the question of the concept's general applicability as I only intend to discuss charismatic authority in an undoubted religious context, where contact with "the sacred" is an appropriate category.

5. The Constructive Impulse of Charisma

I have stated above that the charismatic authority relation is a strongly emotional one, though not irrational in the usual sense of this word,[44] as it is ultimately built on a conviction that the leader stands in an exceptionally close relation to the normative centre of society's symbolic universe or its ultimate *ratio*.[45] From this contact comes the radical charismatic criticism of established religion, morality and society, which repudiates the past and its traditions and questions the validity of the prevailing rationality.

Weber described this destructive and revolutionary impact of charisma[46] but not the other aspect of the same phenomenon: the strong constructive impulse of charisma, which can be described as the "collective effort to establish a charismatically legitimate society—or church, or party, etc.— which will possess a greater authenticity".[47] This is an important point. A charismatic movement should not be interpreted as a kind of rapture or as enthusiastic flight from society to a predominantly emotional, freakish way of communal life. It is an attempt to build the society (church, party) anew, from the "roots", in principle nothing less than the founding anew of society. This accounts for the sacrilegious attitude of the charismatic

42. The term is borrowed from *Cohen* (1972), who criticizes a number of sociologists and political scientists (Worsley, Etzioni, Friedland, Willner, Apter) who come rather close to equating charisma with the personal influence of inspirational political leaders.

43. See especially *Bensman-Givant*'s sharp criticism of Shils and McIntosh (1975: 581–599).

44. *Weber* did not use the word "irrational" of charisma as meaning that this kind of relation lacked all ordered reason, but that it is "foreign to all rules" (1968:244). This "Regelfremdheit" (1976:141) is a radical protest against what is established as "reason". *Deltgen* (1969:421 f) criticizes *Worsley* (1957:267, 272) for not having understood Weber correctly on this point. My own criticism of Weber is that he never refers to the fact that charismatic authority is based on a reason of its own, a "counter-reason" in relation to that prevailing in society, and thus leaves an impression that charisma is "irrational" in the usual sense of the word (i.e. merely emotional, slightly insane).

45. The belief that a person is God's mouthpiece logically presupposes some idea of God and what is characteristic of his communications or in other words, some "knowledge" or body of "reason" to which the behaviour and message of the mouthpiece is related.

46. *Weber* (1968:244 f, 1115 f = 1976:141 f, 657 f).

47. *Shils* (1968:389).

group towards the old order and for the special kind of "proof" the group expects from their leader. *Weber* states that a leader best convinces his followers that he is endowed with charisma, not by performing miracles, but by "bringing well-being to his faithful followers".[48] And this must inevitably have something to do with the continued existence of the group itself.[49] *Eisenstadt* puts it this way:

> . . . a crucial aspect of the charismatic personality or group is not only the possession of some extraordinary, exhilarating qualities, but also the ability, through these qualities, to reorder and reorganize both the symbolic and cognitive order which is potentially inherent in such orientations and goals and the institutional order in which these orientations become embodied.[50]

This concerns the function and the structure of the charismatic group. *Weber* himself maintained that

> . . . charismatic authority does not imply an amorphous condition ("Zustand amorpher Strukturlosigkeit"); it indicates rather a definite social structure with a staff and an apparatus of services and material means that is adapted to the mission of the leader. The personal staff constitutes a charismatic aristocracy composed of a select group of adherents who are united by discipleship and loyalty and chosen according to personal charismatic qualification. For the charismatic subject adequate material contributions are considered a dictate of conscience, although they are formally voluntary, unregulated and irregular; they are offered according to need and economic capacity.[51]

Thus, even the non-routinized charismatic group has a clear differentiation of functions and an incipient hierarchy, even if it is not a rational, "utilitarian" organization. Rather it is a "normative" organization in the eyes of its adherents, i.e. it is regarded both as the result of establishing contact with "the sacred" and the instrument of contact.[52]

The leader's mission is the primary task both for himself and for the group, and this forms the group into an instrument for the divine commission of recreating the social order in some or all vital respects. The existence of the group is not merely an accidental consequence of a general interest in the charismatic leader's message and mission; rather the group is regarded, by the leader and his followers, as an élite, a reality-transforming, more than human group that has priority over all other merely human social obligations.

48. *Weber* (1968:1114 = 1976:656).
49. Cf. *Eisenstadt* (1968a:XXI).
50. *Idem*, p. XL.
51. *Weber* (1968:1119=1976:659 f.).
52. The distinction from *Etzioni* (1961:31, 40 f.).

From this self-understanding it is not far to the conviction that the group has an identity of its own, and a fundamental existence of its own, independent of its several members.[53]

This élite-consciousness is often manifested in a theory of the group as an anticipation or prototype of the new society or Kingdom to come, and in intense missionary zeal.[54] As soon as the charismatic community begins to regard itself in this way, it has begun to turn itself into a new source or repository of charisma, or contact with "the sacred". The importance of this is evident for the continued existence of the charismatic community after the death of the original leader. This point will not be dealt with until the next chapter.[55]

C. CHARISMATIC AUTHORITY IN THE PRIMITIVE CHURCH

Before beginning a comparison of charismatic authority as described above with the phenomena described in Part I I must emphasize the fact that the *theological* question of what Paul means by χαρισμα must be kept strictly apart from the *sociological* question of the occurrence of charismatic authority in the early Christian churches. Certainly *Weber* took the concept "charisma", via *Rudolph Sohm*'s "Kirchenrecht I" (Leipzig 1892), from Paul himself, but in *Weber*'s exposition it is a strictly sociological, analytical and general concept, by no means intended to represent what this word signifies in the New Testament. It is possible and probable that *Weber* was

53. *Stark* (1969:104–106), who points to the self-understanding of the Jerusalem church and Paul's ecclesiology. On the role of group-identification see *Luhmann* (1964:150) and especially *McIntosh* (1970:908), who argues against Weber that identification with an institutional authority (e.g. the charismatic community) is not a transfer from the members' identification with personal authority (e.g. the charismatic leader).

54. *Stark* (1969:98 f) and *Heiler,* who counts the "urge to communication" as one of the fundamental forms of the religious experience and adds: "Dieser Drang bricht im erhöhten Masse dort durch, wo das religiöse Erlebnis bestehende Schranken der Tradition überschreitet und neue Formen der Gottes- und Heilsvorstellung wie der äusseren Gottesverehrung schafft" (1961:550). Religious charismatic groups often have a strong missionary urge, as is evidenced by early Christianity, Islam and Buddhism.

55. Weber's conception of charisma has been criticized for being slightly evolutionistic and not so "value-free" as he himself considered. His distinction between "pure, genuine, primary" charisma on the one hand (i.e. by virtue of natural endowment) and "artificial, depersonalized, routinized" on the other (e.g. hereditary and office charisma) seems to express a negative evaluation of the latter. The same impression is given by a formulation such as "das Charisma in seinen höchsten Erscheinungsformen" (1976:658), and by the remarks on the charisma's "death by suffocation under the weight of material interests" (1968:1120). And it can be questioned whether the lumping together of inspirational leaders as different as Buddha and a berserk really is value-free. *Friedrich* rightly remarks: "Secularists, like Weber, did not even notice that an identification of heterogeneous values implies itself a value of judgment", (1961:19 n. 33).

influenced by *Sohm's* erroneous interpretation of Pauline texts on χαρισμα,[56] but this does not in itself diminish the typological, analytical value of the generalized category of "charismatic authority" that *Weber* has described.[57]

1. A Model of Pure Charismatic (Religious) Authority

In order to facilitate comparison and discussion I shall summarize the previous account in a detailed model of pure charismatic authority in a religious context. Pure charismatic authority is characterized by:

1. *The leader's person and way of life*:

He is considered by himself and by the subordinate members of the group

(a) to have a personal calling direct from God,

(b) to have magical or other superhuman powers, and

(c) to be the group's personal "saviour".

(d) He lives "extraordinarily" ("ausseralltäglich"), has no paid or organized work, no family life, no property and does not conform to traditional custom and belief.

2. *The leader's mission*:

His God-given mission is radical, destructive and innovating; he proclaims a new message of salvation, attacks the old order ("you have heard . . . , but I say"), and formulates rules for a new life. Ultimately his mission aims at founding the whole social order anew.

3. *The relation of the followers to the leader*:

His adherents regard him as a "hero" or superman, participating in divine reality through superior insight, strength, goodness. Their relationship to him is one of devotion, awe and absolute trust and they give priority to his words before those of all others. Obedience and support are the natural manifestations of this attitude.

4. *The behaviour of the charismatic group*:

(a) All believe, obey and support the leader as stated above.

---

56. On Weber's knowledge of New Testament research, see *Winckelmann* (1976: 69 f, 77, 85). That Sohm's exegesis of Paul's letters is one-sided and partly erroneous is today generally recognized, cf. *Linton* (1932), *Stoodt* (1962:16–26, 38–87) and *Dreier* (1972:19–37). *Brockhaus* has shown how the research after Sohm, in spite of all its criticism against him, accepted and transmitted his fundamental postulates: the difference between Spirit and law and the existence of a charismatic initial period of the whole of (or at least the Pauline part of) the Church, and a charismatic church order, (1975:7–94). Weber's conception of the Old Testament prophets has also been modified by later research, *Berger* (1963a).

57. Here I differ from *von Campenhausen* who considers that Weber's categories are developed too schematically to be useful for throwing light on early Christian situations (1969:1 n. 1).

(b) All have experienced an internal revolution and been converted from ordinary life to "the new life", which is manifested in various concrete ways.

(c) All have in common an awareness of belonging to an élite, of being holy and elect, in possession of "salvation" and its consequences.

5. *The differentiation within the charismatic group*:

(A) The outer group, consisting of adherents who continue their ordinary way of life (work, family, property, local traditional life).

(B) The inner group, the "staff", those who share the "extraordinary" existence of the leader:

    (a) They are personally called by the leader to be his disciples and co-workers on the basis of their charismatic qualification.

    (b) They abandon family, occupation, property and tradition to live in a communistic relationship with the leader.

    (c) They are appointed their tasks directly by the leader, none of them has any authority, rank or sphere of competence of his own independent of the leader.

    (d) As a consequence of (a)–(c) the staff has an élite-consciousness of a more accentuated type: they are the élite of the élite, in all respects closely related to the leader.

2. Jerusalem and Paul—A Relation of Charismatic Authority?[58]

No person in the Primitive Church holds a leading position characteristic of pure charisma. Or in plain words: Jesus has no successor.[59] This means that categories 1 to 3 in the model above are, if not empty, filled in a very different way from when Jesus was present in person among his followers. They certainly believe that (a) He was personally called by God, (b) He had superhuman powers and (c) He was and is their personal "saviour". They cherish the memories of His "extraordinary" way of life (d) and His preaching and teaching, instructions and commandments taken together with the totality of His person and life form the centre of the belief- and value-system of this movement (2). They all believe that He did fundamentally reorganize human existence and is radically renewing the Covenant between God and Israel. The relation to the leader (3) is still one of devotion, awe and absolute trust, but is now expressed through confession and cult.

58. The historical evidence for statements in this and following sections and chapters is found in Part I of this book; much of it is general knowledge requiring no detailed proof.

59. As *Weber* expressly stated (1968:1123 = 1976:663).

But the movement is not entirely separated from its leader as it believes that He is alive ("risen from the dead") and actively present in their group through His Spirit. And as is evident from 1 Thess 4:17 and 1 Cor 15:51, for example, Christians still believe in the fifties that they will meet Jesus face to face again within their own lifetime.

Nonetheless we have to state that categories 1 to 3 of the model are not filled by a saviour that is present in person but rather by "the Gospel" and the christology, pneumatology and eschatology of the Church as expressed in its life. After the death and resurrection of Jesus the Primitive Church must therefore be characterized as a charismatic movement at one remove from its *status nascendi*.

Nevertheless it is obviously a charismatic movement as can be seen by (4) the behaviour of the group. Here one could point to a number of common features, such as the belief in an imminent end and salvation, the group's élite-consciousness, the radical attitude to traditional customs and precepts concerning divorce, oaths, the role of women and children extending to a critical attitude towards the temple cult (cf. Acts 7), the necessity of circumcision for salvation and rules about unclean food.

The differentiation of the charismatic group into a "staff" and "ordinary" members (5) is easy to recognize in the Primitive Church. The latter continue to live in their homes with their families, earning their livelihood as before, which enables them to support the staff (wandering "apostles" or "prophets") by giving them food and shelter, money, etc.[60] The church in Jerusalem may have been an exception, as there are some indications that an unusually large proportion of the community lived "charismatically", i.e. without any regular income, in a communistic sharing of property (at least for some time).[61]

The leaders of the Primitive Church regard themselves as belonging to the staff of Jesus, and exhibit the characteristic features of the staff of a charismatic leader (5B):

(a) The leading missionaries (not all missionaries) are considered to have been called personally by the leader to be His disciples, co-workers in His mission. Gal. 2:7–9 and 1 Cor 15:8–10 make it clear that Paul is also acknowledged as having been thus called, as the last in this special group known as "the apostles of Jesus Christ". No one questions the fact that these apostles (and others) had a charismatic qualifica-

---

60. See *Theissen*'s description of the early Palestinian Christianity from a sociological perspective (1977).
61. Cf. Chap. 1, n. 120 above.

tion of their own, they are endowed with superhuman power manifested in miracles, prophecy and wisdom.

(b) A number of them have left occupation, property and family, and the accompanying traditional way of life, in order to devote themselves exclusively to the leader's mission. But the staff is now dispersed throughout different parts of the eastern Mediterranean area; the communistic, communal way of life of the staff probably did not survive the persecution of the Jerusalem church by Herod Agrippa in the early forties. Family ties seem to have been not altogether unimportant, as we see from 1 Cor 9:5 and the possible role of kinship in enhancing James's authority. As discussed above there seems also to have existed a difference between Palestinian missionaries and the group of (Antioch-based?) missionaries to the Gentiles to which Paul and Barnabas belonged: the latter did not observe the principle of charismatic poverty. Their attitude to financial questions is guided by theological and pragmatic rationality.

(c) Characteristic for the top layer of the staff was a pronounced awareness of having been commissioned by the Risen Lord direct. It is on this basis, in part, that Paul justified the non-circumcision practice of the Antiochene church and that the Jerusalem apostles acknowledged this practice. "None of them has any authority, rank or sphere of competence of his own independent of the leader"; this point was emphasized by Paul in his attack on Cephas in Antioch. His criticism was aimed at showing that Cephas had not followed the superior norm "the truth of the Gospel", and consequently had stepped out of the role "subordinated to the authority of Jesus" (Jesus's gospel liberates the Gentiles from the need to "live like Jews" ('Ιουδαΐζειν) while Cephas forces them to do this). The principle of direct dependence on the leader by every staff member also made Paul critical of the designation and status of a secondary type (typically "traditional", in Weber's terminology), that had been accorded his colleagues in Jerusalem from below, from the group, not from the leader Himself.

(d) This direct dependence on the leader is the basis of the élite-consciousness of the staff, manifested in a special title and in a considerable proportion of self-awareness, cf. Rom 15:16–18 and the underlying allusions of Gal 1:15, Rom 1:1. Through the Lord's commission His apostles function as His living representatives and form the unique and indispensable link between the Lord and His Church.[62]

What has so far been said here is a necessary introduction to the question

62. Cf. *Barrett* (1953:18).

indicated in the heading of this section, viz. whether the relations between the church of Jerusalem and Paul can be described as being in any respect a relation of charismatic authority.

At the end of Chapter 2 A I summarized the situation thus: "Paul and the church of Jerusalem stand in a relation of mutual, but not symmetric, independence and responsibility". At the Apostolic Council and when the Collection is delivered it appears that Paul is dependent on the way in which the others of the staff interpret the situation, or to be more precise, on whether they and the Jerusalem church acknowledge him and his work. This is no mere coincidence, but is based on the selfunderstanding of the Jerusalem church and on Paul's theological view of himself in relation to Jesus and the origin of the church in Jerusalem. This church is regarded as the starting point from which all other churches have grown, and so it is only to be expected that the inter-church (or intra-Church) voluntary financial support has Jerusalem as its destination. Another consequence of this Jerusalemite superiority is that Paul has a difficult time fighting those opponents (in Corinth) who most clearly have connections with the leaders of the Jerusalem church.

This state of things has been characterized by *Schlier* in a much-cited dictum: "Jerusalem ist der geschichtliche und moralische Vorort der Kirche, aber nicht der rechtliche".[63] Some would add that this church has some kind of "spiritual leadership"[64] or that it is, even to Paul, the *salvation-historical centre of the Church.*[65]

An adequate discussion of *Schlier*'s statement would have to go deep into the question of what is meant by 'legal' ("rechtlich") and its cognates, but this is outside the scope of this book.[66] It is true, however, that the church in Jerusalem has no traditional or legal-rational authority over Christians in other parts of the Empire; no tradition, or body of doctrine, or law gives it the constitutional right to rule over churches.

But there is no need to discuss the question of Jerusalem's authority in terms of what might have been included in Paul's view of salvation-history and sacred law ("Sakralrecht").[67] If we admit that he "personalized" and

63. *Schlier* (1971:80 f).
64. *Knox* (1955:96 f).
65. *Eckert* (1971:192, 216), cf. *Holtz* (1974:144 f).
66. I must however mention the work of Hans *Dombois*, especially his monumental "Das Recht der Gnade", Witten 1961, and Wilhelm *Steinmüller*, Evangelische Rechtstheologie I–II, Köln 1968, where he gives a detailed survey of the revolutionary development in German Protestant "theology of law" since 1945 by its most prominent scholars. An analysis of how this revolution affects the understanding of the history of the Primitive and Early Church is an important task waiting to be fulfilled.
67. As does *Stuhlmacher* (1968:87 f) in his criticism of *Schlier*'s statement that the earlier gospel and apostolate is naturally superior in authority (1971:68). *Pedersen* takes a position close to Schlier's (1977:112 f).

theologized what was in reality "a meeting of ecclesiastical, rather than merely personal, significance"[68] (Gal 2:1-10), it is only logical to admit the reality and importance of the ecclesiastical significance. Paul may be interpreting the Council, the Collection and his relation to the other apostles from a theological point of view and see them and himself as situated within "a strict salvation-historical", and sacred-legal ("sakralrechtliche"), "system and space of coordinates".[69] But from the point of view of ordinary history he moves within an *ecclesiastical*-legal ("kirchenrechtliche") system and space of coordinates, because this is where everybody else places him.[70]

Or we simply leave out of the question the distinction between the different types of law and say that Paul moves in a social space determined by the charismatic authority of the church in Jerusalem which is greater than that of any other church. In terms of charismatic authority the Jerusalem church, and the Jerusalem apostles and leaders, are perceived by all actors to be in closer contact than the Antiochene church or Paul with the *fons et origo* of all value and order in the Church—Jesus Himself. Charismatic authority it not defined in a body of tradition, doctrine or law, but is nonetheless effective in history—especially in the history of the Primitive Church. I submit that this difference in charismatic authority explains why, as I have shown in Chapter 1, the contacts between Paul and the church in Jerusalem came to manifest, subtly but unmistakably, the superiority of the latter.

3. Paul's Charismatic Authority within His Churches

Paul exercises charismatic authority in his churches. He regards himself, and is regarded by those subject to his authority, as having received a personal call to his apostolate, direct from God (1a).[71]

His superhuman powers (1b) are taken for granted by himself and others (2 Cor 12:12, Rom 15:18 f). But, paradoxically, his power is a power in weakness, it is divine power, clearly separable from his own per-

---

68. *Schütz* (1975:140).
69. *Stuhlmacher* (1968:87 f).
70. The term "sakralrechtlich" is not a very happy one in this context. "Sakralrecht" usually means "the pronouncement of a prophetic, eschatological, divine judgment without respect to persons" (and techniques for bringing about such judgments) as *Schütz* defines the anathema of Gal 1:8 (1975:129). Gal 2:9, which *Stuhlmacher* (1967:7) gives as an example of a "sakralrechtliche" decision, is an agreement come to by human beings, with the help of the Spirit to be sure, but not a divine verdict delivered through prophetic oracle. The term "kirchenrechtlich" would be more appropriate.
71. The one possible exception to this statement is the church in Corinth during the success of the Jewish Christian intruders (2 Cor 10-13).

son.[72] This is something that, according to Weber, belongs to the depersonalized, routinized charisma and not to the pure, original form.

Naturally Paul does not regard himself as the "saviour" (1c) of the Gentiles in the real sense of the word, but in a transferred, sociological sense he undoubtedly functions as such. He is the "minor founder"[73] of a charismatic movement in many different places, he is the "father" of Christians in Corinth, Galatia, Thessalonika, etc. He has "begotten" them and given them the "new life" and led them out of their distress and darkness into light and eternal life. But here, too, it is obvious that Paul clearly distinguishes between the source of his authority and his own person (cf. Gal 1:8, 1 Cor 7:10-12, 25, 2 Cor 4:5-7). He asks, directly and indirectly—through frequent references to the Scriptures, to the normative transmitted tradition, to his readers' own experience of the Spirit—that his addresses develop a relationship of their own with the Gospel, the norm or *ratio* common to him and to them. He wishes to foster his converts to maturity and independence (cf. Rom 12:2, 1 Cor 3:1-3, Gal 5:13a). When they show themselves too impressionable (2 Cor 11:4, 19 f, Gal 3:1) they not only demonstrate their own immaturity and lack of immediate relationship to the Gospel, but they have also thereby discredited Paul's apostolic authority as their behaviour shows that they submitted not to the truth but to Paul's personality, persuasiveness and superficial influence.[74]

This independence of the recipients of the Gospel, which ideally means that "all Christians participate directly in the Gospel itself"[75], does not entail an abolishment of the apostle's authority in the church. He has " . . . a continuing responsibility . . . for the ordered and healthy life of the Christian community . . . ",[76] which includes the duty and the right to judge whether the community has received the Gospel correctly or not. It is precisely because both church and apostle "stand in" the Gospel that the church is to imitate Paul in all his ways, and not vice versa.[77] It is not true that the apostle can exercise authority or assert his power over against the churches only "when and where there is a power vacuum in them by virtue

72. Cf. the discussion above in Chap. 2 B 2, and *Schütz* (1975:272).
73. *Stark* (1969:84).
74. I have borrowed this discussion from *Thielicke* (1958:228 f). Cf. *Schütz* (1975:183–186).
75. *Schütz* (1975:249).
76. *Idem*, p. 250.
77. This point seems to be lost in some of the too sharp formulations *Schütz* makes later; e.g. "Even if the apostolic rank is a charisma, it cannot take precedence over any other charisma which builds up" (p. 258), or "Where they stand 'in' the gospel they stand in the same power as he does and their authority is the same as his" (p. 282).

of the failure of Christians to reflect and embody the power (sc. the Gospel) which originally he made available to them".[78] Paul is their "father" or authoritative head even when the church to which he writes is not in need of correction.

Paul is a celibate, a travelling preacher of Jewish descent but in radical opposition to traditional Torah piety; he has no ordered economy or occupation, he sometimes receives financial support from Christians he has converted, sometimes he stays for months in a town working with his own hands for his living. He is clearly sufficiently deviant to qualify as "extraordinary" (1d), and characteristically he sees his way of life as a consequence of being set aside for the work of the Gospel, which is why he has become a "slave", cf. 1 Cor 9:19–23, 2 Cor 4:5. But that he periodically works for his livelihood is uncharismatic.

The apostle's message agrees with the model (2): he has received it from God, it is about salvation and conversion in the face of the imminent Day of Judgment. And once accepted and believed this message has a life-transforming effect. The message is however not Paul's own gospel in that he could say "You have heard—but I say unto you". Rather it is a transmission of the Christian Gospel about Jesus, whose vital contents are common to all the apostles (1 Cor 15:11) and has, to a certain extent, been preformulated in fixed blocks of tradition (1 Cor 11:23–25, 15:3–7). Further, Paul's message cannot be said to be altogether revolutionary, especially not in the fields of social ethics and politics. He does not demand that his Christians shall practise celibacy or give up their property, he does not attack slavery or class differences within the church. In his paraenesis he uses material from traditional Jewish and popular-philosophical ethics and does not refrain from referring to what is "natural", "proper" or "honourable" in surrounding society (cf. Phil 4:8, 1 Cor 11:13–15).[79]

As regards the followers' relation to the leader Paul, we see from his letters that he expects and receives the estimation that is rightly accorded a founder and "father"—this includes respect, imitation, trust. But we have no indication that the relation was marked by any emotional intensity or hero-worship. Of course, to those he converted to the Christian life Paul is a singular authority, but we need only compare this relation with that existing between Jesus and his disciples to see the difference (cf. Matt 10:32 f with 1 Cor 1:12 f). In the case of Jesus the charismatic leader's person and

---

78. *Ibidem.*
79. Cf. *Austgen* (1966), and *Troeltsch* (1912:51, 60–72) on Paul as socially conservative.

his mission are fused, but this is not the case with Paul. He expressly separates his own person from the source of all authority; he is but an instrument in attaching people to Jesus, he is the messenger of a great Lord and must not be personally over-rated (2 Cor 1:24, 4:5; 1 Cor 3:5–7).

Moreover, when assessing the true character of his (charismatic) authority we must keep in mind that Paul is not the only messenger, missionary or apostle of Christ. Even in the churches he founded other teachers turn up who are Paul's equals and who function in the same charismatic manner (sometimes even in a higher degree). Paul does not withhold the existence of or deny the authority of other "staff members", although he never condones any competition from them. This fact is a further limitation to his own unique authority in his churches: there exists not only authority above Paul (God and Jesus) but also other authority on his own level (other missionaries).

Paul is never in any doubt about the fact that he, like the other apostles, has a right to financial support from his churches (4a). But he and the others in the "Antiochene" group of missionaries to the Gentiles have deliberately abstained from availing themselves of this right, primarily on grounds of missionary tactics. This pragmatic, calculating attitude to being supported by one's followers is not typical of the exercise of pure charismatic authority.

Before examining Paul's staff (5B), we must remember that he began his Christian life as an outsider and possibly also began his career as a missionary by working alone. Later he is incorporated as a junior member into the staff of the Antiochene church and accompanies Barnabas as his colleague and assistant in the early missionary enterprise of this church. After the Council and the Antioch Incident he functions more and more as an independent apostle and a founder of churches. He assembles a group of co-workers or a staff around himself, but even now this staff does not conform wholly to the model of pure charismatic authority.

Some have been personally chosen by the leader himself to be his disciples and assistants (5Ba)—this applies to Timothy and (probably) Titus, and perhaps to Epaphras. But Barnabas, Apollos, Silvanus, Priscilla and Aquila are among those who have not been recruited by Paul, and they work independently of him both before and after their period of cooperation with him.

The group of missionaries around Paul probably share support and other sources of income with him (5Bb), and to carry out their itinerant missionary work they have to leave their homes and families. But the only relationship of this kind of any considerable permanency seems to be that between Timothy and Paul and, to a lesser degree, that between Paul and Titus.

We need not doubt that Paul is the unquestioned leader of the different "teams" of missionaries that form around him during the fifties. At least the junior members receive all their tasks directly from the apostle; he tells them what to do, where to go, he makes them a medium for his own presence and influence in his churches, and it can be said of them that they have no authority, rank or sphere of competence of their own independent of Paul (5Bc). But this statement does not apply to Barnabas, Apollos, Silvanus and some others.

We have no concrete information about whether Paul's staff has any kind of élite-consciousness (5Bb), or even a group consciousness.

4. Charismatic Authority within Local Churches

During Paul's lifetime his churches are not autonomous with an independent leadership worth mentioning. The reason for this is the fact that the real leader of these charismatic communities is Paul himself. He acts in his churches through a combination of personal presence (increasingly intermittent and early ceasing altogether), personal representatives and apostolic letters. In spite of the distance separating leader and group, Paul retains a strong hold over his churches, which he uses at least when it is needed.

The offices of the local church probably do not constitute an integrated leadership, with a hierarchy of cooperation between different offices, such as can be found in the letters of Ignatius or (in part) in the Pastoral Epistles. No office, no single person, seems to have the ultimate responsibility of leading the rest of the church. The προϊστάμενοι have no formally or traditionally defined duties or rights, and as the authority they have cannot be said to be of the pure charismatic type we have to conclude that it is simply based on personal social influence of an ordinary kind. (In Paul's *theological* interpretation this function is a χάρισμα.)

On the other hand, the prophets, glossolalists and miracle workers are persons who have received a "charismatic", supernatural endowment from God. But we cannot with certainty maintain that this entails the exercise of any concrete leadership within the church, except possibly in the common act of worship. Acknowledgement of their supernatural gifts does not necessarily make them leaders of the church.

We observe that Paul sets limits to the exercise of prophecy during the act of worship (1 Cor 14:29–32), and, interestingly enough, the local prophecy is firmly placed under the apostle's authority (1 Cor 14:37–40).

He does not seem to wish this charismatic endowment to be manifested in an extraordinary way of life, but exhorts all brothers "to aspire to live quietly, to mind your own affairs, and to work with your hands, as we charged you" (1 Thess 4:11, in the same letter as that in which he expresses the following request: "Do not quench the Spirit, do not despise prophesying", 5:19 f). 2 Thess 3:6-13 may be interpreted as a criticism of the kind of exercise of charismatic authority within a local church that demands payment of the other members.

The "charismatically" endowed leaders within the church (using "charismatically" in the sociological sense of the word) have no original message or mission of their own. On the contrary, prophecy is a primary example of a gift that edifies the existing community. Although prophetic revelations come from God they are undoubtedly expected to conform to the great truth already transmitted by the apostle—the Gospel. Any teaching which substantially adds to or subtracts from the apostolic Gospel is *eo ipso* false (cf. Gal 1:8). The prophets in Pauline churches are certainly not examples of pure charismatic authority.

The one clear instance we have of the remuneration of local leaders, Gal 6:6, is not a case of spontaneous support of a leader who is regarded with fervent devotion and awe. What we have here is an instruction from a superior authority concerning a lower authority, implicitly referring to a traditional and rational norm of reciprocity.

One should not say, however, that the local leadership we see exercised in the Pauline congregations is in no way "charismatic". After all these leaders have not been appointed prophets, and so on by the apostle, nor have they attained the office by their own efforts. Their supernatural endowment is a fact, recognized by apostle and church alike, and this implies the existence of a certain degree of authority in these persons. Although they are not charismatic leaders of the "pure" type, they can certainly be said to exercise a form of limited, charismatically based group leadership in part of the life of the church.

The comparison made above can be summarized thus: the model of pure, intense charismatic authority is admirable as a description of Jesus and the group around him; in many respects it is a good description of the way of life of the Primitive Church and of the relation between the apostles and the early Christian churches, while it has few counterparts in the authority structure of the local Pauline churches.

Neither Paul nor any of the other apostles and missionaries are in themselves a source of authority as they are all part of a tradition, share in a definite sacred *ratio,* and see themselves as representatives of a more important leader who, to a certain extent and in some ways, is still present. Once again, the Primitive Church is a charismatic movement at one remove from its origin or *status nascendi.*

In Paul's case there are a number of additional features which make him less charismatic (i.e. purely charismatic) than his colleagues:

(a) His personal conduct is marked both by superhuman powers and by very human weaknesses.
(b) He emphasizes strongly that his authority is delegated, and that a distinction must be made between his person and his charisma.
(c) His attitude to money is pragmatic and rational.
(d) His message is identical with the Gospel, an entity which to a substantial degree is independent of the apostle. The consequences in social ethics and politics of his message are not revolutionary (less so than in the Palestinian church[80]).
(e) His staff is not bound to him personally.

This is the type of charismatic authority exercised in the Pauline churches, yet it is strong enough to restrict the charismatic authority of the local leadership to a remarkable extent.

This is not exactly what we should expect when we consider the conventional picture of the early years of the Church—a high-strung eschatological atmosphere and an all-pervading expectation that the end of the world is imminent, a profusion of ecstatic and pneumatic phenomena, a turbulently emotional life characterized by freedom, mobility and spontaneity. Such conditions may have existed, at least in Corinth, but the rather noncharismatic character of charismatic authority in Pauline churches should warn us from being too quick to postulate a theory of development that holds that every church must pass from a chaotic, "charismatic" state to an ordered, non-charismatic one. And then it is a fact that, even if some of the local churches to which Paul is writing have not existed for five years the Church of which they are a part has by this time existed for a whole generation.

My conclusion from the comparison of *Weber*'s typology of authority and the state of the Primitive Church in this chapter is that the authority in the Primitive Church cannot be characterized as purely charismatic but is mixed with traditional and rational elements, i.e. we encounter what *Weber* termed *"routinized charisma"*. We shall analyse this in the next chapter.

80. Cf. *Theissen* (1973, 1977).

CHAPTER 6
The Institutionalization of Charismatic Authority

Weber's designation of the process whereby a charismatic group such as that around Jesus develops into a church with a systematized body of doctrine, cult and organization is "the routinization of charisma" ("Verall-täglichung des Charismas"). I shall begin this chapter with an account of how he describes this process.

A. ROUTINIZATION OF CHARISMA ACCORDING TO WEBER[1]

In its pure form charismatic authority may be said to exist only *in statu nascendi*. It cannot remain stable, but becomes either traditionalized or rationalized, or a combination of both.[2]

The instability of charisma is due to the fact that it is exclusively dependent on the personal qualities of an individual person, the charismatic leader. All the modifications of charisma have

basically one and the same cause: The desire to transform charisma and charismatic blessing from a unique, transitory gift of grace of extraordinary times and persons into a permanent possession of everyday life. This is desired usually by the master, always by his disciples, and most of all by his charismatic subjects.[3]

And when the charisma is to be adapted to everyday life it is inevitably influenced by the dominating forces at work there, in particular economic interests.

The turning point is always reached when charismatic followers and disciples become privileged table companions . . . and subsequently fief-

1. *Weber's* account is found in (1968:246–254 and 1121–1148 = 1976: 142–148 and 661–681).
2. *Weber* (1968:246 = 1976:143).
3. *Idem* (1968:1121 = 1976:661).

holders, priests, . . . party officials . . . , all of whom want to live off the charismatic movement, or when they become employees, teachers and others with a vested occupational interest.[4]

The ordinary adherents become paying members in an organization, the message develops into dogma and law, the staff into a paid hierarchy. So are gradually united the utterly antagonistic forces of charisma and tradition.

Weber devotes most of his account to describing how this change is manifested in the leadership of the group. Often it is the death of the leader and the problem of succession that gives the impulse to the routinization process. There are many different solutions to the problem of succession: the selection of a new charismatic leader who must comply with certain criteria; selection by means of techniques of divine revelation (oracle, lots); designation of the successor by the original leader; designation of the successor by the staff, followed by the acclamation of the community; the successor comes from among the leader's closest relatives (hereditary charisma), charisma is transmitted by ritual means to someone who thereby becomes the successor. The last-mentioned case is an example of the depersonalization ("Versachligung") of charisma: it is transformed into an objective quality that is either transferable or personally acquirable or becomes attached to the incumbent of an office or to an institutional structure.

But the wish to make charisma the permanent possession of everyday life is neither the only motive for routinization nor is it the most important one. "The most fundamental problem is that of making a transition from a charismatic administrative staff . . . to one which is adapted to everyday conditions".[5] The staff needs and develops a consistent administrative practice, with rules for making decisions, the limitation of spheres of competence, and some sort of hierarchy within the staff itself. Moreover it is necessary to develop a fiscal organization for the financial support of the staff and for the movement as such. This type of motive can be called the community's systemic needs, i.e. needs that must be met if the movement is not to disintegrate.

The real driving force of the routinization process is the staff and its strong ideal and material interest in the continuation of the community. Up to this point they have been totally dependent upon the leader, living in an enthusiastic, communistic community of faith. But gradually they desire their position to become ideologically, socially and economically stabilized and they therefore appropriate positions of power and economic advan-

4. *Idem* (1968:1122 = 1976:662).
5. *Idem* (1968:253 = 1976:147).

tages to themselves, and regulate recruitment to the stratum of the group that alone may exercise authority. Charisma now belongs to the staff only, the office-holders, and serves to legitimate their acquired rights.

Charisma is now no longer personal, radical, irrational and anti-economic but "there always remains an extraordinary quality which is not accessible to everyone and which typically overshadows the charismatic subjects".[6]

This justifies the appellation "charisma" although it must now be characterized as "routinized charisma".

B. CRITICISM OF WEBER'S VIEWS

The criticism of *Weber* begins with the last-mentioned point: it is confusing and self-contradictory to combine "routine" and "charisma" in the one concept when, according to *Weber,* they are opposites.[7] It would be more appropriate to just talk about the transformation of charismatic authority into other types of authority (traditional and rational-legal). As it is one gets the impression that there remains some fundamental difference between routinized charisma and traditional, or rational-legal, authority, which is not the case.[8]

Further, *Weber* must be criticized for a fundamental vagueness in defining the nature of routinization, as is manifest in his inability to decide when the process begins and what the leader's role is. The general impression is that this process starts with the death of the leader,[9] but we need only read the quotation above before note 3 to find that *Weber* at times did not exclude the possibility of routinizing intentions in the leader too. In his somewhat later Sociology of Religion[10] *Weber* even writes as follows:

> Primarily, a religious community arises in connection with a prophetic movement as a result of routinization, i.e. as a result of the process whereby either the prophet himself or his disciples secure the permanence of his preaching and the congregation's distribution of grace, hence insuring also the economic existence of the enterprise and those who man it.[11]

6. *Idem* (1968:1135 = 1976:671).
7. *Friedrich* (1961:22), *Willner* (1968:3) and *Tucker* (1968:753).
8. Cf. *Ratnam* (1964:343).
9. "These interests (sc. in the continuation of the community) generally become conspicuously evident with the disappearance of the personal charismatic leader and with the problem of *succession.* The way in which this problem is met—if it is met at all and the charismatic community continues to exist or now begins to emerge . . . ", *Weber* (1968:246 = 1976:143). According to *Bensman-Givant* (1975:580), in almost all historical cases of pure charisma routinization did *not* occur in the lifetime of the leader.
10. On the chronology of Weber's work, see the previous chapter n. 9.
11. *Weber* (1968:452 = 1976:275 f).

But in the last part of *Weber's* work the leader's interest in the continuation of the movement and his role in its routinization is almost entirely excluded. It appears only as one possible solution to the problem of succession, that where the leader designates his successor. This is one of six solutions—the other five are managed by the staff![12]

It would seem that *Weber* did not squarely face up to the problem inherent in the case where the charismatic leader himself is the primary routinizing agent, i.e. he desires to build a lasting community out of the group he has collected around him. Instead, the unavoidable impression we are left with is that the routinization is a kind of afterthought, or unintentional consequence of a diffuse longing for the continuation of charismatic community life. The entire emphasis is placed on the private economic interests of the staff as the really decisive factor while the interest of the leader and of the adherents in the mission as such are merely termed "ideal interests" and then put on one side. The systemic needs of the organization are mentioned in passing but are seen as being subordinated to the staff's struggle to make a living. This leaves unanalysed the important traditionalization and rationalization of the community's doctrine, cult, ethical behaviour, and order of common life, which are independent of the actors' interests. *Weber's* "somewhat bitter 'realism' "[13] causes him to overlook important aspects of the routinization process and substitute a sociological analysis with crude psychologizing about personal motives.[14]

To say this is not to deny the possible influence of personal motives and intentions in historical processes.[15] But it is necessary (a) to include *all* the motives and intentions of the actors, even the conscious, "ideal" ones and (b) to see these in the context of everyday social life and its strong formative influence. The needs of everyday life are operative not only, or even primarily, through the private (economic) interests of the chief actors but, more importantly, through the institutionalizing factors that incessantly mould all human interaction.

12. *Idem* (1968:246–248 = 1976:143–144).
13. *Sternberger* (1968:247).
14. It is after all somewhat naive to state that the Christian Church (or for that matter the movements of Islam or Buddhism) came to exist in its historical form mainly on account of the immediate disciples' interest in consolidating their power positions and economic privileges.
15. Weber's own view on the nature of historical processes does not otherwise seem open for the idea that certain actors can manipulate the development of the movement of which they are a part. Rather, historical processes are a dialectical process between certain ideas and production factors, through the elective affinity between those ideas and certain social strata. Cf. *Berger* (1963a:949 f), *Blau* (1963: 310) and *Hill* (1973:261, 263).

As regards (a) I refer to the criticism of *Weber* that points to the content of charisma or better, the message of the charismatic leader, as being of vital importance for the origin and existence of any charismatic movement.[16] A charismatic movement is characteristically a movement of change. The leader is not idolized or "followed" just because he is considered to be a wonderful person, but because he is one who demonstrates extraordinary qualities "in the process of summoning people to join in a movement for change and in leading such a movement".[17] The leader is considered to be in closer contact with the "roots" of society and the existing order, and ultimately the movement he initiates and leads is aimed at founding a new society itself.

If this is correct we must draw the conclusion that important aspects of the process *Weber* called "routinization" are inherent in the charismatic impulse as such. This constructive charismatic impulse is a collective effort of the whole group, not just an intention in the mind of the leader and his staff. The institutional form of charisma is, from the beginning, an intended and much longed-for manifestation of the authenticity of the charisma itself.[18] Charisma is not merely the victim of routinization[19] but actively seeks institutional manifestation, albeit a radically new one in contrast to existing patterns of authority. This seeking may end in failure and, of course, it has to receive important influence from the hard facts of everyday life, which will eventually transform charismatic authority into other forms of authority. But *Weber* exaggerates the role of secondary motives (the problem of succession and of securing a livelihood) to the virtual exclusion of the institution-building motives inherent in the charisma itself.[20] The dilemmas of institutionalization[21] should not be confused with its driving forces.

As regards (b) we shall now examine institutionalization from a general sociological point of view.

C. INSTITUTIONALIZATION

In sociological theory the concept "institution" does not have a uniform content that is generally agreed upon. It is an analytical concept or way of

16. See Chapter 5, with the literature cited in n. 34.
17. *Tucker* (1968:737).
18. Cf. Chapter 5, nn. 48–50.
19. Cf. *Weber* (1968:1120) on its "suffocation".
20. Cf. *Eisenstadt* (1968a and 1973).
21. *O'Dea* (1963) numbers five such dilemmas, three of them being special forms of the unavoidable contact between charisma and the prosaic elements of everyday life.

viewing society which varies with different theories of society.[22] In the following I choose a view that is based on an anthropologically grounded analysis of human interaction as represented by scholars such as *Bronislaw Malinowski, Arnold Gehlen, Helmut Schelsky* and, in particular, *Peter L. Berger* and *Thomas Luckmann.*

1. The Beginnings of the Institutionalization Process

Human activity is formed by habitualization, even for someone who lives quite alone. Habit causes human behaviour to follow certain well-trodden paths, and these are the precondition for all institutionalization. According to the definition of *Berger-Luckmann*

> Institutionalization occurs whenever there is a reciprocal typification of habitualized actions by types of actors. Put differently, any such typification is an institution.[23]

"Typification" is a mental activity going on in almost every human interaction where the participants continuously classify each other by means of typificatory schemes.[24]

By "types of actors" is meant that certain actions are seen as being distinct from the self. When performing one of these actions a person performs a typical act, e.g. marrying, voting. "We can properly begin to speak of roles when this kind of typification occurs in the context of an objectified stock of knowledge common to a collectivity of actors.—Institutions are embodied in individual experience by means of roles",[25] i.e. by observing roles, playing parts, being aware of these roles and internalizing them. And the representation of an institution in and by roles is representation par excellence on which all other representations (linguistic and symbolic) are dependent.[26]

---

22. Cf. *von Wiese* (1956:298), *Gundlach* (1959:325) and *Schneider* (1964:338). Articles of interest on "institution" in social science dictionaries and encyclopedias are: *Bellebaum* (1959), *Schneider* (1964), *Eisenstadt* (1968b), *Mühlmann* (1969) and *Lipp* (1975).

23. *Berger-Luckmann* (1967:54). This concept of "institution" is broader than that prevailing in contemporary sociology, *idem* p. 197 n. 21. A distinction is usually made between "organization" and "institution": "organization" is a purposive coordination of persons or their activities to achieve certain defined goals, while "institution" is a social construct more deeply grounded than calculated striving for a goal, *Schelsky* (1965a:262), cf. *Bellebaum* (1959:332) and *Schneider* (1964:338). From the discussion in *Luhmann* (1972:277) and *Vaskovics* (1972:328–331) it can be gathered that "institution" is nowadays a general and abstract concept, while "organization" is restricted to signify concrete social phenomena in our own time. *Lipp* even sees an inherent conflict between the two (1975:1017).

24. *Berger-Luckmann* (1967:30–34).

25. *Idem*, p. 73 f. Cf. *Eisenstadt* (1965:31 f, 38) on the continuous "crystallization" of roles.

26. *Berger-Luckmann* (1967:75).

A reciprocal role expectancy such as that described in the definition above is the result of a common history and does not arise immediately. Participation in interaction gradually binds the participants to certain common and separate behaviour patterns, and creates the expectation that these patterns will be encountered. And the longer one participates without opposition and without proposing another course of action, the firmer becomes the consensus on what is demanded of the actors by the interaction.[27] Institutionalization may therefore be said to effect a generalization of consensus, i.e. it expands and confirms actual consensus.[28] In doing this it does not have to build upon an existing consensus about values, etc. but rather the opposite—it is a process that creates consensus about what should be done (activity patterns) and, secondarily, why it should be done (the legitimation of activity through norms and values).[29]

Institutionalized role expectancy need not be accompanied by any formulated norm, still less does it need the support of sanction. Normally, the control exerted by an institution is a primary social control, prior to any special sanction system developed in order to protect the institution in question. And primary social control simply consists of the difficulty of going against what other people expect.[30]

Even two actors work out roles in their interaction, which makes it possible for each of them to predict the other's action and his expectancies. The parties' understanding of the situation and their interaction constitute a unity, an institution.[31] Thus interaction forms an ever-widening "background" of routine actions and predetermined choices against which innovation and division of labour can take place, and this in its turn can become

27. Luhmann has termed this "engagement through presence" and explains "Es entstehen kraft Implikation gemeinsam hingenommene, oft unartikuliert bleibende Selbstverständlichkeiten, für die man Konsens unterstellen kann" (1970:31).
28. Idem, p. 30.
29. Cf. "The meaning of an act is dependent on and arises in an interaction-situation" (the view of G. H. Mead, summarized in Asplund, 1970:138).
30. "Wer sich institutionalisierten Erwartungen entgegenstemmen will, hat das Schwergewichteiner vermuteten Selbstverständlichkeit gegen sich. Er muss vorläufig angenommene Erwartungen, auf die andere sich schon eingelassen hatten, durchkreuzen, greift also deren Selbstdarstellungen an. Ihm obliegt die Last der Initiative, die Last der Verbalisierung und der Explikation. Er muss dafür sorgen, dass der unbemerkt eingelebte Konsens durch erteilten Konsens ersetzt wird. Sein Handeln fällt auf und ist fast unvermeidlich mit Führungsansprüchen verbunden. Es wird ihm persönlich zugerechnet und kann ihn ruinieren, wenn es scheitert. Das Risiko ist entsprechend hoch, oft entmutigend hoch", Luhmann (1969:42).
31. The following view is taken from Arnold Gehlen's theory of institutions, which has influenced Helmut Schelsky, Peter L. Berger and Thomas Luckmann and others. Gehlen belongs to a tradition of biologists and philosophers who have worked at formulating a biologically informed philosophical anthropology. For a critical and systematic description of his influential theories, see Berger-Kellner (1965), Jonas (1966), Dullaart (1975:20–51) and especially Weiss (1971).

institutionalized.[32] This creation of a stable background, or a "social world",[33] which facilitates social life constitutes the institutionalization of social life.

The effects of institutionalization are twofold: (a) It brings social control of various kinds to bear on the individual, which restricts his freedom and inherent capacities. (b) It unburdens him and frees him of the pressure of living in an unstructured world and gives him media for self-governed action which increase his freedom and possibilities.[34] Examples of this twofold effect of institutionalization are a child's acquisition of language, matrimony, the use of money and religious ritual.[35]

2. The Advent of the Third Party

Institutionalization can well be said to begin with the interaction of only two persons,[36] but the addition of a third party to the relationship makes an important difference. The behavioural patterns that developed between the first two acquire a more objective character and are gradually experienced as having a reality of their own, meeting the individual as an exterior and imperative fact. As long as the pattern creators are alone on the scene or dominate it the routinized "background" can be changed or complemented as they are aware of its accidental and non-necessary nature.[37] The next "generation" (in either the literal or transferred sense of the word) experiences the institution as much more massive and opaque, part of the solid, factual structure of the outer world.[38] And then, by means of a mirror-effect, the given patterns or institutions become more of a solid, unchangeable fact for the creators themselves—the product acts back on the producers.[39] The institutionalizing subject becomes increasingly anonymous and is called "one" or "we". And "one" or "we" constitute an undefinable, semi-personal entity which cannot be encountered, questioned or made responsible for anything. Naturally this anonymization of the creative

32. *Schelsky* (1965a:263 f and 1970:19), *Jonas* (1966:23–29), *Berger-Luckmann* (1967:53) and *Lipp* (1975:1013).
33. *Berger-Luckmann* (1967:57).
34. Cf. *Lipp* (1975:1016).
35. Cf. *Berger-Luckmann* (1967:34–46) on language and their remarks on its "reality-generating" quality (p. 153, 178). On the double function of religious rituals, see *O'Dea* (1967:60 f), *Geertz* (1968:27–29) and *Stark* (1969:134 f).
36. *Berger-Luckmann* (1967:55 f), *Luhmann* (1970:31).
37. *Idem*, p. 58. This applies even more to the case where the pattern-creating (or institutionalizing) first generation does not consist of equals in free interaction, but of one innovative or charismatic leader and his devoted followers. Mark 10:13–16 pictures this kind of complementing an established "background".
38. Cf. the difference between "Let us call that little black furry animal c-a-t" and "That is a cat".
39. *Berger-Luckmann* (1967:58 f, 61).

subject makes the institution even more opaque, stable and binding and this includes those who were not original participants.[40]

The creation of a social world, i.e. institutionalization, is a dialectical process—man and his social world interact with each other. Man externalizes words, habits, behavioural patterns, which are then regarded by himself as being objective realities, independent of himself (objectivation). This objectivated world is then retrojected into consciousness by the process of internalization in the course of socialization. This fundamental social dialectic between man and the institutional world operates in its totality only with the appearance of a new generation.

3. Legitimation

The problem of generalizing consensus in societies which grow in size and complexity cannot be solved by interaction in small groups. It is solved by the use of two connected "mechanisms": (1) the generalization of the fundamental belief- and value-systems ("Sinngrundlagen") of institutions and (2) the institutionalization of the institutionalization process.[41]

The first mechanism consists of the abstraction of principles and an ethos from the institutional behavioural pattern, and is more generally known as "legitimation". Through legitimation the institutional world can be explained and justified by recourse to a theory or "myth", and this is done when the third party or new generation appears.

> . . . the expanding institutional order develops a corresponding canopy of legitimations, stretching over it a protective cover of both cognitive and normative interpretation. These legitimations are learned by the new generation during the same process that socializes them into the institutional order.[42]

Analytically it is possible to distinguish between many different levels of legitimation which overlap empirically. At the first level legitimation is built into the vocabulary.[43] The second level of legitimation consists of simple and pragmatic theoretical propositions in a rudimentary form often given in the form of proverbs, moral maxims, legends and songs. The third level consists of explicit theories legitimating a whole institutional sector; a body of knowledge such as this is frequently entrusted to specialists.[44]

40. *Luhmann* (1970:33).
41. *Idem*, p. 34.
42. *Berger-Luckmann* (1967:62). Cf. the title of *Berger*'s sociology of religion: "The Sacred Canopy" (1969).
43. *Idem*, p. 94. I follow their account on legitimation (pp. 92–104) in this paragraph.
44. *Idem*, p. 77 f.

The fourth level of legitimation is constituted by "symbolic universes", bodies of theoretical tradition that integrate different provinces of meaning and encompass the institutional order in a symbolic totality, an all-embracing frame of reference.

The dialectical relation between man and institutions tends to be forgotten and when this happens the institutions are said to be "reified". "Reification is the apprehension of human phenomena as if they were things, that is, in non-human or possibly supra-human terms".[45] The social world produced by man is regarded as being formed by forces outside his control. Both the institutional order as a whole and segments of it (separate institutions and roles) can be apprehended in reified terms, and normally this way of understanding one's world is the original and "natural" one. Enlightened awareness of the human-made character of the social world is a comparatively late development in history and in individual biography.[46]

4. Cumulative Institutionalization

Normally when we talk about institutions we refer to social formations that are more complex than the simple results of dyadic interaction described above as the beginning of institutionalization. Such complex institutions are the result of cumulative institutionalization. To take one oversimplified example only, the institution of matrimony may have begun as a tendency to form dyadic, hetero-sexual groups. Once such a group has been formed it engenders new conditions for action and new needs that must be satisfied. It becomes a family, with children and property of its own, customs of its own, etc. and so causes new, derived (or secondary) institutions to crystallize.[47] The family grows into a developed social institution that satisfies both basic bio-psychological needs and derived cultural needs that man himself has created. Its function refers to a synthesis of needs and must consequently be termed a synthesis of functions.[48] The needs that cause

45. *Idem*, p. 89. "Objectivation" includes awareness that the institutionalized behaviour in question is a human product, and is thus not identical with reification.

46. "It would also be a mistake to look at reification as a perversion of an originally non-reified apprehension of the social world, a sort of cognitive fall from grace. On the contrary, the available ethnological and psychological evidence seems to indicate the opposite, namely, that the original apprehension of the social world is highly reified both phylogenetically and ontogenetically", *Berger-Luckmann* (1967:90). Cf. *Berger* (1969:86, 92).

47. See *Malinowski* (1944:171 f), quoted in *Schelsky* (1965b:37, with n. 11, and 1970:17 f). Malinowski was the first to replace earlier simple co-classifications of bio-psychological needs and social institutions with a more differentiated theory, *Schelsky* (1970:13 f).

48. *Schelsky* (1970:19). Most types of needs are satisfied not by one institution only but by a number of institutions with equivalent functions. *Schelsky* gives a

institutions to develop secondary institutions may be the product of technical innovations or new learning in society (e.g. a more complete legitimation). This confirms the general statement that the relation between knowledge and its social base is a dialectical one.[49] This permanent institutionalization is an important factor in stabilizing the institution; an institution that does not develop is already on its way to disintegrating.[50]

A special case of this cumulative institutionalization is seen when the process becomes reflexive and we encounter the institutionalization of the institutionalization process. The institutionalization process becomes doubled, or divided into two parts. The first part is the visible and definable one where the anonymous institutionalizing subject ("God", the "spirit", "society", "the will of our people") is given possibilities of communication in the form of interpretation privileges, offices and corresponding official procedures (which are institutionalized). Through them the "subject" acts, formulates binding decisions and defines consensus. The other, invisible part of the same process takes place in the elementary processes of socialization and forming of public opinion. The latter part of the institutionalization process legitimates the former.[51]

The distinction between custom and law is an example of this "double" form of institutionalization. Custom is a body of norms or rules that is actually followed in practice, i.e. institutionalized behaviour. Law is custom that has been "re-institutionalized at another level", overtly restated in order to make it amenable to the activities of legal institutions. While custom is a simple institutionalization of norms, law is a double institutionalization of them.[52]

Luhmann characterizes this reflexive mechanism of double institutionalization (together with the occurrence of higher levels of legitimation) as a kind of "cultural mutation". This is first observed in the transition from primitive, archaic societies to the early higher cultures of antiquity.[53]

Law is not the only case of double institutionalization. Other examples are provided by the political and sacral institutions (in the limited sense of this term), for instance the authority of church leaders in doctrinal,

---

graphical representation of institutional hierarchy (institutions of the first, second order, etc.) and functional equivalence in (1965:40), reprinted in (1970:20).

49. *Schelsky* (1970:25 f), *Berger-Luckmann* (1967:87, 95).
50. "Ein gleichbleibender, blosser Bestand institutioneller Formen ist nach den dynamischen Gesetzlichkeiten der Stabilität von Institutionen bereits ihr Niedergang", *Schelsky* (1965b:45).
51. *Luhmann* (1970:34).
52. *Bohannan* (1965:34–37).
53. *Luhmann* (1970:34).

cultic and disciplinary matters,[54] or even the existence of specific rules for how to treat those who deviate from a given norm of belief or conduct.[55]

5. The Role of the Élite in Institutionalization

Primary institutionalization of the kind first described comes about by itself, as it were, and is a natural consequence of human interaction with time. This is not the case with those more complex reflexive re-institutionalization mechanisms that *Luhmann* pertinently names "cultural mutations". They may or may not appear at all, and when they do, they may take on widely differing forms, as is witnessed by the enormous cultural, religious and institutional variety manifested in human history. Institutionalization above the primary level is fundamentally "open" which means that within certain structural limits it is largely a process of innovation, creating new interaction and organization patterns, new norms and ways of thinking.[56]

It is generally agreed that individual human striving and thought cannot as a rule act directly upon the institutional structure or the working of social mechanisms. A new idea, for instance, must first be communicated to others and become a factor in a social movement or group interaction in order to eventually become institutionalized.[57] It is also more or less agreed that the existence of certain broad demographic, economic and social conditions and various potential needs within broader groups and strata of society is not in itself sufficient to bring about the necessary institutionalization.[58]

The rise and growth of the empires of antiquity provide examples of how this complex institutionalization comes about. In general

> . . . the development and institutionalization of new types of political or economic organizations or enterprises is greatly dependent on the emergence of various entrepreneurs who are able to articulate new goals, set up new organizations, and mobilize the resources necessary for their continuous functioning.[59]

54. "Ganz andere Lösungen bahnen sich in Gesellschaften an, in denen die Religion zum Ort der Problemlösung wird, also sie als Sinngrundlage der Institutionen abstrahiert . . . und in denen die Institutionalisierung der Institutionalisierung sich deshalb primär auf den Prozess religiöser Exegese und Verkündigung beziehen muss, der dann weder von der politischen Herrschaft noch vom Recht getrennt werden kann.", *Luhmann* (1970:34 n. 12).

55. *Luhmann* (1969:43 f).

56. *Eisenstadt* (1968b:414).

57. *Idem* (1965:35–38), *Jonas* (1966:46) and *Schelsky* (1970:17, 26).

58. *Eisenstadt* (1968b:413).

59. *Eisenstadt, ibidem.* Cf. *Bohannan* (1965:38) on the role of the "sovereign", and *Lachmann* (1970:78 f).

The "entrepreneurs" are an active élite able to offer solutions to the new range of problems by verbalizing the collective goals and norms, establishing organizational frameworks and leading this process of innovation (political entrepreneurs, if successful, become new emperors and their entourages). The result of entrepreneurial activity is not predetermined—the entrepreneurs may have widely differing intentions vis-à-vis the group or society, they may have to compete with other entrepreneurs who offer alternative forms of institutionalization and they may be only partially successful or may even fail altogether.[60]

The interesting thing about the role of an entrepreneurial élite from our point of view is that it seems to provide a good description of the role of charismatic leaders and their staffs in creating new institutional structures.[61] But even here we see no direct individual influence on the existing institutional structure. The new institutionalization makes a detour over men's devotion to a great leader and his great ideas.[62] The primary aim of a charismatic movement is not to create a political or religious organization, but to reorganize the fundamentals of life. The idea, vision or programme, in short the mission has priority over everything else and the resulting institution is only an embodiment of this mission. To use *Weber*'s distinction institutions are value-rationally ("wertrational") oriented and not instrumentally rational ("zweckrational") i.e. they are not purposive organizations in the modern meaning of the word. They are primarily although not exclusively, "determined by a conscious belief in the value for its own sake of some ethical, aesthetic, religious or other form of behaviour, independently of its prospects of success".[63]

D. ROUTINIZATION AND INSTITUTIONALIZATION

1. Routinization Redefined

The most important thing we learn from this account of institutionalization from a sociological point of view is that "routinization" represents a pervasive and ubiquitous quality of social life as such. Institutionalization is not a process that may arise after a time but is a process that inevitably

60. *Eisenstadt* (1965:15 f, 35); " . . . we have to recognize that in any given situation adequate institutional arrangements may fail to crystallize", *Eisenstadt* (1968b: 414).

61. *Eisenstadt* expressly refers to the work of Weber on charismatic leadership in this connection and adds: "The development of such charismatic personalities or groups constitutes perhaps the closest social analogy to 'mutation' " (1965:55)—cf. n. 53 above.

62. This is an important element in Gehlen's theory of institutions, *Jonas* (1966:50 ff), and has influenced *Schlesky* (1970:23).

63. *Weber* (1968:24 f = 1976:12). Cf. above n. 23.

starts almost as soon as human interaction begins and continues for as long as the group, association or society exists.

It is also important to notice that this process is not primarily governed by purposive efforts from the actors but by the latent and powerful laws of consensus generalization inherent in the nature of human interaction. This means that the process of institutionalization will have begun long before any actor makes a conscious effort to organize or stabilize the group. Of course this applies to charismatic communities, too—the daily intercourse with the leader quickly establishes a number of expectations of what he is going to do, say or prescribe, what his staff is expected to do, etc. It is not until somebody pauses to reflect over what has happened that it becomes obvious that a group has now been formed, with a doctrine, vision or mission of its own, its own ethos and way of life and with a rudimentary internal organization of a decidedly aristocratic nature. This may well happen during the lifetime of the original leader—the inspired, intense, extraordinary *status nascendi* of charisma.

I think it was this obvious fact of incipient institutionalization taking place *within* the *status nascendi* that caused *Weber* to state that religious charismatic communities arose as a result of routinization ("Veralltäglichung"). But according to his own sociological definition charisma is not a type of individual psychological equipment but a social phenomenon, viz. a group of followers attributing charismatic endowment to their leader. Charisma does not exist without a charismatic community, and consequently charisma as a social phenomenon does not exist except in a routinized form![64]

I propose that the problem involved in this contradiction be solved by making a distinction between institutionalization and routinization. Institutionalization is the whole process of consensus generalization, structural solidification, legitimation, etc., whereas routinization is part of a secondary phase in this general process, viz. a change in the set of personal motives of the actors.

> Routine actions are those which are governed mainly by motives of moderate, personal attachment, by considerations of convenience and advantage, and by anxiety to avoid failure in conforming to the immediate expectations and demands of peers and superiors. Routine actions are not simply repetitive actions; they are uninspired actions . . .[65]

64. This confusion reveals that Weber, at least in his sociology of religion, thought of charisma as an objective fact in personal psychology and not only as a social phenomenon.
65. *Shils* (1968:387).

A religious charismatic group is characterized by completely different motives such as intense devotion to the leader, a deliberate repudiation of economic or other personal advantages, a strong feeling of having been called by God to a new life and of receiving continuous, immediate contact with His directives.[66] However, while this high-strung state does preclude "routine actions" (i.e. uninspired actions) it does not preclude the process of "reciprocal typification of habitualized actions by types of actors", the growth of roles and generalized consensus or in other words, institutionalization.

Even when, at a later stage in the development of a charismatic group, routine increasingly asserts itself and considerations of personal interest, expediency, traditional loyalties again become more prominent, this "routinization" is not the only factor operating. As *Weber* conceded, but did not sufficiently stress, the sheer logic of group life and group development demands systematization and rationalization irrespective of the staff's private interests. And, what he perhaps stressed even less and what is perhaps more important, the "ideal interests" of the leader and the group make the dispersion and institutionalization of charisma imperative.[67] Even the mission itself, the "spreading of the message"[68] entails formulation of the message, techniques of transmitting it, ethical and ritual instruction for converts and children and consequently the whole process of explaining,

66. The criterion that distinguishes between routine and inspired action is the distance from "ultimate" sources of legitimacy; in religious terms, from God or the Spirit. Inspired action is thought by the actor to derive "its impetus immediately, intensively, and unalloyedly from direct contact with 'ultimate' sources of legitimacy", while routine action is motivated by non-transcendental factors, *Shils, ibidem.* Cf. *Berger's* distinction between "sect" and "church": the former is based on the belief that the spirit is immediately present, while the latter believes the spirit to be remote (1954:474).

67. *Shils* makes the distinction between the deliberate *dispersion* of charisma and a less intentional but unavoidable *attenuation* of it. The latter term denotes a state where a "high", charismatic norm of conduct (e.g. equality or saintliness) is mixed with "low", routine motives and thus not exclusively respected. Dispersion of charisma means spreading the particular charismatic sensitivity (belief and conduct) to a larger number of people and institutions, and of course this also produces an attenuation of charisma (1968:389).

68. Bryan *Wilson* has shown that (Christian) sects who have a strong missionary zeal and aim at converting the world are particularly subject to denominationalizing tendencies or more simply, to become like churches (1959).

The distinction between "sect" and "church", which originated in the work of Weber and Troeltsch, has been lavishly employed and developed in the sociology of religion. In spite of intense work in this field, the classificatory and methodological shortcomings of this distinction are undeniable and render it unusable, cf. the criticisms by *Berger* (1954), *Johnson* (1963) and *Eister* (1967 and 1973). This is why, after having worked for some time with these categories on the NT material, I chose to put them aside as unfruitful.

justifying, defending and systematizing the group's life, doctrine and history (i.e. legitimation).[69]

To sum up: what *Weber* saw as one process, routinization, must be differentiated analytically and redefined as above. Institutionalization is the term denoting the whole process, and is present from the very inception of the charismatic movement whereas routinization is only part of the process. And as routinization proper increasingly sets in as an institutionalizing factor it operates alongside other established factors, such as the laws of consensus generalization, the ideal interests of the group and the systematic needs of the group.[70]

2. The Institutionalization of Charismatic Authority

The charismatic person is a creator of a new order as well as the breaker of routine order. Since charisma is constituted by the belief that its bearer is effectively in contact with what is most vital, most powerful, and most authoritative in the universe or in society, those to whom charisma is attributed are, by virtue of that fact, authoritative.[71]

Charisma is typically manifested in authority relations, and consequently the institutionalization (*Weber:* "routinization") of charisma is identical with the institutionalization of a certain kind of authority. And it is this I shall now analyse from the point of view described in the previous section

(a) Primary institutionalization

In the "pure", intense and concentrated state the vital contact with the source of authority is thought to reside in a certain person and this belief gives the person a high degree of revolutionary "counter-authority".[72] Gradually this authority flows over into the charismatic leader's characteristic message, his instructions and his way of life and the institutions formed by him or arising from interaction with him. Charisma thus is diffused into the group, its customs, rituals, doctrine, verbal tradition, ethos, order of

69. Cf. *Carl Mayer*'s criticism of Weber: "What is lacking is the question concerning the nature of religious sociation as such, or, more precisely, the problem posed by religious sociation as a religious necessity", cited from *Berger* (1954:471).

70. *Berger* mentions that a "change of pressure" takes place during the history of a "sect". "At first, when the sect is *in statu nascendi*, . . . the religious motif largely determines the inner social structure of the sect . . . Later, however, as the spirit recedes into remoteness and the sect hardens, as it were, into ecclesiastical forms, the pressures predominate in the other direction, from the social to the religious; the church makes its peace with the world and is invaded by the latter's social realities, norms, institutions (1954:480).

71. *Shils* (1968:387).

72. Cf. *Hennen-Prigge* (1977:30).

preference designed by the leader, and this kind of charisma-diffusion is as unavoidable as the discharge from a charged wire when touched by a conductive object. Even *Weber* admitted that this process of "depersonalization" ("Versachligung") may begin during the lifetime of and through the action of the original charismatic leader.[73]

As long as the leader is alive everything in the life of the group is under his direct control and has authority (or charisma) only because and in so far as the leader supports it with his own authority. He is the charismatic entrepreneur in relation to the charisma-hungry segment of society which responds to his call, his verbalization of their innermost aspirations in a new message and his salvific leadership. His entrepreneurial activity takes the form of creating a community into which charisma is discharged as it were. And all the time this group is becoming structurally solidified or institutionalized.

(b) Secondary institutionalization

When the leader disappears the group is not left in a state devoid of authority, but with a social construct, whose different parts have a derived, and now independent, authority of their own. The leader's words, his message and example, the rituals and institutions he created now enjoy more authority than before, as he is not there to complete, interpret or change them. But all these authoritative parts of charismatic group life need to be unified and placed in relation to one another so as to be accessible to the group. This is done by means of a secondary institutionalization which transforms unconsolidated verbal tradition into a body of normative texts, ways of living and a typical ethical "atmosphere" into a formulated code of behaviour and a paraenetical teaching tradition, community rites into organized forms of worship. The most important change is that the former staff of assistants become new leaders of the group, responsible for teaching, decision-making and development.

Cumulative institutionalization or re-institutionalization is necessary for the stability and continued functioning of the primary institution itself. If it failed to develop, this would imply stagnation and possibly eventual dissolution of the institution. The situation after the death of the original leader is characterized by acute new needs which call for new institutional structures. Secondary institutionalization is the answer to this call. It may have

73. "There are no established administrative organs. In their place are agents who have been *provided with charismatic authority by their chief* or who possess charisma of their own" (my italics), *Weber* (1968:243 = 1976:141), and cf. the leader's action of designating his own successor (1968:247 = 1976:143).

been planned and started by the original leader himself, it may be the result of new initiative from the staff, or be wholly unplanned and haphazard,
the result of competing interests and proposed solutions. It may even be a
combination of all these possibilities. In any case it is not possible to state
with any confidence that the private (economic) interests of the staff comprises the most important motive force in this development. But *Weber* is
undoubtedly right when he ascribes the decisive influence in this charisma-
transforming process to the actions of the group élite. They serve as an
entrepreneurial élite of the second order, consolidating the internal organization of the group that was created by the primary entrepreneurial enterprise.

This is why the staff do not formulate fundamentally new goals and
norms, or invent totally new forms of group life but conserve, expound,
develop and systematize what has already been given. Their work is aimed
at preserving the original group and fulfilling its mission, and consequently
their authority is of necessity traditional and rational and can by no means
be purely charismatic, resting within themselves only.

This second-generation charismatic authority may well exhibit all other
characteristics of charismatic authority: a personal call from the deity,
supernatural powers, an extraordinary, irrational and anti-economic way of
life exciting a high degree of devotion and reverence from other believing
followers. But it is invariably bound to the tradition and *ratio* imparted by
the original leader.

The process of the depersonalization of charismatic authority is not a
mere transfer of originally personal charisma to other persons and institutions. This diffusion also means that charisma becomes diluted and weakened or, to put it in *Peter Berger's* terms, that the spirit has receded and
can now be reached only through media such as representatives, offices,
holy traditions and rituals. Thus the institutionalization of charismatic authority is a medialization of contact with the "spirit". This is an important
transformation of authority, unavoidable if authority is to survive at all[74]
and necessary from the point of view of the institution or charismatic group
itself, but nevertheless bringing about a great difference in the life of the
group.

Thus the institutionalization of charismatic authority invariably implies
its rationalization and traditionalization—*Weber* was quite right there. But
he underrated the complexity of factors and motives at work in the process.

74. Cf. n. 50 above, and *Shils* (1968:389) and *Eisenstadt* (1968b:413 f).

The former staff certainly has a key-role as an entrepreneurial élite of the second order, but their enterprise is governed not only by the "routinization" of their own motives but also by the systemic needs arising from the life and history of the movement as such, and by the movement's "ideal interest" or fundamental vision.

E. THE INSTITUTIONALIZATION OF CHARISMATIC AUTHORITY IN THE PRIMITIVE CHURCH

Sociologically the Primitive Church cannot be called a creation *de novo,* a totally new enterprise; there is too much continuity between the group that is seemingly brought to an end by the death of Jesus and the group that arises in Jerusalem as the result of His resurrection appearances. In reality it is the same group continuing in a very different manner.

The primary institutionalization has thus already begun in the group around Jesus. To describe this lies outside my task here. Suffice it to say that if this group existed as early as a year before the death of Jesus there would have been ample time for the laws of consensus generalization to mould the interaction of this group and develop its social structure. We can also note in passing the remarkable likeness between what we know about this group and *Weber's* description of a charismatic community.

The authority of Jesus has been exercised within this group (and outside it) which implies that His authority has been diffused and "stored" in His words and body of teaching, His characteristic ethos and way of life, His way of praying, of breaking bread and worshipping the Father, and in the immediate group of disciples that has shared His life and works with Him in His mission.

There seems to be good reason for believing that the active part in the process of secondary institutionalization that began after the death and resurrection of Jesus was played by His former staff, that group of disciples some of which came to be called "apostles of Jesus Christ".[75] They are simply the leaders of the "church" in Jerusalem during its early days, recognized as such both within the group and outside it. From our point of view they act as the entrepreneurial élite of the second order, institutionalizing the fruits of the primary institutionalization. Within a few years we see the emergence of a developed system of doctrine, cult and organization, a group exhibiting missionary zeal and a strong sense of their uniqueness (they regard themselves as "the holy, the elect of God, *qahal*/ἐκκλησια).

75. See e.g. *von Campenhausen* (1969:12–29).

1. The Jerusalem Church and Paul

Paul visits the Jerusalem church, or rather Cephas, three years after his conversion at a time when this church has existed for about five years.[76] It is the consensus of New Testament scholarship that he there encountered a religious group which had reached a fairly high degree of development in doctrinal tradition, teaching, cultic practice, common life and internal organization.[77]

The Jerusalem church treasured its tradition from and about Jesus which included His teachings, instructions and commandments and His life, death and resurrection. This was the primary content of its missionary preaching, internal instruction and theological work. Very early the kerygma was given typical patterns, and different kerygmatic formulas such as we find in 1 Cor 15:3–7 were formulated. The church had a christologically determined tradition concerning their interpretation of the Scriptures,[78] and a group of persons engaged in this work, among whom we may presume were "the apostles of Christ".[79] The missionary zeal of the church had at the time of Paul's conversion caused the rise of the church in Damascus and very soon also of the church in faraway Antioch in northern Syria. There Greek-speaking Jewish Christians who had been expelled from Jerusalem had begun to make converts among the Gentiles without first requiring them to become Jews by the act of circumcision. Thus the Church was, even before Paul's time, pluralistic in regard to the observance of the Torah.

The very fact of this missionary zeal witnesses to a remarkable consciousness of the group's distinctive character and value or in other words it witnesses to a church-consciousness. The first Christians did not regard themselves as a sect or party within Judaism, but rather as the beginning of its total renewal, a renewed Israel constituted by those who believed that Jesus was Messiah and who had received the first-fruits of the coming Kingdom through the effusion of the Holy Spirit. This is also why the Jerusalem Christians, apart from their participation in the worship of synagogue and temple, from the very beginning had their own initiation rite, baptism in the name of Jesus, a sacral meal of their own and a cultic tradition of their own (*Abba, maranatha,* and the Lord's Prayer are reflections of this). As the uniting and governing factor in this élite-conscious, charismatic group, which while awaiting the parousia of Christ Jesus, shared a

76. *Goppelt* (1966:152 f), *Hengel* (1972a:44).
77. The following two paragraphs contain general knowledge that can be obtained from any of the existing textbooks on the earliest period of Church History. Here it is sufficient to point to *Goppelt* (1966:17–41) and *Conzelmann* (1969:30–47).
78. See *Hengel* (1972a).
79. *Gerhardsson* (1961:224 f, 244 f).

κοινωνια that may have included a common central fund and communistic sharing of incomes, Paul knew that he would find the apostles, with Cephas at their head. From the beginning of the Church's existence after Easter this collegium of plenipotentiaries had enjoyed an undisputed role of leadership, both in the mission directed outwards and in the inwardly directed functions of teaching and governing.

In the light of this development it would not be an exaggeration to say that by the time Paul visited Cephas in Jerusalem the church had become institutionalized and had taken on its fundamental, first-generation pattern.[80] Of course doctrine, cult and organization did continue to develop during the period up to the death of the first generation (c. A.D. 60–70), but the fundamental pattern remained the same.

The part of this fundamental pattern that is of greater interest to us in this context is the existence of a limited group of plenipotentiary representatives of the Risen Lord, the apostolate in Jerusalem. It is not a group of leaders that gradually emerges from the larger group of believers as a result of interaction, but is one of the founding facts of the Church itself and this on two counts: (a) This was the very kernel of the Church, the beginnings from which it grew. (b) The apostolate was considered to have been constituted by the Risen Lord Himself, who had thus given His staff a unique and unassailable authority right from the start.[81]

But the Jerusalem church and the Jerusalem apostolate did not remain the only church or group of apostles. New churches emerged in Damascus and Antioch as early as the thirties, the church in Antioch in its attitude towards Gentiles representing something so strikingly new, that it has with some justification been characterized as a second start.[82] This church if any could have claimed an independent authority of its own. But it did not, because it was vitally dependent on the previous institutionalization of the Jerusalem church from which it had received its creed, christology, cult and sacraments and partly even its organization. This dependence is manifested in a number of ways: Barnabas, who was foremost in the Antiochene group of prophets and teachers (Acts 13:1) had been sent to Antioch by the apostolate of Jerusalem which can be compared with other similar visits by prophets sent from Jerusalem, Acts 11:27 and 15:32 (= Gal 2:12?). The church in Antioch supported the mother church in Jerusalem both before and after the Apostolic Council and they wished to receive the ver-

---

80. *Hengel* has rightly stressed the astonishingly short time needed to formulate the fully developed christology we meet in the Pauline Epistles (1972a:45, 63 ff).
81. Cf. *von Campenhausen* (1969:13 f, 22 f).
82. *Goppelt* (1966:42).

dict of this church in the question of the circumcision of Gentiles, and, lastly, they abandoned their own practice of shared meals at the request of Jerusalem (Gal 2:11–14).

In the previous chapter I argued that this dependence is a manifestation of the fact that the church in Jerusalem had greater charismatic authority than any other church because of its closer contact with the origin of the Church. In view of the fundamental unity of the Church it may even be somewhat anachronistic to compare different churches, as the multiplicity of church*es* is in itself a secondary phenomenon. During the thirties and forties the unity of the Church created no problem and it is only the growing number of Gentiles in the Antiochene church that gives rise to apprehension in Jerusalem. The Council and the Collection are measures taken to guard the unity of the Church against disuniting factors both inside and outside the Church, which by this time (c. A.D. 50) were beginning to make their influence felt.[83] Sociologically, these measures are part of the institutionalization process and have the character of adjustment to new conditions and needs which arise as the result of the previous institutionalization of the community. It can be added that the situation began to change more drastically during the decade following the Council, and the dissolution of the Jerusalem church in the late sixties as a result of the first Jewish War (A.D. 66–70) put an end to its already waning supremacy. But this lies outside the scope of this investigation.

In the light of the preceding discussion even the heading of this section can appear slightly absurd: "Paul" and "the Jerusalem Church" are scarcely comparable entities! At every point of his history where Paul comes into contact with this church he meets the fact of an institution into which he was grafted by a very special secondary institutionalization. The primary institutionalization was not restructured by his advent, and the closeness of the other apostles to Christ must be admitted by Paul as part of the definition of his own apostolate. Their chronological priority does not nullify his late calling, and his enormous capacity for work and missionary achievements do not reduce their role to insignificance. Thus we must conclude that even if all apostles of Christ are equals theologically they are not equals sociologically, i.e. they do not have the same amount of authority.

The relation between Paul's apostolate and the apostolate in Jerusalem (together with this church as a whole, as described in Chap. 1) shows us that historical and social facts determine the theology of the apostolate.

---

83. Cf. *Munck* (1954, passim), *Goppelt* (1966:119 f), *von Campenhausen* (1969: 33 f).

This theology is part of the legitimation of the movement, which in its turn is part of the institutionalization process continuously at work. Expressed in other words the institutionalization of charismatic authority includes Paul's theology of the apostolate. Not even Paul's theology can be placed apart as an independent commentary from the institutionalization process as it is an integral part of this process, in dialectical interaction with other factors. Therefore, the supremacy of Jerusalem and its apostles over the Gentile churches and their apostles (notably Paul) during the period we are investigating is not merely a theological idea or a moral obligation but an institutionalization of its charismatic authority. And its institutionalization makes it a solid fact in the social life of the Church.

2. The Institutionalization of Paul's Authority

In the previous chapter Paul was characterized as a "minor founder", a person who launches an enterprise, who makes a new founding within an existing tradition without breaking with its fundamental institutions or values (as St. Francis did). The difference between Paul as a minor founder and Jesus as the major founder is above all the following: (a) Their view of themselves—Paul never comes near to making implicit messianic claims for himself. (b) Their relation to existing tradition also differs—Paul does not radically reinterpret the Christian tradition in the way Jesus interpreted Jewish tradition. And a third difference (c) lies in their respective intentions—Paul does not only aim at preaching a message wherever he comes, but wants to plant or found a Christian church with a definite cultic, ethical and doctrinal tradition (cf. 1 Cor 3:6, 10 f), whereas the intentions of Jesus concerning the organizing of a church were not so specific.

When Paul comes to a new town in Asia Minor or Greece he does not simply represent God or Jesus Christ but also the Christian Church which by then is the result of about one generation's institutionalization of the charismatic group that had formed around Jesus. Phenomena such as praying in the name of Jesus, celebrating the Eucharist, baptizing and instructing converts, reading and expounding the Holy Scriptures of Israel in the Christian manner, or inculcating Christian ethos regarding the treatment of wives, children, slaves, money do not arise more or less unintentionally from the interaction of the group of adherents to Paul. They are given elements in a sacred tradition or order which the apostle plants from the very beginning into the life of the group. He does not create these institutions and the theology intrinsic in them from day to day, but transmits formulated traditions and customs that are binding even for himself.

The emphasis on "tradition" does not of course mean that Paul's task

consisted of introducing a detailed system of doctrine, cult and organization in every new place he came to. Even after one generation's institutionalization the tradition was relatively "open" and variable, especially in
regard to new conditions and problems. Different apostles or missionaries
within the same tradition may go different ways in the continuous process
of institutionalization. But the starting point is always the common fund of
invariable, institutionalized fundamental elements or patterns ("the Gospel"), and their importance in Paul's mission should not be underrated.[84]

Paul's authority vis-à-vis his churches is not traditional or rational-legal
in spite of his dependence on tradition, as it is in no way based upon the
prior tradition or *ratio* of his converts. Paul's role in relation to his Christian converts is the same, *mutatis mutandis,* as that of Jesus in relation to
his adherents—he mediates a closer contact with the vital, sacred centre of
existence through his articulation of their needs and aspirations, of the new
goals and norms, and through his guidance to a new order and a new life.
He is, in short, a charismatic entrepreneur who offers an answer to peo-
ples' need for salvation. And his answer takes the form of the transmission
of a certain charismatic tradition that encompasses all dimensions of
human life.

If we turn to the institutionalization of apostolic authority in Pauline
churches it must be stated at the outset that it is somewhat complex.

We cannot disregard the plain, fundamental fact that by reason of being
the founder of these churches Paul is the authority par excellence in them.[85]
All they know of Jesus, the Christian faith, worship and Christian ethics
they have received from him. He is the main source of information and
contact with sacred *ratio*. This is corroborated by references in his letters
to his actual relationship with his churches. In general they give a picture of
impressive apostolic authority and a person who is not afraid to exercise it.

But there are numerous factors in the life of these churches which contribute to a limitation of Paul's authority. Some of them are connected with
the fact that the charisma Paul is mediating is institutionalized in phenomena outside his own person—the apostolate of Christ encompasses many
others beside Paul, the fundamental christological doctrine and tradition
from and about Jesus arose largely prior to and independent of Paul, and
so on. Other preachers and teachers may turn up in Paul's churches and
present the same message as Paul does, and what is more important may

84. Cf. *K. Berger* (1977c:130, 132).
85. *von Campenhausen* (1969:45). Naturally Paul is not quite alone, as is seen
from Phil 3:17 and his frequent use of "we", etc. But 1 Cor 4:15 f and Gal 4:19
show that his position is nonetheless unique.

offer alternative solutions to problems. This diminishes Paul's authority as it makes the churches more independent of him and makes it possible for them to judge the work of Paul (1 Cor 4:3–5).

This possibility also emerges from the fact that once Christians have become fully initiated in the charismatic tradition, they are familiar with it too, and can use it as a means of controlling and criticizing the apostle, or can claim some measure of independence from him. Naturally, this tendency is strengthened where a church is richly endowed with pneumatic gifts. These gifts are regarded as providing direct contact with the "Spirit" or Christ himself, which augments self-confidence even to the point of opposing the founding "father" himself.

In addition to this inevitable limitation of authority that is a result of the nature and historical context of church-founding, Paul himself contributes in more than one way to limit his own authority.

(a) He makes it absolutely clear to his churches that his authority is delegated from a higher source of authority to which, in principle, they themselves have direct access (cf. 1 Cor 3:5–9, 21b–23). It is typical of Paul that he makes a clear distinction between his own person and the divine gift of grace that makes possible his special service to God in the Church.[86] And the apostle makes no secret of the fact that there are many others who enjoy the same degree of authority as he himself does (1 Cor 9:1–12, 15:3–11).[87]

(b) Paul chooses to regard himself as "father" of the churches he has founded. This is of course a role that includes a high degree of authority in contemporary society, but it is interesting to see what this choice excludes and what it can develop into. Paul does not regard himself in relation to his converts as a "prophet", a person whose every word is a divine communication, or as "head" or "chief". In the choice of the "father" image it is the personal and cordial relationship between father and child that is stressed while the element of order and obedience is not. A father loves his children and he therefore brings them up and cares for them in all their needs; the children in their turn love their father with a feeling of trust and pay him due respect and obey him without being continually asked to do so. In the choice of this

86. *Schütz* (1975:184 f, 272).
87. But it is obvious that contact with these persons and their alternative form of institutionalization did shake the then uncomplicated authority relation between Paul and his churches and necessitates complementary legitimation. Gal and 1–2 Cor are examples of this.

image lies also Paul's expectation that his Christians will grow and develop into maturity and independence (cf. 1 Cor 3:1–2). A father does not want his children to remain babes all their life, for ever dependent on him, and this side of the relation between Paul and his converts is often seen in the trust the apostle places in his readers and in his wish that they will attain to the full freedom of God's children.[88] This view of himself as a father helps to explain Paul's mildness and his unassuming conduct, which contrasts so sharply with that of other persons with charismatic authority (e.g. 2 Cor 10:10–12, 11:20 f).

(c) It is worth noticing in this context that Paul abstains from his right to financial support, an otherwise natural manifestation of authority (not only charismatic authority). Paul explains this by pointing to his parental role (2 Cor 12:14b "I seek not what is yours but you; for children ought not to lay up for their parents, but parents for their children"). That is, he emphasizes a side of parenthood which is not concerned with authority.

(d) Without ever letting go his hold on his churches, Paul implicitly rationalizes his authority in the way he motivates and explains his admonitions and instructions.[89] The aim and effect of always analysing ethical and other problems from the point of view of their relation to "the Gospel", that basic instruction that the converts have already received, is to make them capable of applying this sacred *ratio* to other situations and problems. The intended result is that the local churches with their own knowledge of and access to sacred *ratio* will make independent decisions and direct their own development (cf. Rom 12:2, Phil 1:9–11). Here we observe a diffusion of apostolic authority taking place simply in the apostle's way of criticizing faults and answering questions, as this builds up the readers' knowledge and capacity for correct analysis and judgment. The apostle's letters are thus both an exercise of apostolic authority and at the same time a diffusion of this authority into the local churches. And they can therefore be characterized as a re-institutionalization of the primary institutionalization which took place during the founding period.[90] The apostolic authority is on its way to becoming a theological tradition (this contains the germ of canon formation), and on its way to becoming

---

88. *Gerhardsson* (1971:55–76) gives a vivid description of how important this really was to Paul.

89. It is to *Schütz*'s credit that he has shown this in his criticism of Weber (1975: 273–278).

90. Cf. n. 54 above on double institutionalization in a religious context.

accessible to and applicable by the local churches themselves (which contains the germ of the later development of offices in the Church).

This self-chosen limitation of Paul's authority is not a sign of weakness, but is part of his programme. It is based on a deep appreciation of the freedom and inherent capacity of local churches to conduct their own lives and attain a state where they will not need apostolic supervision. But this was not always the outcome. It can for instance be argued that it is this voluntary limitation of apostolic authority that lies behind the conflict between Paul and the church in Corinth in 2 Cor 10—13. The intruders seem to have exhibited signs of a more purely charismatic authority, and one decisive factor in their successful attempt of ousting Paul from his position of authority was that he had never set himself up as their absolute leader. Even if Paul was more "pneumatic" or conspicuously endowed with Spirit than appears at first from his letters, he had no wish to live up to this church's expectations of a powerful charismatic leader endowed with superhuman powers, in all ways demonstrating his closeness to the divine sphere.[91] This attitudinal incongruity weakened the relation of authority between Paul and the church in Corinth and prepared the ground for the insubordination and opposition that the intruders desired and effected.

The cause of this attitudinal incongruity is probably that the sophisticated theological rationalization of Paul's apostolate we find in 2 Cor 10—13 had not been communicated to or understood by the Corinthians. This theology of apostolic authority is not a description of the "sociology" of apostolic authority.[92] The Corinthians have gone by what they have seen and heard from Paul and interpreted this with the help of their own role expectations. And if one does not know and understand Paul's theological interpreting principles, his conduct probably did appear somewhat incon-

91. "An apostle, they thought, must be (not necessarily a 'divine man' . . . but certainly) a powerful and imposing person, standing out for all the rights he could possibly claim, performing miracles, and accepting the adulation and support of those whom he was able to impress", *Barrett* (1973b:322). On Paul as a "pneumatic", see *Ellis* (1974).

92. A fact of which not only Paul but also *Schütz* seems insufficiently aware, when the latter confines his discussion of "the sociology of apostolic authority" (defined 1975:249) to the "implicit *theory* of order embedded in the articulation of apostolic authority", p. 263 (my italics). In *Schütz's* own definition the "sociology of apostolic authority" is the structure of a historical community and its relationship to Paul; that is, concrete social phenomena. ('Sociology' here stands for "social life, context, reality", much as "the psychology of Paul" is used of his interior life, not his theory of human behaviour.) It is true that Paul thinks of charisma more as Edward Shils does, and that his opponents have a more Weberian view of it, but simply pointing out this does not explain why actual authority relations between Paul and the Corinthians deteriorated.

sistent. The fault lies in part with Paul himself as his behaviour was actually ambiguous (cf. once again 2 Cor 10:10) and it cannot be denied that theory and reality sometimes diverged considerably.[93]

The fact that Paul managed to win back his Corinthians and re-establish his authority in this church is a measure of the strength and resilience of institutionalized authority relations.

3. Local Intra-church Institutionalization of Authority

I shall concentrate here on the question of Paul's participation in the institutionalization of intra-church authority as this will give a clear picture of the process.

There are few indications that Paul "instituted" any local offices in the churches he founded, but the point is worth discussing. In Chapter 3 I discussed Paul's probable strategy of providing a basis for his work in a new place by concentrating on converting some rich, house-owning God-fearer or Jew (such as Stephanas, Gaius and Crispus in Corinth, cf. 1 Cor 1:14–16) from the local synagogue. In the churches where the apostle stayed for a long time (Corinth, Ephesus) it is reasonable to assume that the type of non-pneumatic leader-functions described in 1 Cor 12—14 emerged while the apostle was actually there and that they were found in the thin stratum of wealthy, educated and capable Christians. A primary institutionalization of the Lord's Supper in private homes, of worship with elements of prophecy, instruction, exhortation and prayers certainly occurred during these months when the apostle was present in person. And 1 Cor 12 makes it hard to believe that this development should have passed unnoticed by Paul, or that those who functioned as leaders during the act of worship (prophets, teachers, hosts) when he was present should have stopped performing these functions when he left them. One can perhaps even suspect some gentle Pauline prodding behind Stephanas's service to the community, and it does not seem unreasonable to assume that some sort of responsibility was transferred to capable and responsible Christians when the apostle eventually had to leave. This is not to postulate the occurrence of any formal training or ordination by imposition of hands. But the fact that the laying on of hands seems to have existed in the contemporary church (cf. Acts 13:1–3) ought to warn us from stating with confidence that it cannot have occurred. To sum up: it cannot be excluded that Paul participated in the institutionalization of intra-church authority even during the initial stage, but this assumption represents only an educated guess.

93. Compare, for instance, 1 Cor 5:3–5 with 2 Cor 1:24 and 4:5, and see in general Paul's financial relations with Corinth and how he explains them.

A number of other factors not connected with Paul's theological thinking and his intentions were more important in this process.

(a) To these belongs the development of the pneumatic gifts. In Corinth they led to a distribution of and exercise of authority within the church that Paul could not accept. We see Paul working at interpreting speaking in tongues and prophecy in such a way as will put them in line with other functions; and he sets limits, not only to the display of gnosis and "inspiration" of a general kind, but also to that of genuine spiritual gifts, both through direct regulation (1 Cor 14: 26–40) and through the introduction of higher criteria for their use and evaluation, such as "love, upbuilding" and "order" (ἀγαπη, οἰκοδομη, ταξις).[94] Precisely this effort shows indirectly that this type of phenomenon is a constructive factor in the institutionalization of authority and one that operates independent of the apostle.

(b) Another of these factors is the aspect of time itself—the person who was the first to be converted in a place is called the "first-fruit", and apparently enjoys a certain degree of authority on behalf of this fact. There are sociological reasons for this as those who are the first members of a group, through their interaction, set the direction for the institutionalization of the subsequent life of the group. They formulate the language for expressing the experiences of the beginning, they become the apostle's special assistants and function as transmitters of the socialization of later converts. But here the biblical view of first-fruits as being of special importance and promise has probably also come into play: a first-fruit is always called to serve the Lord and put himself at His service.[95]

(c) But chronological priority is no more the only important aspect of the institutionalization of authority here than in the case of Paul and the Jerusalem apostles. "I worked harder than any of them", wrote Paul (1 Cor 15:10), and capacity for work and the amount of service rendered are surely of decisive importance in the field of intra-church authority too, as we can see from 1 Thess 5:13 and 1 Cor 16:15 f. In principle anybody could devote himself to working for the church in whatever way lay open for him or her, but it stands to reason that some Christians had greater possibilities than others. A slave in a heathen household was not in a position to spend a considerable

94. On the concept of "upbuilding" in Paul's argument see *Daube* (1971:226–231).
95. *Brockhaus* (1975:111, 124).

amount of time, money and energy in the service of the church, whereas men like Stephanas or Crispus were. Moreover they probably had education, administrative ability and initiative and a certain amount of influence in the local government and the civic community. It may not have been the rule that only wealthy and free men became the leaders (προΐσταμενοι, or ἐπισκοποι) of the local church but it would be sociologically naive to deny the importance of individual competence for this selection. And "competence" is not only a question of personal intelligence or devotion but also of social position.

Naturally, this observation does not imply that social standing was a criterion that was directly and consciously applied in the selection of leaders, neither by Paul nor anybody else. The "selection process" is none other than the institutionalization of group life which with time inevitably results in the emergence of a leading stratum as this answers to the needs of the group. As the apostle is not consciously directing this process it may be called "a development from below"[96], i.e., it comes from the church itself. But within the local church considered as a heterogeneous social group this is rather a development from "above" coming from the higher stratum of those who are capable of taking this responsibility and are willing to do so.

It can be presumed that all these factors cooperate in the intra-church institutionalization of authority formed by the laws of consensus generalization. The results may differ from church to church, as we can see even from the fragments of information we have in the Pauline letters. There we see that in Philippi there are two groups of office-holders with titles and in Cenchreae we meet a διακονος, while in the neighbouring Corinth we have both titled and untitled functionaries, and a divided community life witnessing to a lack of effective leadership. It is evident that the institutionalization process is fundamentally "open" and need not lead to uniform result.

Paul's attitude to this institutionalization is positive. In all cases we know of he supports and recognizes the existing local officials (1 Thess 5:12 f, Gal 6:6, 1 Cor 16:15 f, Rom 12:3–8, 16:1 f, Phil 1:1),[97] primarily on the ground of their usefulness, the development thereby receiving a consolidating legitimation. The content of this apostolic legitimation is simply that these persons contribute to building up the church and so participate in a function that the apostle himself fulfills in his churches. What they are doing is ultimately commissioned by God, and must therefore be accepted

96. *Laub* (1973:85), *Hoffmann-Eid* (1975:215).
97. *Brockhaus* (1975:125) et al.

as mediating a contact with him. Consequently the apostle does not merely refer to pragmatic usefulness or to personal sacrifice as being worthy of respect but lends these functions something of his own authority.

The clearest example of this is Paul's interpretation of different functions in the local church, including both pneumatic and purely practical functions, as being gifts of the Holy Spirit ($\chi\alpha\rho\iota\sigma\mu\alpha\tau\alpha$). Functions of responsibility and leadership that are not extraordinary are given a "spiritual" meaning. Theologically this can be characterized as the "charismatization" of the incipient institutionalization of authority. But the interesting thing about it sociologically is that this is a de-charismatization or "rationalization" of the process as it legitimates social phenomena from the body of sacred *ratio*. Thus we find Paul institutionalizing local church authority by rationalizing it.

It is important that the term "legitimation" is understood correctly— it does not imply mere justification of what has happened. In Corinth, where this theological interpretation was used for the first time, the situation that has developed is in no way accepted or justified by the apostle. The institutionalization process has up till now been unsatisfactory both from a practical and from an ideological point of view. Several necessary tasks have not been performed because of the lack of a united and active leadership, and what leadership there is builds on false premises. The apostle's theology of charisma consequently has an obviously corrective purpose. But it is not the existence of leadership that is corrected, nor is it the flowering of pneumatic gifts but their perverted development. And the guiding principle set before the Corinthians is the image of cooperation between "members" who have different functions (of varying importance) and where subjection between members is a natural thing (cf. 1 Cor 16:15 f). The function of apostolic legitimation is here to bar certain possible but undesirable developments in the institutionalization of local authority and to open up (or declare open) other developments. Paul's essential contribution to the institutionalization of intra-church authority is not to be found in its inception, where his activity seems to have been of moderate extent. And the development which took place during his absence was governed by non-theological factors, largely independent of his intentions, as they were of an ordinary social nature. But the secondary, theological rationalization that he effects by his acknowledgement of what has happened, and through the formulation of his theology of charisma, has undoubtedly been an essential factor in the subsequent development of the offices in the church. Not because Paul's theology of charisma was understood and passed on as it was first formulated (this seems not to have been the case[98]), but because his rationalization of authority-functions facilitates and leads up to their institutionalization, i.e. the development of offices.[99] The separation of charisma from charisma-bearer, which *Weber* saw as a precondition for the development of the Roman Catholic ministry where a person receives his charisma by entering the ministry,[100] was anticipated by Paul.

Consequently we cannot say that the institutionalization of intra-church authority or the inception of offices occurs independently of Paul, even if he did not "institute" them in any simple sense of the word. The actual social structures are not directly influenced by Paul's thinking or ideas, but the fact that the apostle does indeed legitimate the development involves the consolidation or institutionalization of the institutionalization process.

---

98. *Herten* (1976:84–87, 89).

99. " . . . allerdings ist ja wohl nichts sicherer, als dass nicht seine Rechtfertigungs-lehre, sondern seine Konzeptionen der Beziehung zwischen Pneuma und Gemeinde und die Art der relativen Anpassung an die Alltagsgegebenheiten der Umwelt damals wirklich rezipiert wurden", *Weber* (1976:310 = 1968:511).

100. *Weber* (1968:248 f, 1139 f = 1976:144, 674). Cf. already 1 Tim 4:14.

CHAPTER 7

Conclusion: Authority in the Primitive Church

A. THE STRUCTURE OF AUTHORITY IN THE PRIMITIVE CHURCH

1. The Church as a Structure of Authority

My investigation of the distribution of power in the Primitive Church in Part I and the subsequent analysis of the structure of authority in Part II would seem to permit the conclusion that the Primitive Church constitutes a structure of authority. This implies that the numerous relations of super-ordination and subordination that can be found in the Pauline texts are with few exceptions based neither on coercion nor on a utilitarian constellation of interests but on a belief in legitimacy shared by all parties. The asymmetric distribution of power that we can observe is justified by socially valid norms and beliefs concerning the legitimacy of this lack of symmetry.

But the statement that the Primitive Church constitutes an authority structure also implies that the many different authority relations are not mere isolated occurrences of authority but are interrelated parts of an organic whole. All authority is considered as ultimately flowing from the same source, viz. the Founder of the Church, and this is recognized as being the basis for the legitimacy of the exercise of authority in the Church.[1] This is why all local churches stand in a relation to one another as parts of one and the same Church. All local leaders, itinerant mission-aries and apostles stand in relation to others on the same or another level. More will be said below on this type of "charismatic" authority.

---

1. Cf. *Stanley*'s distinction between the source of authority and the exercise of authority in the Church (1967:566). See further *Williams* (1950:22 f, 110, 112), *Gerhardsson* (1961:294), *Roloff* (1965:124 f) and *Delorme* (1974:316–323).

2. The Structure of the Church at Different Levels

As regards the highest, "global" (German "gesamtkirchliche") level I have
stated with some emphasis that Paul has not the same status as the church
in Jerusalem or the apostolate in this church. On a number of occasions it
appears that he is permanently dependent in some respects on this centre
of the Church. This dependence is a result of the manner in which he was
incorporated into the Church—while still a persecutor of the Church he
was called by the Risen Lord to be His apostle, to be a witness to the
Gentiles, and not at the same time and place as the other apostles of Christ.
In addition to these biographical factors it is also of importance that up to
c. A.D. 50 his position in the Church is determined by the fact that he is a
leader in and a missionary (or "apostle") of the church in Antioch—a
church that considers itself bound in vital respects to its point of origin, the
church in Jerusalem, as we can see from Gal 2:1–14. Paul develops dy-
namically into a person with a role in and influence in the Church far ex-
ceeding that of Barnabas, for instance, but is nonetheless marked by his
beginnings. The relation between Paul and the church in Jerusalem can be
characterized as being an institutionalized charismatic authority relation,
where the institutionalized charisma of Jerusalem dominates the relation,
although the authenticity and independence of Paul's charismatic authority
is also acknowledged by this church.

At the regional level we can observe Paul exercising his authority over
some of his missionary assistants and over the churches he founded. Some
of his co-workers are colleagues rather than assistants (for instance Barnabas, Silvanus and Apollos), and there are reasons for considering that he
did not exercise unrestricted authority over his "staff". But in the churches
that he founded his charismatic authority is of wide range and great intensity. He acts there as the personal representative of God and Christ mediating the new life in a complete transformation of the spiritual, intellectual,
moral and social life of the believers. We can note, however, a self-imposed
limitation of apostolic authority. The newly converted (Gentile) Christians
interpret his authority in an unsophisticated fashion, primarily valuing his
"magical" powers and his proximity to the sacred, whereas Paul himself
interprets it by means of sophisticated theological rationalization. As long
as the relation between church and apostle is harmonious this attitudinal
incongruity does not affect the relation as it is the generally prevailing interpretation (that of the local church) that determines the relation. But
Paul's rationalization of his own authority serves also to weaken it, and
under the impact of hostile criticism and rivalry from impressive intruders
this leads to a temporary deterioration of the authority relation as such in

the church of Corinth. The ensuing conflict is one indication of the inter-dependence of different relations (or levels) within the authority structure as a whole—Paul's standing in Jerusalem affects, adversely, his standing in Corinth.

At the local level I have argued that we can observe a functional differentiation which within a short time becomes institutionalized, i.e. develops into offices. This differentiation arises largely by itself, influenced by pneumatic and social differences within the local congregation but without much organization on the part of Paul. As long as Paul is present or active in his churches the local offices remain undeveloped, although the institutionalization of the functions of prophesying, teaching, leadership, caring for and helping the members of the church where this is needed goes on continuously. Although we know most about this process in the Corinthian church, this church cannot be considered typical of the Pauline churches; it is a fact that institutionalization can develop along different lines in different churches. Paul's attitude to the development of local leadership is positive and he helps to consolidate it by authoritatively putting pneumatic and non-pneumatic functions on the same basis as being manifestations of the Spirit in the church. The apostle's anti-enthusiastic endorsement has of course a strongly institutionalizing effect on the emerging local offices.

B. THE NATURE OF AUTHORITY IN THE PRIMITIVE CHURCH

1. Charismatic Authority

The most important basis for the legitimate exercise of power or, in other words, for the exercise of authority in the Primitive Church is proximity to the sacred (Christ and His Spirit). Temporal, geographical and personal proximity to the sacred origin endows a person with an exalted status as compared with persons who are otherwise like him. This applies in a number of cases: to the relation between the Jewish Christians in Palestine and the Gentile Christians in the diaspora; the relation between the apostles of Christ in Jerusalem who had known Jesus before Easter and the apostle Paul; the relation between Paul, the founder, and Apollos in Corinth; and that between the "first-fruit" Stephanas and the rest of the church in Corinth. And the esteem enjoyed by James in Jerusalem is certainly not unrelated to the fact that he is a brother of the Lord.

But the fact of having known Jesus personally (or of being one of the first converts in a place) is not in itself sufficient to accord any person a position of authority in the Church (or church). The really crucial form of proximity to the sacred is that of being in close contact with sacred *ratio*, the divine Word: apostles, prophets and teachers are the real "authorities" during the first years of the Church. The most powerful manifestation of charisma is to have received the commission to preach the Gospel from the Lord himself or to mediate divine revelation direct from the Spirit, or to expound the Holy Scriptures and transmit the Jesus-tradition. Of course performing miracles of healing and speaking in tongues are also considered important manifestations of endowment with the Spirit but, except for possible short-lived aberrations in the Corinthian church, we never hear of authoritative leadership based on the possession of these gifts.

But Paul surpasses the authority of Barnabas in spite of the fact that the latter had belonged to the original circle of Christians in Jerusalem and was a leader of the church in Antioch before Paul even arrived there. In speaking about himself in relation to the other apostles (and resurrection witnesses) Paul declares that he has "worked harder than any of them" (1 Cor 15:10), and (it might be added) has achieved a greater missionary success than any of them. Service and the capacity for work is thus also an important basis on which to be acknowledged as having authority in the Church. In 1 Cor 9:2 (cf. 2 Cor 3:2 f) Paul concludes from the existence of the church in Corinth that he is an apostle. We can observe the same principle at work in the emergence of "working authorities"[2] in the local Pauline churches. It is not only pneumatic gifts that manifest contact with the Spirit but also non-pneumatic functions of serving the church.

To anyone familiar with the Weberian typology of authority and the distinction it makes between traditional, rational-legal and charismatic authority it is obvious that *charismatic authority* is the predominant type in the Primitive Church, based mainly as it is on the endowment of divine or extraordinary gifts. But as we saw in Part II the Church must also be characterized as an institutionalized charismatic movement, since it exhibits elements of traditional and rational-legal authority. Even the founders of churches, such as Paul and Barnabas, refer to a common history and transmit a tradition, "the Gospel", containing a number of given elements of doctrine (christology, eschatology), cult (baptism, the Eucharist, the Lord's Day) and organization (the apostolate commissioned by Christ, the central role of the church in Jerusalem). Thus we must add another characteristic to the description of the nature of authority in the Primitive Church.

2. Institutionalized Authority

As in any other permanent human group there is a continuous process of institutionalization going on in the Primitive Church: behaviour, language

2. *Brockhaus* (1975:124).

and other forms of expression (rites, symbolic actions), modes of procedure, missionary techniques, categories of theological interpretation—all of these become increasingly stabilized and traditional. It is an inevitable process at work in all parts of the life of the Church, and is especially apparent in everyday activities such as rearing children in Christian families, the instruction of new converts, the act of worship, the propagation of the Gospel and polemics. The process of institutionalization is in principle "open", i.e. may proceed in many directions, and this partly explains the variety of institutional solutions to the needs of the churches in different regions and also why, for instance, local church leadership can develop differently in Corinth and Philippi.

As institutionalization is "open" the latest part of the process is always the most insecure one, until it has become part of the stabilized "background" of the social world in question it is open to criticism and change. There is a time when the practice of not circumcising Gentile converts can still be attacked at the top level of the Church and when Paul has apprehensions about the outcome. But once the decision has been made (at the Apostolic Council), the non-circumcision of Gentiles becomes an irreversible, institutionalized fact in the life of the Church. Conversely, the insecurity of Paul's own standing in Jerusalem (shown by the Judaistic attacks on his work and by his own apprehension concerning the reception of the Collection in Jerusalem, Rom 15:31) indicates that his position has not been clearly and fully institutionalized.

I stated above that proximity to sacred *ratio* is the foremost basis of authority in the Primitive Church. In combination with the time factor (temporal proximity to the sacred) this means that sacred tradition is of great importance in the Church. Any new custom, invention or revelation must be fundamentally in accordance with existing sacred tradition. Examples of this can be found at all levels of Church life: local custom, prophecy or gnosis must conform to what the apostle considers to be true and upbuilding (Gal 1:8, 1 Cor 5:1–5, 8:1 f, 10:23, 14:37 f),[3] and must sometimes also conform to the general practice of the Church (1 Cor 7:17, 11:16, 14:34). The preaching of Apollos and other teachers in Corinth must accord with the foundation Paul has laid (1 Cor 3:10 f)[4], and Paul's own "gospel" must at one point in his career be laid before the notables of Jerusalem to receive their approval (Gal 2:2, 6).

The result is that as time passes the institutionalization of Church life

3. Cf. the discussion of *Delorme* on how emerging offices are received by the existing community of believers (1974:329–342).
4. On this "foundation", see *Gerhardsson* (1961:295, 302 f) and *Roloff* on "Grundkerygma" (1965:92, 104, 134 f n. 320).

and of authority becomes increasingly less free to develop in any possible direction. Cult, doctrine and organization do not simply develop out of free interaction between members of small independent local groups of Christians. On the contrary, what we see is a controlled process of development although it is not controlled by any one person or central institution but by a corporate tradition which guides the emerging functional differentiation and its institutionalization.[5]

This "controlled" institutionalization is the outcome of cumulative institutionalization. At times this crystallizes out in special acts of authoritative interpretation such as the Apostolic Council, or in a period of extensive secondary institutionalization. The prime example of the latter phenomenon is the period following the resurrection of the Lord, when His highly personal, supernatural and radical authority is medialized, i.e. institutionalized in the form of media such as the verbal Jesus-tradition, the Christian ethos and code of behaviour, the cult, the group of plenipotentiaries. All these institutions are considered to mediate the authority of the Lord, and this re-institutionalization of the previous primary institutionalization of charismatic group life naturally has a consolidating and direction-defining effect on the life of the Church that is profound and unalterable.

The sacred tradition that Paul transmits to the churches he founds is the result of this process, and the conversion of these new Christians is thus an incorporation into the life of a Church that has already attained to a fairly high degree of institutionalization. Still there is ample scope for continued (or tertiary) institutionalization within the local church as, for instance, the institutionalization of local leadership and authority. As we see in 1 Cor 12—14 there is a certain degree of restriction—Paul's rationalizing interpretation of the development of authority in this church contains an unmistakable element of control, he modifies some parts of local institutionalization at the same time as he consolidates it. Here as always legitimation follows the facts, explaining, justifying, modifying and endorsing them.[6]

3. Dialectical Authority

In studying the phenomenon of authority within the Primitive Church we can observe a dialectic operating at different levels. Opposing forces or elements interact without cancelling each other in a constant process of interplay or feedback.

5. " . . . no single individual, not Peter or Paul or Mark or John, was ever in a position entirely to *control* the Gospel by his own understanding of it. It is in *'the life of the Church'* (or 'the Spirit' or 'the Paraclete') that the real springs of the history lie . . . ", *Dix* (1953:110).
6. *Berger-Luckmann* (1967:67–72, 93, et passim), *Martin* (1972:19).

The *nature* of authority as such, as discussed in Chapter 4, is dialectical in that it is based upon the opposing elements of insight and trust and is inevitably transformed into another type of relationship if it is based exclusively on one of these grounds. In charismatic authority the dialectic between the charismatic leader's message and his personal extraordinary qualities has often been discussed, both factors being needed if charismatic authority is to emerge and be maintained.

It is obvious that the *exercise* of authority in the Primitive Church is of a dialectical character. In her analysis of life in the local Pauline churches *Jaubert* finds the dialectical principle at work in a number of contexts. In the building up of the church, in brotherly exhortation and correction, in discerning the truth of the Spirit, in caring for other Christians, in mutual submission—everywhere "a kind of dialectic is established between the responsibility of all and the charge of some".[7] All Christians are responsible for and to a degree capable of performing these vital functions, but this never abolishes the need for special charges or offices which are expected to entail a greater degree of responsibility and capability in these respects. Congregation and office-holders can only function soundly if they recognize and act in accordance with this mutual, but asymmetric dependence.

Something of the same dialectic is found in the relation between the apostle Paul, who has a unique calling to preach the Gospel to the Gentiles, and all others who "labour" at the same task, in particular his co-workers. The latter cannot work independently of the apostolic "foundation", but they themselves by no means lack spiritual authority.

In the development or *institutionalization* of authority the dialectical principle is conspicuously at work. If we consider the church in Corinth this seems at first sight not to be the case, as persons with ecstatic-pneumatic gifts apparently dominate the interior life of the congregation at the expense of those endowed with other gifts. But Paul's corrective comments on this state (1 Cor 12—14) show us how he envisaged a healthier (and perhaps also more typical) development of local authority: many have received gifts, all share in the responsibility of using their gifts to build up the church, pneumatic and non-pneumatic gifts alike are spiritual gifts of grace and therefore valuable and indispensable to the one "Body" that is the church. This is no mere utopian programme even if it is not a description of actual conditions in the Corinthian church. Paul's intervention as

---

7. "Une sorte de dialectique s'instaure ainsi entre la responsibilité de tous et la charge de certains", *Jaubert* (1974:25), and see the whole section pp. 23–28.

such must be considered to give the interplay of pneumatic and non-pneumatic gifts an impulse in the right direction. Paul's letter helps to start the
dialectical process whereby a sound institutionalization of local authority
will develop.

This practice of giving instruction by letter is also evidence of the dialectic existing between apostle and local church or, more precisely, between
apostolic intention and social reality in a local church. What Paul is confronted with in Corinth is in part at least the result of his own founding
and the concomitant transmission of contact with the sacred, and on that
account is neither wholly commendable nor wholly condemnable. Paul
knows that he has transmitted powers over which he does not have control.
In spite of the fact that the gifts of speaking in tongues, of prophecy, wisdom, etc. have been abused they must be accorded respect as genuine manifestations of the Holy Spirit, and cannot simply be repudiated. What is
needed is not to re-found the church but to correct a one-sided institutionalization of gifts that have some genuine authority. Thus true institutionalization of authority in the local church is effected through the dialectical
interplay between the greater, institutionalized apostolic authority and the
lesser, emergent local authority.

The authority relation between Barnabas and Paul develops in a similar
fashion, as does that between Paul and the leaders of the Jerusalem church.
Paul's charisma is evident to all parties and lies behind his dynamic authority. But his authority cannot be isolated from its context, as the truth is that
it develops in constant interplay with older and consequently more institutionalized authority. In the case of Barnabas Paul eventually separated
from him without denying his authority, as theologically and sociologically
they were equals. But in the case of the relation existing between Paul and
the church of Jerusalem there was not such separation; Paul continues to
be internally and externally bound to this church. I consider that a separation between Paul and Jerusalem similar to that between Paul and Barnabas would have been theologically and sociologically impossible. Paul
could not deny that the authority of the Jerusalem church and of the first
apostles was a superior charismatic authority that placed them closer to the
source of all authority, the Lord Himself. Thus even a form of separation
that entailed not repudiation of their authority but only missionary activity
totally independent of the church in Jerusalem would have amounted to a
separation from the source of authority of that church. On the other hand
it was also impossible for the Jerusalem leaders to deny Paul's charismatic
authority and the authenticity of his calling as an apostle of Christ with a
special commission to preach to the Gentiles (Gal 2:7–9). In short, Paul

needs the recognition of the Jerusalem apostles and they cannot withhold this recognition—a clear example of the dialectical nature of authority in the Primitive Church.

Lastly we have to take into account the dialectical character of the institutionalization process itself, which was discussed above in Chapter 6. The institutionalization of charismatic authority was there shown to be a complex dialectical process between factors such as the "ideal interests" of the members of the charismatic group (their missionary zeal, their vision of or programme for the future as well as their theology), the "routinization" of their motives (getting a livelihood off the charismatic movement becomes important), and the systemic needs of the movement (the needs of keeping the group going financially, organizationally, etc.).

C. METHODOLOGICAL CONCLUSIONS

If this investigation has achieved nothing else it has at least shown the complexity of authority in the Primitive Church—a charismatic form of authority that is continuously being institutionalized and reinstitutionalized through the dialectical interactions of persons, institutions and social forces at many different levels within the structure of the Church. But as it is not very helpful to summarize by listing an agglomeration of abstract nouns I will attempt to point to some methodological consequences.

1. The Fallacy of Idealism

Idealism in historical research can be roughly described as the view that the determining factors of the historical process are ideas and nothing else, and that all developments, conflicts and influences are at bottom developments of, and conflicts and influences between ideas. This conception can scarcely be said to be represented in a thorough-going fashion in any of the scholarly works cited in this investigation, but my contention is that a degree of unconscious idealism has nonetheless influenced even some of the best of them, such as *Bultmann* (1953), *von Campenhausen* (1969), *Hainz* (1972), *Käsemann* (1942, 1955, 1960), *Schütz* (1975) and *Schweizer* (1959). To be sure historical phenomena are analysed and described with great diligence and care—the attentive reader will have noticed that on most points of historical fact there is no fundamental disagreement between these works and my work. But the methodologically fateful step comes with the next stage of the work, where the historical phenomena are often interpreted as being directly formed by underlying theological structures. These structures are found by a sophisticated analysis of the texts where the New Testament author (for instance Paul) comments theo-

logically on the phenomena in question (e.g. 1 Cor 12 on pneumatic gifts).
Thus what is in reality a secondary reaction (Paul's theology of charisma)
on primary, concrete phenomena in the social world (the pneumatic gifts
in Corinth) is misinterpreted as being the structuring principle of that
social world.[8] This confusion between phenomena and descriptions of
these phenomena is due to a fundamental deficiency in methodology. What
is missing in this type of theologically determined historical reconstruction
is an awareness of the continuous dialectic between ideas and social structures. Social life is determined by social factors, including the opinions and
consequently the theology of the actors. Paul's theology of charisma probably did have an effect on the Corinthian church, but not before it had been
formulated and certainly not in any simple, straightforward fashion as if
ideas could act directly on social structures.

Another example of this confusion is the attempt to reconstruct the conflict between Paul and the church in Corinth that we observe in 2 Cor 10—
13 as being an almost purely theological conflict between different chris-
tologies and other theoretical conceptions.[9] When discussing the import of
the Collection some authors conclude that here can exist no legal or authoritatively binding relation between the Jerusalem church and the Gentile
churches unless expressed in a positive law or a formulated theory (theological statement) about it—an influence from idealistic methodology. And
when the attempt is made to determine the real Pauline church order or
polity by analysing how Paul motivates and interprets relations of obedience and the nature of his instructions[10], or by analysing his theology of
charisma while expressly disregarding the historical information available
on Paul's actual exercise of authority[11], we must point out still another
occurrence of idealistic fallacy.

It is a fallacy because it analyses only part of the historical reality while

8. *Brockhaus* summarizes his history of the research on ministry and charisma since
1880: "Was bei allen diesen . . . Arbeiten immer wieder auffällt, ist, dass sie me-
thodisch zu wenig differenzieren zwischen einer Rekonstruktion der Gemeindefunk-
tionen in den frühchristlichen—oder auch nur den paulinischen—Gemeinden einer-
seits und der Exegese der Stellen, an denen Paulus von Charismen spricht, ander-
erseits", (1975:93, cf. p. 95).
9. Cf. the approach of *Georgi* (1964), *Schmithals* (1965) and *Betz* (1972).
10. See the programmatic declaration of *von Campenhausen* (1957:31–33) that it
is by analysing Paul's reasons ("Begründungen") for and interpretations of his instructions that one can find the original church order or church law. As *Dombois*
points out in his criticism of von Campenhausen (1961:66 f, 150) this means that
only the thinking of the subject himself (Paul) confers a legal character on any action
or instruction, while his actions in themselves are considered non-legal in character.
See also his similar criticism of *Käsemann's* distinction between pneumatic and traditional law, *Dombois* (1961:152 f, 800–802).
11. *Schütz* refers to "an implicit theory of order embedded in the articulation of
apostolic authority" and finds the letters are not in themselves sufficient to answer the

considering this to be the entire or essential reality. But Paul's theological thinking is only part of the dialectical process by which authority is institutionalized in the Church. It is not even the primary part of the process as it began before he arrived on the scene and is throughout determined by many other persons and factors. Of course it is perfectly legitimate to analyse Paul's theology, for instance concerning what it says about his apostolic authority. But if one adds anything about his actual apostolic authority the step has been taken from studying the history of ideas to studying the history of concrete social facts which makes it necessary for the investigator to take into account what actually happened between Paul and his churches. To state this is not to make a mistake in the opposite direction, which may be termed the materialistic fallacy, where it is maintained that all ideas are only superstructures of purely social processes determined by economic, political and social forces only. (As far as I can see this type of fallacy does not mar New Testament scholarship today.) Both these simplifications, the idealistic and the materialistic, are countered by a methodological stance that takes into account the dialectic between ideas and facts, theology and social structure characterizing the history of the Primitive Church.[12]

2. A Dialectical Approach

It is necessary to advance from a purely theological investigation of what was thought about these phenomena by the then actors to an investigation of the actual structure of authority. It is also necessary to advance from a purely "historical" account of the phenomena to an analysis of the nature of authority in the Primitive Church. The interdependence and dialectical development of theology and social structure is the central fact that must be taken as a starting point for historical research.

I have argued that the authority structure in the church is an "organic" system, where the different constituents are bound to one another in mutual, but not symmetric dependence.[13] This means that no authority rela-

---

question of "what could and could not emerge from Paul's conception of authority" (1975:263). To be sure they give us historical information on how Paul acted in this respect, "yet no amount of such detail would reveal the outline of an 'order' in its full scope" (p. 264)—that is, no amount of historical information would be sufficient to reveal a Pauline church 'order'. If that is the case one wonders whether "the Pauline church order" is (or even could be) a historical phenomenon at all or if it is something that will for ever belong to the world of ideas.

12. Cf. K. Berger (1977b:219). Drane (1975) is a good example of the trend in recent scholarship to see Paul's theology as developing dialectically through contact with actual history in the different churches.

13. I have borrowed this useful concept from Jaubert (1974:26). This is also the source of its use by Sesboué (1974:370).

tion should be treated in complete isolation from other authority relations if it is to be understood correctly. Paul's standing in Galatia or Corinth in the mid-fifties is affected by his standing in Jerusalem and by what was there agreed upon more than five years previously—to mention but one example of how the authority relations in the Church are interrelated.

I have also argued that the nature of authority is such that it is in itself a social phenomenon, not a theological interpretation of social phenomena. To be sure authority in the Primitive Church is predominantly charismatic, i.e. connected with sacred *ratio,* but this does not alter the fact that it is socially determined and socially determining and is part of the continuous institutionalization process of this historical movement. This means that moral ideals or theological conceptions have singularly little influence in comparison with institutionalized authority as long as they are only one man's idea, even if that man be Paul. I am not denying the considerable effect Paul's theology had on the Church, but merely pointing out that it does not and cannot operate directly on historical processes. Paul's theology becomes effective in Church life only in so far as he is part of its authority structure.

I have not ventured to forward any detailed criticism of the historical and theological work of others concerning church order in the Primitive Church. Rather this investigation constitutes the prolegomena to a relevant historical and theological analysis of the subject. I believe, however, that I have shown by the type of analysis undertaken in Part II of this investigation that historical research in this field would profit by undertaking to analyse social structures before moving on to theological structures. And as theology is or should be concerned with reality I consider that a historical investigation taking into account the complexity of reality with its constant dialectic between ideas and social structures would also result in an improvement of the theological analysis of church order in the Primitive Church.

Bibliography

All abbreviations of journals, series, lexica and editions follow "Theologische Realenzyklopädie. Abkürzungsverzeichnis zusammengestellt von Siegfried Schwertner", Berlin-New York 1976, Part V, which is an improved version of S. *Schwertner, Internationale Abkürzungsverzeichnis für Theologie und Grenzgebiete, 1974 (IATG).*

Agrell, Göran
    1976   Work, Toil and Sustenance. An Examination of the View of Work in the New Testament, Taking into Consideration Views Found in Old Testament, Intertestamental and Early Rabbinic Writings, Lund, 1976.

Allo, E.-B.
    1935   Saint Paul, Première Épitre aux Corinthiens, 2. ed. (EtB), Paris, 1935.

Arendt, Hannah
    1970   Om våld, Stockholm, 1970.

Asplund, Johan
    1970   "George Herbert Mead" (in J. Asplund (ed.), Sociologiska teorier. Studier i sociologins historia, 3. ed., Stockholm, 1970, 132–147).

Austgen, Robert J.
    1966   Natural Motivation in the Pauline Epistles, Notre Dame, 1966.

Bachrach, Peter–Baratz, Morton S.
    1972   Makt och fattigdom. Teori och praktik. Stockholm, 1972.

Barrett, C. K.
    1953   "Paul and the 'Pillar' Apostles" (in Studia Paulina. FS (=Festschrift) J. de Zwaan, Haarlem, 1953, 1–19).
    1963   "Cephas and Corinth" (in Abraham unser Vater. Juden und Christen im Gespräch über die Bibel. FS O. Michel, ed. by Betz-Hengel-Schmidt (AGSU 5), Leiden, 1963, 1–12).
    1964   "Christianity at Corinth" (BJRL 46, 1964, 267–297).
    1969   "Titus" (in Neotestamentica et Semitica. FS M. Black, ed. by Ellis-Wilcox, Edinburgh, 1969, 1–14).
    1970   *"Pseudapostoloi* (2 Cor 11, 13)" (in Mélanges Bibliques. FS B. Rigaux, Gembloux, 1970, 377–396).

1971   "Paul's Opponents in II Corinthians" (NTS 17, 1971, 233–254).

1973a   A Commentary on The First Epistle to the Corinthians (BNTC), 2 ed., London, 1973.

1973b   A Commentary on The Second Epistle to the Corinthians (BNTC), London, 1973.

Bauer, Walter

1958   Griechisch-Deutsches Wörterbuch zu den Schriften des Neuen Testaments und der übrigen urchristlichen Literatur, 5. ed., Berlin, 1958.

Bellebaum, Alfred

1959   "Institution. III. Die Institution in soziologischer Sicht" (StL, vol 4, 1959, 330–334).

Bendix, Reinhard

1960   Max Weber. An Intellectual Portrait, London, 1960.

1971   "Charismatic Leadership" (in R. Bendix–G. Roth, Scholarship and Partisanship: Essays on Max Weber, Berkeley, 1971, 170–187).

Bensman, Joseph–Givant, Michel

1975   "Charisma and Modernity: The Use and Abuse of a Concept" (Social Research 42, New York, 1975, 570–613).

Berger, Klaus

1970   "Zu den sogenannten Sätzen heiligen Rechts" (NTS 17, 1970, 10–40).

1977a   "Almosen für Israel. Zum historischen Kontext der paulinischen Kollekte" (NTS 23, 1977, 180–204).

1977b   Exegese des Neuen Testaments. Neue Wege vom Text zur Auslegung, Heidelberg, 1977.

1977c   "Wissenssoziologie und Exegese des Neuen Testaments (Kairos 19, 1977, 124–133).

Berger, Peter L.

1954   "The Sociological Study of Sectarianism" (Social Research 21, New York, 1954, 467–485).

1963a   "Charisma and Religious Innovation: The Social Location of Israelite Prophecy" (ASR 28, 1963, 940–950).

1963b   Invitation to Sociology. A Humanistic Perspective, Harmondsworth, 1963.

1969   The Sacred Canopy. Elements of a Sociological Theory of Religion, Garden City, 1969.

1965   –Kellner, Hansfried, "Arnold Gehlen and the Theory of Institutions" (Social Research 32, New York, 1965, 110–115).

1967   –Luckmann, Thomas, The Social Construction of Reality. A Treatise in the Sociology of Knowledge, Garden City, 1967.

Bernsdorf, Wilhelm

1969   "Autorität" (in W. Bernsdorf (ed.), Wörterbuch der Soziologie, 2. ed., Stuttgart, 1969, 73–77).

Betz, Hans Dieter

1972   Der Apostel Paulus und die sokratische Tradition. Eine exegetische Untersuchung zu seiner "Apologie" 2 Korinther 10—13 (BHTh 45), Tübingen, 1972.

Bierstedt, Robert

1954   "The Problem of Authority" (in M. Berger (ed), Freedom and Control in Modern Society, New York, 1954, 67–81).

Binder, Hermann

1976   "Die angebliche Krankheit des Paulus" (ThZ 32, 1976, 1–13).

Bjerkelund, Carl J.
1967   *PARAKALÔ*. Form, Funktion und Sinn der parakalô-Sätze in den
       paulinischen Briefen (BTN 1), Oslo, 1967.
Blau, Peter M.
1963   "Critical Remarks on Weber's Theory of Authority" (Amer. Polit.
       Sci. Rev. 57, Menasha, 1963, 305–316).
1964   Exchange and Power in Social Life, New York, 1964.
Bochénski, J. M.
1974   Was ist Autorität? Einführung in die Logik der Autorität (HerBü
       439), Freiburg i. Br., 1974.
Boer, Willis Peter de
1962   The Imitation of Paul. An Exegetical Study, Kampen, 1962.
Bohannan, Paul
1965   "The Differing Realms of Law" (Amer. Anthropologist, Spec. Publ.,
       vol 67, part 2, Menasha, 1965, 33–42).
Bonnard, Pierre
1953   L'épître de saint Paul aux Galates (CNT(N)9), Neuchatel-Paris,
       1953.
Bornkamm, Günther
1956   "Herrenmahl und Kirche bei Paulus" (ZThK 53, 1956, 312 ff; now in
       Studien zu Antike und Urchristentum, Ges. Aufsätze, Bd II (BEvTh
       28), München, 1963, 138–176).
1959   *"presbys ktl"* (ThWNT 6, 651–683), Stuttgart 1959.
1966   "Das missionarische Verhalten des Paulus nach 1 Kor 9, 19–23 und
       in der Apostelgeschichte" (in Studies in Luke-Acts. FS O. Schubert,
       ed. by Keck-Martin, Philadelphia, 1980, 194–207; now in Geschichte
       und Glaube II, Ges. Aufsätze IV (BEvTh 53), München, 1971, 149–
       161).
1969   Paulus (UB 119 D), Stuttgart 1969.
1971   "Der Römerbrief als Testament des Paulus" (in Geschichte und
       Glaube II, Ges. Aufsätze IV (BEvTh 53), München, 1971, 120–139).
Bourke, Myles M.
1968   "Reflections on Church Order in the New Testament" (CBQ 30, 1968,
       493–511).
Braun, Herbert
1966   Qumran und das Neue Testament I—II, Tübingen, 1966.
Brockhaus, Ulrich
1975   Charisma und Amt. Die paulinische Charismenlehre auf dem Hinter-
       grund der frühchristlichen Gemeindefunktionen, 2. ed., Wuppertal,
       1975.
Brown, Raymond E.
1974   The Virginal Conception & Bodily Resurrection of Jesus, London,
       1974.
Brown, Raymond E.–Donfried, Karl P.–Reumann, John (eds.)
1973   Peter in the New Testament. A Collaborative Assessment by Protes-
       tant and Roman Catholic Scholars, Minneapolis-New York, 1973.
Brox, Norbert
1969   Die Pastoralbriefe (RNT 7:2), 4. ed., Regensburg, 1969.
Budillon, Jean
1971   "La première épitre aux Corinthiens et la controverse sur les minis-
       tères" (Istina 16, Paris, 1971, 471–488).

Bultmann, Rudolf
1953   Theologie des Neuen Testaments, Tübingen, 1953.
Bultmann, Rudolf
1959   review of Munck, Johannes, Paulus und die Heilsgeschichte, Aarhus-København, 1954 (ThLZ 84, 1959, 481–486).
Burchard, Christoph
1970   Der dreizehnte Zeuge. Traditions- und kompositions-geschichtliche Untersuchungen zu Lukas' Darstellung der Frühzeit des Paulus (FRLANT 103), Göttingen, 1970.
Burton, E. de Witt
1921   A Critical and Exegetical Commentary on the Epistle to the Galatians (ICC), Edinburgh, 1921.
Campenhausen, Hans von
1941   "Recht und Gehorsam in der ältesten Kirche" (ThBl 20, 1941, 279–95, now in Aus der Frühzeit des Christentums, Tübingen, 1963, 1–29).
1957   "Die Begründung kirchlicher Entscheidungen beim Apostel Paulus" (SHAW 1957:2, now in Aus der Frühzeit des Christentums, Tübingen, 1963, 30–80).
1969   Ecclesiastical Authority and Spiritual Power in the Church of the Three First Centuries, London, 1969.
Cartwright, Dorwin
1965   "Influence, Leadership, Control" (in J. G. March (ed.), Handbook of Organizations, Chicago 1965, 1–47).
Catchpole, David R.
1977   "Paul, James and the Apostolic Decree" (NTS 23, 1977, 428–444).
Cerfaux, Lucien
1965   La Théologie de l'Église suivant saint Paul, 3. ed. (UnSa 54), Paris, 1965.
Chadwick, Henry
1959   The Circle and the Ellipse. Rival Concepts of Authority in the Early Church, Oxford, 1959.
Chevallier, Max-Alain
1966   Esprit de Dieu, paroles d'hommes. Le rôle de l'esprit dans le ministères de la parole selon l'apôtre Paul, Neuchatel, 1966.
Cohen, D. L.
1972   "The Concept of Charisma and the Analysis of Leadership" (PolSt 20, 1972, 299–305).
Cohen, Jere–Hazelrigg, Lawrence E.–Pope, Whitney
1975   "De-Parsonizing Weber: A Critique of Parson's Interpretation of Weber's Sociology" (ASR 40, 1975, 229–241).
Colson, Jean
1962   "Der Diakonat im Neuen Testament" (in K. Rahner–H. Vorgrimler (eds.), Diaconia in Christo. Über die Erneuerung des Diakonates (QD 15–16), Freiburg, 1962, 3–22).
Conzelmann, Hans
1969a Der erste Brief an die Korinther (KEK 5), Göttingen, 1969.
1969b Geschichte des Urchristentums (GNT 5), Göttingen, 1969.
Cothenet, Édouard
1972   "Prophetisme dans le Nouveau Testament", (DBS 8, Paris, 1972, 1222–1337).

Dahl, Nils Astrup
1967   "Paul and the Church at Corinth according to 1 Corinthians 1—4" (in Christian History and Interpretation. FS J. Knox, ed. by Farmer–Moule–Niebuhr, Cambridge, 1967, 313–336).
Dahlström, Edmund
1966   "Exchange, Influence and Power" (Acta sociologica 9, Copenhagen, 1966, 237–284).
Daube, David
1959   "Concessions to Sinfulness in Jewish Law" (JJS 10, 1959, 1–13).
1971   "Pauline Contributions to a Pluralistic Culture: Recreation and beyond" (in Miller, Donald G.–Hadidian, Dikran Y. (eds.), Jesus and man's hope, vol II, Pittsburgh 1971, 223–245).
Dautzenberg, Gerhard
1969   "Der Verzicht auf das apostolische Unterhaltsrecht. Eine exegetische Untersuchung zu 1 Kor 9" (Bib. 50, 1969, 212–232).
1975   Urchristliche Prophetie. Ihre Erforschung, ihre Voraussetzungen im Judentum und ihre Struktur im ersten Korintherbrief (BWANT 104), Stuttgart, 1975.
Davies, W. D.
1974   The Gospel and the Land: Early Christianity and Jewish Territorial Doctrine, Berkeley-London 1974.
Delorme, Jean
1974   "Diversité et unité des ministères d'après le Nouveau Testament" (in J. Delorme (ed.), Le ministère et les ministères selon le Nouveau Testament. Dossier exégétique et réflexion théologique, Paris, 1974, 283–346).
Deltgen, Florian
1969   "Was kann unter einer 'Bewegung' verstanden werden?" (KZS.S 13, 1969, 410–429).
Dias, Patrick V.
1967   Vielfalt der Kirche in der Vielfalt der Jünger, Zeugen und Diener (ÖF.E 2), Freiburg i.Br., 1967.
Dibelius, Martin
1937   " 'Bischöfe' und 'Diakonen' in Philippi" (HNT 11, Tübingen 1937, 60–62, now in Kertelge (ed.), Das kirchliche Amt im Neuen Testament, Darmstadt 1977, 413–417).
Dix, Gregory
1953   Jew and Greek. A Study in the Primitive Church, London, 1953.
Dobschütz, Ernst von
1910   Die Thessalonicher-Briefe (KEK 10), 7. ed., Göttingen, 1910.
Dodd, Charles Harold
1953   "ENNOMOS CHRISTOU" (in Studia Paulina. FS J. de Zwaan, Haarlem, 1953, 96–110).
Dombois, Hans
1961   Das Recht der Gnade. Ökumenisches Kirchenrecht I (FBESG 20), Witten, 1961.
Donfried, Karl P.
        See Brown, Raymond E.–Donfried, Karl P.–Reumann J.
Drane, John W.
1975   Paul, Libertine or Legalist? A Study in the Theology of the Major Pauline Epistles, London, 1975.

Dreier, Ralf
  1972   Das kirchliche Amt. Eine kirchenrechtstheoretische Studie (Jus Eccl
         15), München, 1972.
Dullaart, Leo
  1975   Kirche und Ekklesiologie. Die Institutionenlehre Arnold Gehlens als
         Frage an den Kirchenbegriff in der gegewärtigen systematischen
         Theologie (GT.S 16), München-Mainz, 1975.
Dungan, David L.
  1971   The Sayings of Jesus in the Churches of Paul. The Use of the Synop-
         tic Tradition in the Regulation of Early Church Life, Oxford, 1971.
Dupont, Jacques
  1967   Études sur les Actes des Apotres (LeDiv 45), Paris, 1967.
Eckert, Jost
  1971   Die urchristliche Verkündigung im Streit zwischen Paulus und seinen
         Gegnern nach dem Galaterbrief (BU 6), Regensburg, 1971.
Ehrhardt, Arnold
  1969   The Acts of the Apostles. Ten Lectures, Manchester, 1969.
Eid, Volker
         See Hoffman, Paul–Eid, Volker.
Eisenstadt, Shmuel Noah
  1965   "The Study of Processes of Institutionalization, Institutional Change,
         and Comparative Institutions" (in Essays on Comparative Institutions,
         New York, 1965, 3–40).
  1968a "Introduction. Charisma and Institution Building: Max Weber and
         Modern Sociology" (in Max Weber, On Charisma and Institution
         Building. Selected papers ed. by S. N. Eisenstadt, Chicago-London,
         1968, IX–LVI).
  1968b "Social Institutions" (IESS, vol 14, New York-London 1968, 409–
         429).
  1973   "Tradition and Social Structure" (in Tradition, Change and Moder-
         nity, New York, 1973, 119–150).
Eister, Alan W.
  1967   "Toward a Radical Critique of Church-Sect Typologizing: Comment
         on 'Some Critical Observations on the Church-Sect Dimension' "
         (JSSR 6, 1967, 85–90).
  1973   "H. Richard Niebuhr and the Paradox of Religious Organization: A
         Radical Critique" (in C. Y. Glock–Ph.E. Hammond (eds.), Beyond
         the Classics? Essays in the Scientific Study of Religion, New York,
         1973, 355–408).
Ekeh, Peter P.
  1974   Social Exchange Theory. The Two Traditions, London, 1974.
Ellis, E. Earle
  1971   "Paul and His Co-Workers" (NTS 17, 1971, 437–452).
  1974   " 'Spiritual' Gifts in the Pauline Community" (NTS 20, 1974, 128–
         144).
Emmet, Dorothy
  1972   Function, Purpose and Powers. Some Concepts in the Study of Indi-
         viduals and Societies, 2. ed., London, 1972.
Etzioni, Amitai
  1961   A Comparative Analysis of Complex Organizations. On Power, In-
         volvement, and their Correlates, New York, 1961.

Fascher, Erich
  1937a "Timotheos" (PRE, 2. Reihe, Band VI, Stuttgart 1937, 1342–1354).
  1937b "Titus" (PRE, 2. Reihe, Band VI, Stuttgart 1937, 1579–1586).
Filson, Floyd V.
  1939 "The Significance of the Early House Churches" (JBL 58, 1939, 105–112).
Fitzmyer, Joseph A.
  1970a "Acts of the Apostles", introduction and commentary on chapters 6–28 (JBC, vol II, art. 45:1–8, 35–119), London, 1970.
  1970b "A Life of Paul" (JBC, vol II, London, 1970, art. 46).
  1970c "The Letter to the Galatians" (JBC, vol II, London, 1970, art. 49).
Fjärstedt, Biörn
  1974 Synoptic tradition in 1 Corinthians. Themes and clusters of theme words in 1 Corinthians 1—4 and 9, Uppsala, 1974.
Forkman, Göran
  1972 The Limits of the Religious Community. Expulsion from the religious community within the Qumran sect, within Rabbinic Judaism, and within Primitive Christianity (CB. NT 5), Lund, 1972.
Fridrichsen, Anton
  1947 The Apostle and his Message (UUA 1947:3), Uppsala, 1947.
Friedland, William H.
  1964 "For a sociological concept of charisma" (Social Forces 43, Baltimore, 1964–65, 18–26).
Friedrich, Carl J.
  1958 "Authority, Reason and Discretion" (in C. J. Friedrich (ed), Authority (Nomos I), Cambridge, Mass., 1958, 27–48).
  1960 "Politische Autorität und Demokratie" (ZPol 7, 1960, 1–12).
  1961 "Political Leadership and the Problem of the Charismatic Power" (The Journal of Politics 23, Gainsville, 1961, 3–24).
  1963 Man and His Government. An Empirical Theory of Politics, New York, 1963.
  1964 "Authority" (in J. Gould–W. L. Kolb (eds.), A Dictionary of the Social Sciences, New York, 1964, 42–44).
  1972 Tradition and Authority, London, 1972.
Friedrich, Gerhard
  1963 "Die Gegner des Paulus im 2. Korintherbrief" (in Abraham unser Vater. Juden und Christen im Gespräch über die Bibel. FS O. Michel, ed., by Betz-Hengel-Schmidt (AGSU 5), Leiden, 1963, 181–215).
  1970 "Das Problem der Autorität im Neuen Testament" (in G. Krems–R. Mumm (eds.), Autorität in der Krise, Regensburg-Göttingen, 1970, 9–50).
Fries, Heinrich
  1970 "Autorität in der Krise" (in G. Krems–R. Mumm (eds.), Autorität in der Krise, Regensburg—Göttingen, 1970, 51–78).
Fürst, Heinrich
  1963 "Paulus und die 'Säulen' der jerusalemer Urgemeinde (Gal 2,6–9)" (in Studiorum paulinorum Congressus, II (An Bib 18), Romae, 1963, 3–10).
Funk, Robert W.
  1967 "The Apostolic Parousia: Form and Significance" (in Christian His-

tory and Interpretation. FS J. Knox, ed. by Farmer–Moule–Niebuhr, Cambridge, 1967, 249–268).

Gager, John G.
1975 Kingdom and Community: The Social World of Early Christianity, Englewood Cliffs, 1975.

Gasque, Ward
1975 A History of the Criticism of the Acts of the Apostles (BGBE 17), Tübingen, 1975.

Geertz, Clifford
1968 "Religion as a Cultural System" (in M. Bainton (ed.), Anthropological Approaches to the Study of Religion, London Crawley, 1968, 1–46).

Georgi, Dieter
1964 Die Gegner des Paulus im 2. Korintherbrief. Studien zur religiösen Propaganda in der Spätantike (WMANT 11), Neukirchen-Vluyn, 1964.
1965 Die Geschichte der Kollekte des Paulus für Jerusalem (ThF 38), Hamburg-Bergstedt, 1965.

Gerhardsson, Birger
1961 Memory and Manuscript. Oral Tradition and Written Transmission in Rabbinic Judaism and Early Christianity (ASNU 22), Uppsala. 1961.
1963 "Die Boten Gottes und dei Apostel Christi" (SvEÅ 27, 1963, 89–131).
1971 "Bibelns ethos" (in G. Wingren (ed.), Etik och kristen tro, Lund, 1971, 15–92).

Gewalt, Dietfried
1971 "Neutestamentliche Exegese und Soziologie" (EvTh 31, 1971, 87–99).

Givant, Michael
See Bensman, Joseph–Givant, Michael.

Gnilka, Joachim
1968 Der Philipperbrief (HThK 10:3), Freiburg . . . , 1968.
1969 "Geistliches Amt und Gemeinde nach Paulus" (Kairos 11, 1969, 95–104).

Goppelt, Leonhard
1965 "Kirchenleitung in der palästinischen Urkirche und bei Paulus" (in Reformatio und Confessio. FS W. Maurer, ed. by F. W. Kantzenbach–G. Müller, Berlin-Hamburg, 1965, 1–8).
1966 Die apostolische und nachapostolische Zeit (KIG 1A), 2. ed., Göttingen, 1966.

Grässer, Erich
1976– "Actaforschung seit 1960" (ThR 41, 1976, 141–194, 259–290 and
1977 42, 1977, 1–68).

Granger, Gilles
1973 "Geschehen und Struktur in den Wissenschaften vom Menschen" (in H. Naumann (ed.), Der moderne Strukturbegriff, Darmstadt, 1973, 207–248).

Greek New Testament
1975 Ed. by K. Aland, M. Black, C. M. Martini, B. M. Metzger and A. Wikgren, 3. ed., Stuttgart, 1975.

Greeven, Heinrich
1952/ "Propheten, Lehrer, Vorsteher bei Paulus. Zur Frage der 'Ämter' im
1953 Urchristentum" (ZNW 44, 1952/53, 1–43, now in Kertelge (ed.),
Das kirchliche Amt im Neuen Testament (WdF 439), Darmstadt,
1977, 305–361).

Grelot, Pierre
1971 "Sur l'origine des ministères dans les églises pauliniennes" (Istina 16,
Paris 1971, 453–469).
1974 "Les épîtres de Paul: la mission apostolique" (in J. Delorme (ed.),
Le ministère et les ministères selon le Nouveau Testament. Dossier
exégétique et réflexion théologique, Paris, 1974, 34–56).

Gundlach, Gustav
1959 "Institution. I. Die Institution in sozialphilosophischer Sicht" (StL,
vol 4, Freiburg, 1959, 324–327).

Gutierrez, Pedro
1968 La Paternité Spirituelle selon saint Paul, Paris, 1968.

Haas, Pieter de
1972 The Church as an Institution. Critical studies in the relation between
theology and sociology, Apeldoorn, 1972.

Haenchen, Ernst
1965 "Petrus-Probleme" (in Gott und Mensch. Ges. Aufsätze, Tübingen,
1965, 55–67).
1971 The Acts of the Apostles. A Commentary, Oxford, 1971.

Häring, Hermann
1972 Kirche und Kerygma. Das Kirchenbild in der Bultmannschule (ÖF.
E 6), Freiburg i. Br., 1972.

Hahn, Ferdinand
1974 "Der Apostolat im Urchristentum. Seine Eigenart und seine Voraussetzungen" (KuD 20, 1974, 54–77).

Hainz, Josef
1972 Ekklesia. Strukturen paulinischer Gemeinde-Theologie und Gemeinde-
Ordnung (BU 9), Regensburg, 1972.
1976a "Die Anfänge des Bischofs- und Diakonenamtes" (in J. Hainz (ed.),
Kirche im Werden, München 1976, 91–108).
1976b "Amt und Amtsvermittlung bei Paulus" (in J. Hainz (ed.), Kirche
im Werden, München, 1976, 109–122).

Harnack, Adolf von
1897 "Barnabas" (RE, vol II 1897, 410–413).
1910 Entstehung und Entwickelung der Kirchenverfassung und des Kir-
chenrechts in den zwei ersten Jahrhunderten, Leipzig, 1910.
1924 Die Mission und Ausbreitung des Christentums in den ersten drei
Jahrhunderten, I–II, 4. ed., Leipzig, 1923–24.

Hartmann, Heinz
1964 Funktionale Autorität. Systematische Abhandlung zu einem soziologischen Begriff (Soziol. Gegenwartsfragen, Heft 22), Stuttgart, 1964.

Hasenhüttl, Gotthold
1969 Charisma. Ordnungsprinzip der Kirche (ÖF. E 5), Freiburg . . . ,
1969.

Heiler, Friedrich
1961 Erscheinungsformen und Wesen der Religion (RM 1), Stuttgart,
1961.

Hengel, Martin
1972a "Christologie und neutestamentliche Chronologie. Zu einer Aporie in
      der Geschichte des Urchristentums" (in Neues Testament und Ges-
      chichte. Historisches Geschehen und Deutung im Neuen Testament.
      FS O. Cullman, ed. by H. Baltensweiler–B. Reicke, Zürich-Tübingen,
      1972, 43–67).
1972b "Die Ursprünge der christlichen Mission" (NTS 18, 1972, 15–38).
Hennen, Manfred–Prigge, Wolfgang-Ulrich
1977 Autorität und Herrschaft (EdF 75) Darmstadt, 1977.
Héring, Jean
1949 La première Épître de Saint Paul aux Corinthiens, (CNT(N) 7),
      Neuchatel-Paris, 1949.
Herten, Joachim
1976 "Charisma—Signal einer Gemeindetheologie des Paulus" (in J. Hainz.
      (ed.), Kirche im Werden, München, 1976, 57–90).
Heyl, Cornelius-Adalbert von
1963 "Autorität (ESL, 4. ed., Stuttgart, 1963, 129–132).
Hill, Michael
1973 "Max Weber (1864–1920)" (ET 84, 1972–73, 260–265).
Hoffmann, Paul–Eid, Volker
1975 Jesus von Nazareth und eine christliche Moral. Sittliche Perspektiven
      der Verkündigung Jesu (QD 66), Freiburg . . . , 1975.
Holl, Karl
1928 "Der Kirchenbegreiff des Paulus in seinem Verhältnis zu dem der
      Urgemeinde" (orig. in SPAW.PH 1921, 920–947; then reprinted in
      Holl's "Ges. Aufsätze zur Kirchengeschichte, II" Tübingen, 1928, 44–
      67, and lastly in K. H. Rengstorf (ed.), Das Paulusbild in der neueren
      deutschen Forschung (WdF 25), 2. ed., Darmstadt, 1969, 144–178.
      As customary I refer to the page numbers of the 1928 publication).
Holtz, Traugott
1966 "Zum Selbsverständnis des Apostels Paulus" (ThLZ 91, 1966, 321–
      330).
1974 "Die Bedeutung des Apostelkonzils für Paulus" (NT 16, 1974, 110–
      148).
Hurd Jr., John Coolidge
1965 The Origin of 1 Corinthians, London, 1965.
Hyldahl, Niels
1977 "Den korintiske situation—en skitse" (DTT 40, 1977, 18–30).
Iserloh, Erwin
1974 "Prophetisches Charisma und Leitungsauftrag des Amtes in Spannung
      und Begegnung als historisches Phänomen" (in W. Weber (ed.),
      Macht–Dienst–Herrschaft in Kirche und Gesellschaft, Freiburg, 1974,
      143–153).
Jaubert, Annie
1974 "Les Épîtres de Paul: le fait communautaire" (in J. Delorme (ed.),
      Le ministère et les ministères selon le Nouveau Testament. Dossier
      exégétique et réflexion théologique, Paris, 1974, 16–33).
Jervell, Jacob
1971 "Der Brief nach Jerusalem. Über Veranlassung und Adresse des
      Römerbriefes" (StTh 25, 1971, 61–73).
1976 "Der schwache Charismatiker" (in Rechtfertigung. FS E. Käsemann,

ed. by Friedrich–Pöhlmann–Stuhlmacher, Tübingen-Göttingen, 1976, 185–198).

Jewett, Robert
1971 "The Agitators and the Galatian Congregation" (NTS 17, 1971, 198–212).

Johnson, Benton
1963 "On Church and Sect" (ASR 28, 1963 539–549).

Jonas, Friedrich
1966 Die Institutionenlehre Arnold Gehlens (Soziale Forschung und Praxis 24). Tübingen, 1966.

Käsemann, Ernst
1942 "Die Legitimität des Apostels. Eine Untersuchung zu II Korinther 10—13" (ZNW 41, 1942, 33–71, now in K. H. Rengstorf (ed.), Das Paulusbild in der neueren deutschen Forschung (WdF 25) 2. ed., Darmstadt, 1969, 475–521). I refer to the page numbers of the original publication.
1952 "Die Johannesjünger in Ephesus" (ZThK 49, 1952, 144–154, now in Exegetische Versuche und Besinnungen I, 6. ed., Göttingen, 1970, 158–168).
1955 "Sätze heiligen Rechtes im Neuen Testament" (NTS 1, 1954/55, 248–260, now in Exegetische Versuche und Besinnungen II, 3. ed., Göttingen, 1970, 69–82).
1960 "Amt und Gemeinde im Neuen Testament" (in Exegetische Versuche und Besinnungen I Göttingen, 1960; cited after 6. ed., 1970, 109–134).
1974 An die Römer (HNT 8 a), 3. ed., Tübingen, 1974.

Kaplan, Abraham
See Lasswell, Harold D.–Kaplan, Abraham.

Karrer, Otto
1953 Um die Einheit der Christen. Die Petrusfrage. Ein Gespräch mit Emil Brunner, Oskar Cullmann, Hans von Campenhausen, Frankfurt a.M., 1953.

Kasting, Heinrich
1969 Die Anfänge der urchristlichen Mission. Eine historische Untersuchung (BEvTh 55), München, 1969.

Kellner, Hansfried
See Berger, Peter L.–Kellner, Hansfried.

Kertelge, Karl (ed.)
1977 Das kirchliche Amt im Neuen Testament (WdF 439), Darmstadt, 1977.

Kieffer, René
1977 Nytestamentlig teologi, Lund, 1977.

Kilpatrick, G. D.
1959 "Galatians 1, 18, *Historēsai Kēfan*" (in New Testament Essays. Studies in Memory of Th. W. Manson ed. by A. J. B. Higgins, Manchester, 1959, 144–149).

Das *kirchliche* Amt im Neuen Testament
See Kertelge, Karl.

Kirk, J. Andrew
1972– "Did 'Officials' in the New Testament Church receive a Salary?" (ET
1973 84, 1972–73, 105–108).

Knox, John
1955   The Early Church and the Coming Great Church, New York-Nash-
        ville, 1955.
Koester, Helmut
1971   " 'GNOMAI DIAPHOROI'. The Origin and Nature of Diversifica-
        tion in the History of Early Christianity" (in Robinson, M.–Koester,
        H., Trajectories through Early Christianity Philadelphia, 1971, 114–
        157).
Kraft, Heinrich
1975   "Die Anfänge des geistlichen Amts" (ThLZ 100, 1975, 81–98).
Kretschmar, Georg
1964   "Ein Beitrag zur Frage nach dem Ursprung frühchristlicher Askese"
        (ZThK 61, 1964, 27–67).
Kümmel, Werner Georg
1973   Einleitung in das Neue Testament, 17. ed., Heidelberg, 1973.
Küng, Hans
1967   Die Kirche (ÖF. E 1), Freiburg . . . , 1967.
Kugelmann, Richard
1970   "The First Letter to the Corinthians" (JBC, vol II, London, 1970, art.
        51).
Kuss, Otto
1971   Paulus. Die Rolle des Apostels in der theologischen Entwicklung der
        Urkirche (Ausleg. u. Verkündigung III), Regensburg, 1971.
Lachmann, L. M.
1970   The Legacy of Max Weber. Three Essays, London, 1970.
Larsson, Edvin
1964   "Paulus och den hellenistiska fösamlingsteologin. Ett blad i den
        vetenskapliga dogmbildningens historia" (SvEÅ 28–29, 1964, 81–
        110).
1976   "Beslutsprocessen i urkyrkan" (in Kyrkans beslutande organ. Om
        ämbetsstruktur och representationsstruktur i kyrkan, Lund, 1976, 5–
        25).
Lasswell, Harold D.–Kaplan, Abraham
1950   Power and Society. A framework for Political Inquiry, New Haven,
        1950.
Laub, Franz
1973   Eschatologische Verkündigung und Lebensgestaltung nach Paulus.
        Eine Untersuchung zum Wirken des Apostels beim Aufbau der
        Gemeinde in Thessalonike (BU 10), Regensburg, 1973.
1976   "Paulus als Gemeindegründer (1 Thess)" (in J. Hainz (ed.), Kirche
        im Werden, München . . . , 1976, 17–38).
Lemaire, André
1971   Les ministères aux origines de l'Église. Naissance de la triple hiérar-
        chie: évêques, presbytres, diacres (LeDiv 68), Paris, 1971.
1974   "Les épîtres de Paul: le diversité des ministères (in J. Delorme (ed.),
        Le ministère et les ministères selon le Nouveau Testament. Dossier
        exégétique et réflexion théologique, Paris, 1974, 57–73).
Linton, Olof
1932   Das Problem der Urkirche in der neueren Forschung. Eine kritische
        Darstellung (UUA 1932, 1:2) Uppsala, 1932.
1949   "The Third Aspect. A Neglected Point of View. A Study in Gal. i–ii
        and Acts ix and xv" (StTH 3, 1949, 79–95).

1970   Pauli mindre brev (Tolkning av NT IX), 2. ed., Stockholm, 1970.

Lipp, Wolfgang
1975   "Institution. I. Soziologisch" (EStL, Stuttgart, 1975, 1011–1018).

Löning, Karl
1974   "Herrschaft Gottes und Befreiung des Menschen II" (in W. Weber
       (ed.), Macht–Dienst–Herrschaft in Kirche und Gesellschaft Freiburg
       . . . , 1974, 47–60).

Lønning, Inge
1972   'Kanon im Kanon'. Zum dogmatischen Grundlagenproblem des neu-
       testamentlichen Kanons (FGLP 43), Oslo-München, 1972.

Loewenstein, Karl
1965   Max Webers staatspolitische Auffassungen in der Sicht unserer Zeit,
       Frankfurt a.M.—Bonn, 1965.

Lohse, Eduard
1964   "*Sīon ktl;* C. Zion—Jerusalem im Neuen Testament" (ThWNT 7,
       Stuttgart, 1964, 326–338).
1968   Die Briefe an die Kolosser und an Philemon (KEK 9:2) Göttingen,
       1968.

Luckmann, Thomas
       See Berger, Peter L.–Luckmann, Thomas.

Lütcke, Karl-Heinrich
1968   'Auctoritas' bei Augustin. Mit einer Einleitung zur römanischen
       Vorgeschichte des Begriffs (TBAW 44), Stuttgart, 1968.

Luhmann, Niklas
1964   "Zweck—Herrschaft—System. Grundbegriffe und Prämissen Max
       Webers" (Der Staat 3, Berlin, 1964, 129–158).
1969   "Normen in soziologischer Perspektive" (Soziale Welt 20, Göttingen,
       1969, 28–48).
1970   "Institutionalisierung. Funktion und Mechanismus im sozialen System
       der Gesellschaft" (in H. Schelsky (ed.) Zur Theorie der Institution,
       Düsseldorf, 1970, 27–41).
1972   "Die Organisierbarkeit von Religionen und Kirchen" (in J. Wössner
       (ed.), Religion im Umbruch, Stuttgart, 1972, 245–285).

McIntosh, Donald
1970   "Weber and Freud: On the Nature and Sources of Authority" (ASR
       35, 1970, 901–911).

Malinowski, Bronislaw
1944   A Scientific Theory of Culture and other essays, Chapel Hill, 1944.

Maly, Karl
1967   Mündige Gemeinde. Untersuchungen zur pastoralen Führung des
       Apostels Paulus im 1. Korintherbrief (SBM 2) Stuttgart, 1967.
1969   "Paulus als Gemeindegründer" (in J. Schreiner (ed.), Gestalt und
       Anspruch des Neuen Testaments, Würzburg, 1969, 72–95).

Marshall, I. Howard
1970   Luke: Historian and Theologian, Exeter, 1970.
1973   "Palestinian and Hellenistic Christianity: Some Critical Comments
       (NTS 19, 1972/73, 271–287).

Martin, Jochen
1972   Die Genese des Amtspriestertums in der frühen Kirche (Der Priester-
       liche Dienst III, QD 48), Freiburg . . . , 1972.

Martin Roderick
1971   "The concept of power: a critical defence" (BJS 22, 1971, 240–256).

Michel, Otto
1966   Der Brief an die Römer (KEK 4), 4. ed., Göttingen, 1966.
Minn, H. R.
1972   The Thorn that Remained. Materials for the Study of St. Paul's Thorn
        in the Flesh: 2 Cor XII, vv 1–10, Auckland, 1972.
Mühlmann, Wilhelm Emil
1962   Homo creator. Abhandlungen zur Soziologie, Anthropologie und
        Ethnologie, Wiesbaden, 1962.
1969   "Institution" (in W. Bernsdorf (ed.), Wörterbuch der Soziologie, 2.
        ed., Stuttgart, 1969, 466–468).
Mühlsteiger, Johannes
1977   "Zum Verfassungsrecht der Frühkirche" (ZKTh 99, 1977, 129–155
        and 257–285).
Munck, Johannes
1947   "La vocation de l'Apôtre Paul" (StTh 1, 1947, 131–145).
1954   Paulus und die Heilsgeschichte (AJut 26:1), Aarhus-København,
        1954.
Mussner, Franz
1974   Der Galaterbrief (HThK 9), Freiburg . . . , 1974.
1976   Petrus und Paulus—Pole der Einheit. Eine Hilfe für die Kirchen (QD
        76), Freiburg . . . , 1976.
Naumann, Hans, (ed.)
1973   Der moderne Strukturbegriff (WdF 155), Darmstadt, 1973.
Nickle, Keith F.
1966   The Collection. A Study in Paul's Strategy (SBT 48), London, 1966.
O'Dea, Thomas F.
1963   "Sociological Dilemmas: Five Paradoxes of Institutionalization" (in
        Sociological Theory, Values and Sociocultural Change, FS P. A.
        Sorokin ed. by E. A. Tiryakian, London, 1963, 71–89).
1967   Religionssociologi, Stockholm, 1967.
Odeberg, Hugo
1953   Pauli brev till korintierna, (Tolkning av Nya Testamentet VII), 2.
        ed., Stockholm, 1953.
Oepke, Albrecht
1973   Der Brief des Paulus an die Galater, 3. ed., rev. by J. Rohde (ThHK
        9), Berlin, 1973.
Pedersen, Sigfred
1977   "Die Kanonfrage als historisches und theologisches Problem" (StTh
        31, 1977, 83–136).
Pesch, Rudolf
1971   "Structures du ministère dans le Nouveau Testament" (Istina 16,
        Paris, 1971, 437–452).
Peter in the New Testament
        See Brown, R. E.–Donfried, K. P.–Reumann, J.
Pfammatter, Josef
1960   Die Kirche als Bau. Eine exegetisch-theologische Studie zur Ekkle-
        siologie der Paulusbriefe (AnGr 110), Roma, 1960.
Piaget, Jean
1971   Structuralism, London, 1971.
Pieper, Karl
1926   Paulus. Seine missionarische Persönlichkeit und Wirksamkeit (NTA
        12), Münster i.W., 1926.

Plummer, Alfred.
  See Robertson, Archibald–Plummer, Alfred.
Prigge, Wolfgang-Ulrich
  See Hennen, Manfred–Prigge, Wolfgang-Ulrich.
Rad, Gerhard von
  1965   Theologie des Alten Testaments II, Die Theologie der prophetischen
          Überlieferungen Israels, 4. ed., München, 1965.
Ratnam, K. J.
  1964   "Charisma and Political Leadership" (PolSt 12, 1964, 341–354).
Reicke, Bo
  1957   "The Constitution of the Primitive Church in the Light of Jewish
          Documents" (in K. Stendahl (ed.), The Scrolls and the New Testa-
          ment, New York, 1957, 143–156).
  1959   *proistēmi* (ThWNT 6, Stuttgart, 1959, 700–703).
Reumann, John
  See Brown R. E.–Donfried, K. P.–Reumann, J.
Ridderbos, Herman
  1975   Paul: An Outline of His Theology, Grand Rapids, 1975.
Riesenfeld, Harald
  1968   "De kvantitativa metodernas begränsade räckvidd i bibelutläggningen"
          (SvEÅ 33, 1968, 83–100).
Rigaux, Béda
  1956   Saint Paul. Les Épitres aux Thessaloniciens (EtB), Paris-Gembloux,
          1956.
Robertson, Archibald–Plummer, Alfred
  1911   A Critical and Exegetical Commentary on the First Epistle of St. Paul
          to the Corinthians (ICC), Edinburgh, 1911.
Robinson, James M.
  1971   "The Dismantling and Reassembling of the Categories of New Testa-
          ment Scholarship" (in Robinson, J. M.–Koester, H., Trajectories
          through Early Christianity, Philadelphia, 1971, 1–19).
Robinson, John A. T.
  1976   Redating the New Testament, London, 1976.
Rohde, Joachim
  1976   Urchristliche und frühkatholische Ämter. Eine Untersuchung zur
          frühchristlichen Amtsentwicklung im Neuen Testament und bei den
          apostolischen Vätern (ThA 33), Berlin, 1976.
Roloff, Jürgen
  1965   Apostolat—Verkündigung—Kirche. Ursprung, Inhalt und Funktion
          des kirchlichen Apostelamts nach Paulus, Lukas und den Pastoral-
          briefen, Gütersloh, 1965.
  1977   "Amt, Ämter, Amtsverständnis. IV. Im Neuen Testament" (TRE vol
          II, Berlin, 1977, 509–533).
Sampley, J. Paul
  1977   " 'Before God, I do not lie' (Gal. I.20), Paul's Self-Defence in the
          Light of Roman Legal Praxis" (NTS 23, 1977, 477–482).
San Juan Jr., E.
  1967   "Orientations of Max Weber's Concept of Charisma" (The Centen-
          nial Review of Arts and Science 11, 1967, 270–285).
Schelsky, Helmut
  1965a   "Ist die Dauerreflexion institutionalisierbar? Zum Thema einer mo-

dernen Religionssoziologie" (in Auf dem Suche nach Wirklichkeit. Ges. Aufsätze, Düsseldorf-Köln, 1965, 250–275).

1965b "Über die Stabilität von Institutionen, besonders Verfassungen. Kulturanthropologische Gedanken zu einem rechtssoziologischen Thema" (in Auf dem Suche nach Wirklichkeit. Ges. Aufsätze, Düsseldorf-Köln, 1965, 33–55).

1970 "Zur soziologischen Theorie der Institution" (in H. Schelsky (ed.), Zur Theorie der Institution, Düsseldorf, 1970, 9–26).

1975 Die Arbeit tun die anderen. Klassenkampf und Priesterherrschaft der Intellektuellen, Opladen, 1975.

Schille, Gottfried
1966 Anfänge der Kirche. Erwägungen zur apostolischen Frühgeschichte (BEvTh 43), München, 1966.

Schlier, Heinrich
1971 Der Brief an die Galater (KEK 7), 14. ed., Göttingen, 1971.
1977 Der Römerbrief. Kommentar (HThK 6), Freiburg . . . , 1977.

Schmid, Josef
See Wikenhauser, Alfred–Schmid, Josef.

Schmiedel, Paul W.
1899a "Apollos" (EB(C), vol I, London, 1899, 262–264).
1899b "Barnabas" (EB(C), vol I, London, 1899, 484–487).
1903 "Silas, Silvanus" (EB(C), vol IV, London, 1903, 4514–4521).

Schmithals, Walter
1963 Paulus und Jakobus (FRLANT 85), Göttingen, 1963.
1965 Paulus und die Gnostiker (ThF 24), Hamburg, 1965.
1967 review of D. Georgi, Die Geschichte der Kollekte des Paulus für Jerusalem, Hamburg, 1965 (ThLZ 92, 1967, 668–672).
1975 Der Römerbrief als historisches Problem (StNT 9), Gütersloh, 1975.

Schnackenburg, Rudolf
1971 "Apostel vor und neben Paulus" (in Schriften zum Beuen Testament. Exegese im Fortschritt und Wandel, München, 1971, 338–358).

Schneider, Louis
1964 "Institution" (in J. Gould–W. L. Kolb (eds.), A Dictionary of the Social Sciences, New York, 1964, 338).

Schrenk, Gottlob
1938 "thelō, thelēma, thelēsis" (ThWNT 2, Stuttgart, 1938, 43–63).

Schürmann, Heinz
1968 "Das Testament des Paulus für die Kirche. Apg 20, 18–35" (in Traditionsgeschichtliche Untersuchungen, Düsseldorf, 1968, 310–340).

1970 "Die geistliche Gnadengaben in den paulinischen Gemeinden" (in Ursprung und Gestalt. Erörterungen und Besinnungen zum Neuen Testament, Düsseldorf, 1970, 236–267, now in Kertelge (ed.), Das kirchliche Amt im Neuen Testament (WdF 439), Darmstadt, 1977: 362–412).

1977 " ' . . . und Lehrer'. Die geistliche Eigenart des Lehrdienstes und sein Verhältnis zu anderen geistlichen Diensten im neutestamentlichen Zeitalter" (in Dienst der Vermittlung (EthST 37), Leipzig, 1977, 107–147: separately publ. with enlarged notes and new numeration 1–44, used here).

Schütte, Heinz
1974 Amt, Ordination und Sukzession im Verständnis evangelischer und

katholischer Exegeten und Dogmatiker der Gegenwart sowie in Dokumenten ökumenischer Gespräche, Düsseldorf, 1974.

Schütz, John Howard
1974   "Charisma and Social Reality in Primitive Christianity" (JR 54, 1974, 51–70).
1975   Paul and the Anatomy of Apostolic Authority (MSSNTS 26), Cambridge, 1975.

Schulz, Siegfried
1976   "Die Charismenlehre des Paulus. Bilanz der Probleme und Ergebnisse" (in Rechtfertigung. FS E. Käsemann, ed. by Friedrich-Pöhlmann-Stuhlmacher, Tübingen-Göttingen, 1976, 443–460).

Schweizer, Eduard
1955   "Die Bekehrung des Apollos, Ag. 18, 24–26" (EvTh 15, 1955, 247–254).
1959   Gemeinde und Gemeindeordnung im Neuen Testament (AThANT 35), Zürich, 1959.

Selwyn, Edward Gordon
1969   The First Epistle of St. Peter. The Greek Text with Introduction, Notes and Essays, London, 1969.

Sesboué, Bernhard
1974   "Ministères et structure de l'Église. (Réflexion théologique à partir du Nouveau Testament)" (in J. Delorme (ed.), Le ministère et les ministères selon le Nouveau Testament. Dossier exégétique et réflexion théologique, Paris, 1974, 347–417).

Seyfarth, Constants–Schmidt, Gert
1977   Max Weber Bibliographie: eine Dokumentation der Sekundärlitteratur, Stuttgart, 1977.

Shils, Edward
1965   "Charisma, Order and Status" (ASR 30, 1965, 199–213).
1968   "Charisma" (IESS, vol 2, New York, 1968, 386–390).

Skjevesland, Olav
1976   Kirken i det Nye Testamente. En innføring, Oslo, 1976.

Sohm, Rudolph
1892   Kirchenrecht I. Die geschichtlichen Grundlagen (Systemat. Handb. d. deutschen Rechtswiss., hrsg v K. Binding, 8:1), Leipzig, 1892.

Spencer, Martin E.
1973   "What is charisma?" (BJS 24, 1973, 341–354).

Spicq, C.
1952   L'Épître aux Hébreux. I. Introduction (EtB), Paris, 1952.
1969   Saint Paul, Les Épîtres Pastorales (EtB), 4. ed., Paris, 1969.

Staab, Karl
1969   Die Thessalonicherbriefe. Die Gefangenschaftsbriefe (Reg. NT 7:1), 5. ed., Regensburg, 1969.

Stanley, David M.
1959   " 'Become Imitators of me': The Pauline Conception of Apostolic Tradition" (Bib. 40, 1959, 859–877).
1967   "Authority in the Church: A New Testament Reality" (CBQ 29, 1967, 555–573).

Stark, Werner
1969   The Sociology of Religion. A Study of Christendom, vol IV. Types of Religious Man, London, 1969.

Stauffer, Ethelbert
1960   "Petrus und Jakobus in Jerusalem" (in Begegnung der Christen. FS
       O. Karrer ed. by M. Roesle–O. Cullmann, 2. ed., Stuttgart-Frankfurt
       a.M., 1960, 361–372).
Steinmüller, Wilhelm
1968   Evangelische Rechtstheologie. Zweireichelehre, Christokratie, Gna-
       denrecht, I–II, Köln, 1968.
Sternberger, Dolf
1959   Autorität, Freiheit und Befehlsgewalt (Walter Eucken Institut. Vor-
       träge und Aufsätze 3), Tübingen, 1959.
1968   "Legitimacy" (IESS, vol 9, New York-London, 1968, 244–248).
Stolle, Volker
1973   Der Zeuge als Angeklagter. Untersuchungen zum Paulus-Bild des
       Lukas (BWANT 102), Stuttgart . . . , 1973.
Stoodt, Dieter
1962   Wort und Recht. Rudolf Sohm und das theologische Problem des
       Kirchenrechts (FGLP 10. Ser., 23), München, 1962.
Streeter, Burnett Hillman
1929   The Primitive Church, studied with special reference to the origins of
       the Christian Ministry, London, 1929.
Strelan, John G.
1975   "Burden-Bearing and the Law of Christ: A Re-examination of Gala-
       tians 6:2" (JBL 95, 1975, 266–276).
Strobel, August
1974   "Das Aposteldekret in Galatien: Zur Situation von Gal I and II"
       (NTS 20, 1974, 177–190).
Stuhlmacher, Peter
1967   "Erwägungen zum ontologischen Charakter der *kainē ktisis* bei
       Paulus' (EvTh 27, 1967, 1–35).
1968   Das paulinische Evangelium I. Vorgeschichte (FRLANT 95), Göt-
       tingen, 1968.
1971   "Evangelium—Apostolat—Gemeinde" (KuD 17, 1971, 28–45).
Suggs, M. Jack
1967   " 'The Word is Near You': Romans 10:6–10 Within the Purpose of
       the Letter" (in Christian History and Interpretation. FS J. Knox ed.
       by Farmer–Moule–Niebuhr, Cambridge, 1967: 289–312).
Suhl, Alfred
1975   Paulus und seine Briefe. Ein Beitrag zur paulinischen Chronologie
       (StNT 11), Gütersloh, 1975.
Theissen, Gerd
1973   "Wanderradikalismus. Literatursoziologische Aspekte der Überliefe-
       rung von Worten Jesu im Urchristentum" (ZThK 70, 1973, 245–271).
1974a "Soziale Schichtung in der korinthischen Gemeinde" (ZNW 65, 1974,
       232-273).
1974b "Soziale Integration und sakramentales Handeln" (NT 16, 1974, 179–
       206).
1974c "Theoretische Probleme religionssoziologischer Forschung und die
       Analyse des Urchristentums" (NZSTh 16, 1974, 35–56).
1975a "Die Starken und Schwachen in Korinth. Soziologische Analyse eines
       theologischen Streites" (EvTh 35, 1975, 155–172).
1975b "Die soziologische Auswertung religiöser Überlieferungen. Ihre me-

thodologischen Probleme am Beispiel des Urchristentums" (Kairos 17, 1975, 284–299).

1975c "Legitimation und Lebensunterhalt: Ein Beitrag zur Soziologie urchristlicher Mission" (NTS 21, 1975, 192–221).

1977 Soziologie der Jesusbewegung. Ein Beitrag zur Entstehungsgeschichte des Urchristentums (TEH 194), München, 1977.

Thielicke, Helmut
1958 Theologische Ethik II/2: Ethik des Politischen, Tübingen, 1958.

Troeltsch, Ernst
1912 Die Soziallehren der christlichen Kirchen und Gruppen (Ges. Schriften, vol 1), Tübingen, 1912.

Tucker, Robert C.
1968 "The Theory of Charismatic Leadership" (Daedalus 97, Boston, 1968, 731–756).

Vaskovics, Laszlo
1972 "Religion und Familie—Soziologische Problemstellung und Hypothesen" (in J. Wössner (ed.), Religion im Umbruch, Stuttgart, 1972, 328–352).

Vielhauer, Philipp
1975 "Paulus und die Kephaspartei in Korinth" (NTS 21, 1974–75, 341–352).

Vögtle, Anton
1977 "Kirche und Amt im Werden" (MThZ 28, 1977, 158–179).

Weber, Max
1968 Economy and Society. An Outline of Interpretive Sociology, vol 1–3. Ed. by Guenther Roth and Claus Wittich, New York, 1968.

1976 Wirtschaft und Gesellschaft. Grundriss der verstehenden Soziologie. Fünfte, rev. Aufl. mit textkritischen Erläuterungen hrsg. v. Johannes Winckelmann, I–II, Tübingen, 1976.

Weiss, Johannes
1917 Das Urchistentum. Herausg. und ergänzt von Rudolf Knopf, Göttingen, 1917.

Weiss, Johannes
1971 Weltverlust und Subjektivität. Zur Kritik der Institutionenlehre Arnold Gehlens (Sammlung Rombach N.F. 11), Freiburg, 1971.

Wendland, Heinz-Dietrich
1970 Ethik des Neuen Testamentes. Eine Einführung (GNT 4), Göttingen, 1970.

Westerholm, Stephen
1978 Jesus and Scribal Authority (CB. NT 10), Lund, 1978.

Widengren, Örjan
1977 Power and Influence in Social Relationships. A Conceptual Analysis, Uppsala, 1977.

Wiese, Leopold von
1956 "Institutionen" (HDSW, Stuttgart, 1956, vol. 5, 297–299).

Wikenhauser, Alfred–Schmid, Josef
1973 Einleitung in das Neue Testament, 6. ed., Freiburg i. Br., 1973.

Wilckens, Ulrich
1964 *"Stylos"* (ThWNT 7, Stuttgart, 1964, 732–736).

1974 "Über Abfassungszweck und Aufbau des Römerbriefs" (in Rechtfertigung als Freiheit. Paulusstudien, Neukirchen-Vluyn, 1974, 110–170).

Williams, Ronald Ralph
1950 Authority in the Apostolic Age. With Two Essays on the Modern Problem of Authority, London, 1950.

Willner, Ann Ruth
1968 Charismatic Political Leadership: A Theory (Center of International Studies, Princeton Univ., Research Monogr. 32), Princeton, 1968.

Wilson, Bryan, R.
1959 "An Analysis of Sect Development" (ASR 24, 1959, 3–15).

Wilson, Stephen G.
1973 The Gentiles and the Gentile Mission in Luke-Acts (MSSNTS 23), Cambridge, 1973.

Winch, Peter G.
1958 "Authority" (in The Aristotelian Society. Suppl. Vol. 32, London, 1958, 225–240).

Winckelmann, Johannes
1976 Erläuterungsband zu Max Weber, Wirtschaft und Gesellschaft I–II 5. ed., Tübingen, 1976.

Wolpe, Harold
1968 "A Critical Analysis of Some Aspects of Charisma" (So cR 16, 1968, 305–318).

Worsley, Peter
1957 The Trumpet Shall Sound. A Study of 'Cargo' cults in Melanesia, London, 1957.

Index of Biblical References

225

Index of Early Christian Literature

Index of Modern Authors

229